THE FUTURE OF
JAZZ

THE FUTURE OF
JAZZ

by   Will Friedwald

Ted Gioia

Jim Macnie

EDITED BY   Peter Margasak
YUVAL TAYLOR

Stuart Nicholson

Ben Ratliff

John F. Szwed

Greg Tate

Peter Watrous

K. Leander Williams

Library of Congress Cataloging-in-Publication Data
Friedwald, Will, 1961–
    The future of jazz / by Will Friedwald . . . [et al.];
edited by Yuval Taylor.
        p.   cm.
Includes bibliographical references and index.
ISBN 1-55652-446-3
1. Jazz—History and criticism. 1. Taylor, Yuval. 11. Title.
ML3506.F74 2002
781.65'0112—dc21

                                                    2002001315

Cover and interior design: Lindgren / Fuller Design
© 2002 by A Cappella Books
First Edition
Published by A Cappella Books
an imprint of Chicago Review Press, Incorporated
814 North Franklin Street
Chicago, Illinois 60610
ISBN 1-55652-446-3
Printed in the United States of America

5 4 3 2 1

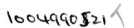

CONTENTS

INTRODUCTION

Maybe the future of jazz has always been in question. God knows the music has weathered enough crises over the past hundred years: the transformation from swing to sweet music in the 1930s; the perceived threat of bebop in the 1940s; the decline in its popularity concomitant with the ascendancy of rock 'n' roll; the turning away of its core audience, African Americans, in favor of rhythm and blues; the split engendered by the rise of free jazz in the 1960s; the introduction of nonacoustic instruments; the watering-down effect of fusion and "smooth jazz" in the late 1970s and thereafter; the tension between Wynton Marsalis's camp and jazz's cutting edge in the late 1980s; and so on.

But in the past year or two we've had strong intimations that jazz's past may have become more important than its future—particularly in Ken Burns's widely seen documentary *Jazz: A History of America's Music*, and in the sales figures for jazz recordings, which overwhelmingly favor reissues of old records over new ones.

So, as this year may mark the centenary of the art form (Jelly Roll Morton claimed to have invented jazz in 1902), I thought it appropriate to ask ten leading jazz critics to ruminate on the state of the art and where it's heading.

Choosing these critics was no easy task. Jazz writers are probably the most eloquent of music writers, and there's no shortage of them. But while eloquence was indeed my primary consideration when coming up with my wish list, other factors were also important. I wanted a representation of a variety of viewpoints, geographical bases, and races, and I hope I was successful on that score: among these critics are at least two who shun rock 'n' roll and at least three who were weaned on the stuff; at least three who have come to the defense of Wynton Marsalis and several who have openly attacked him; one practicing academic; three practicing musicians; two African Americans; and, while six are based in New York, there's also one in Chicago, one in England, one in Connecticut, and one in California. I also wanted relatively young writers with their ears to the pulse, writers who frequent jazz clubs and festivals and talk regularly to jazz musicians, writers with catholic tastes and a broad knowledge of the musical world outside jazz. (Unfortunately, while some of the best writers about jazz are female, they all seem to be jazz historians; finding female critics who fit my criteria proved to be a task beyond my capacity—although the fault may well be my own for not casting a wide enough net.) Of course, not everyone I asked wanted to or was able to participate; and there were many others I would like to have asked as well if the project had been able to accommodate more than ten critics.

The task I assigned these writers was as follows: to write a relatively long piece on one particular aspect of jazz's future, and to respond with shorter pieces to the other nine critics' ruminations on their topics. Responses were encouraged to be off-the-cuff and conversational. The bulk of the book was written via e-mail, without which this approach would probably not have been possible. After receiving the initial essays, I fired them off to the critics at approximately ten-day intervals and waited for the responses to come in. With some exceptions, the book you're holding is a chronological transcript of what was written, so that comments in the later chapters may reflect the contents of earlier ones. In addition, the writers were given the opportunity, once all the essays and responses were in, to add further comments.

Five of the topics center on kinds of jazz: mainstream jazz, jazz-rock, repertory jazz, vocal jazz, and free jazz. The other five deal with other themes: jazz and race, improvisation and composition, the business of jazz, jazz's relationship to the rest of the world, and educational and media institutions and infrastructures. I hope that no topic vital to jazz's future has been overlooked. For an extra bit of fun at the end of the volume, I asked each writer to pick a year in this new century and speculate about the state of jazz in that year, thus jointly composing a *cadavre-exquis* narrative of the future of jazz.

Despite my high expectations, I have been consistently surprised and delighted by the contributions herein. Many of the writers were willing to go through several drafts in order to refine their ruminations; nevertheless they all seem fresh to me, genuine reactions to divisive topics. Some critics are more optimistic than others; some are more forward-looking, some more concerned with jazz history; some like to deal with specific artists, others with the big picture; some banter, others preach. But none of them, to my mind, at least, takes the easy way out by dispensing truisms or playing devil's advocate. What you'll find in this book is the result of intelligent writers honestly grappling with difficult issues.

I would like to acknowledge the invaluable help of Ben Ratliff with shaping the book and suggesting contributors, as well as Gary Giddins for his initial suggestions, and the staff of Chicago Review Press for their advice and support.

Yuval Taylor

THE FUTURE OF
JAZZ

GAMES AND THOUGHT AND GRACE

MAINSTREAM JAZZ

PETER WATROUS

A few years ago I exited the salt mine of jazz criticism, leaving it to others. I grew tired of writing essays about trends, reviewing records with all the enthusiasm of a knee reacting to a doctor's rubber hammer.

I had left music a few decades earlier, after graduating from the prestigious Guitar Institute of Technology. Jazz education, outside of a few well-known places, was seeing its dawn. We didn't really work from books. We worked from handouts, handwritten missives that the teachers had begun to organize from the inchoate, general jazz knowledge available orally, passed on from teacher to student, from better player to enthusiastic lesser players.

Twenty years later, I started playing again. I was just as bad as I was when I was in school—actually worse—but this time I had a lot of written help. In the intervening years, people have published mountains of books on how to play jazz. There are small hills of books on just how to apply the pentatonic scale, books on playing outside, books on blues, books on comping, books on the melodic minor scale, books on the harmonic minor scale. There are theory books, harmony books. There are nearly a hundred Jamey Aebersold Play-A-Long records.

Monks, working in dimly lit rooms late at night, have transcribed the great solos of virtually every great player to be placed in front of a microphone, along with plenty who maybe should have stayed home.

And most of the thousands of books are roughly the same. They treat the same material—blues, rhythm changes, diatonic harmony, quartal harmony, harmony based on minor scales—in roughly the same way. All indications, if one uses jazz literature to point to pedagogy, is that all jazz players must work through a uniform system to arrive at improvisational fluidity. That is, everyone from Louis Armstrong through Henry Threadgill to Pat Metheny has used a foundation, a way of thinking, that's roughly the same.

Which argues that there is a mainstream of music, if one thinks of the mainstream as majority practice. My salt mine, a fairly prestigious one, gave me access to what was considered the upper level of the jazz world: concerts where world-famous jazz musicians played for lots of money, clubs where the best jazz musicians worked. God is in the details: that is, at that level, musicians all have their styles. But from a distance, the foundation—the way people were thinking—was consistent.

Now I take lessons. My teacher, a virtually unknown guitarist with near-perfect technical skills, had introduced me to the vast underbelly of jazz in New York—and really, around the world: a universe almost completely self-contained, filled with seemingly thousands of working, virtually unknown jazz musicians with near-perfect technical skills, except the singers. They range in age from recent college graduates to people in their forties.

They work in restaurants and small jazz clubs, across the city and in the outer boroughs. They work in New Jersey. They work weddings and sometimes escape on cruise ships to play for dancers. They work Broadway shows and play in jam sessions or at people's houses to keep their grasp of the jazz language tight. They are mostly concerned about the same stuff: good time feel, playing well within the restraints of tunes, learning tunes, getting better jobs, recording. They mostly have a grasp on what they need to improve. And they wrangle with the quandary of coming into originality in a music that, one, is really hard to play, and, two, places as much a premium on correctness as it does originality.

And, by and large, issues that obsess jazz writers—pushing the envelope, stirring the gumbo, breaking the rules, ad nauseam—don't have any bearing on the world of most jazz musicians, in part because intrinsically the task of playing jazz well comes with the challenge of balancing originality and correctness, and everyone is trying to beat the challenge.

That is: one of the glories of jazz has been what might be called the Miracle of Substitutional Transformation. By which I mean: jazz musicians have traditionally messed everything up. That is: melodies changed, overlooked, made better. Silence and syncopation used to juice a laggard melody, fills to fill in the blank slate of whole notes. Lines or melodies to suggest harmonic movement where there was none. Riffs to restructure the rhythmic movement of a piece.

And harmony. It reminds me of what a blues musician once said about his peer, Gatemouth Brown: "Gatemouth can do more with a guitar than a monkey can do with a peanut." Translated into the present, that means that jazz musicians, within the limits of conventional harmony, have produced a century of thought about what could be done with the mild two-five-one chord movement, with the one-four-five movement of the blues. There is a long list with options, from the simplest to the most arcane and harsh, that can take a lifetime to learn. And they all suggest alteration, they all suggest independence, mobility, assertion, imagination. In even the politest piano trio, if one listens carefully, and if the pianist is thinking, the dance between what is there in the material and what course the musicians are taking makes the music bristle with tension. One hears the echoes of the willful disruption and disregard for authority that has always characterized one side of American life. And so mainstream music, average jazz practice, the majority speaking, can be seen as radical, a continuous process of upheaval, the supremacy of improvisation and movement, of grace over stasis. (Well, let's say that the last sentence is a bit of a lie. But it's an example of how jazz's political implications are often oversimplified; for days, weeks, months, years, and centuries before the seemingly illegal ascendance of George W. Bush, jazz musicians have been pursuing their individuality, their radicalness, and it didn't stop him one bit. I guess one can push that poor bit of harmony around all one wants, but it is still a metaphorical transgression. And finally, everybody still plays it, mostly, and studies it, and attacks it, and changes it. But jazz convention, the same poor little changes, are what everything, and everybody, finally refers to.)

I haven't been very specific, because being specific in jazz writing is to invite stumbling over a trip wire and setting off a detonation. But let me try. The mainstream jazz practice I'm talking about takes its stylistic cues from the mid-1950s on, often ignoring free improvisation, and swing tone and velocity. It's based on the idea that more vocabulary is better. And it's not so vocal, like swing and free improvisation. It has lasted half a century and will probably last a few more decades, at least in style. The intellectual and improvisational systemic foundation, as I've said, will last as long as anybody's interested. And the reason is simple. Jazz in this form is a perfect game system, like baseball or chess. You might as well ask when baseball will give up the ghost as wonder about jazz's future.

Mainstream jazz, while it is about the rhetoric of emotion, the outward exhibition of emotional states, is also thoroughly a game, with all the invention that a good game allows. A jam session is rarely about exhibiting emotion; it is about showing off prowess and invention, about Sonny Stitt cycling in fourths through the first four measures of a blues or "I Got Rhythm" and not making it sound mechanical. Like baseball, mainstream jazz, within strict limits, has an endless set of possibilities and lengths of performance. The blues form is like boxing in that each chorus opens up cleanly like a new round, part of a whole performance, but capable of standing on its own and limitless in its possibilities. And as in chess, strategy—the implications and suggestions, the shadows that propose, that direct motion—makes jazz listenable.

For those of us in a constant minority, the minority of liking jazz for its language, the grace of that athleticism can be enough; I can listen to Sonny Stitt all day long just to admire his use of the bebop scale. When the athleticism joins with the sort of substitutional intellect of a Benny Golson or Sonny Rollins or James Moody, to name three saxophonists of almost the same generation, we are blessed. They embody

4

a century of hard work and thought by geniuses. And even more, their invention, the slickness of their play, can cast warm light in the dimmest, failing chambers of the cold heart.

But we're a minority, and for all the gifted players out there—from Sonny Rollins to David Berkman, from Tommy Flanagan to Nasheet Waits, from Jackie McLean to Bruce Barth, Steve Wilson, Jason Moran, and whoever else—perhaps it's their sense of the game, of the power of invention, that postpones the search for drama that attracts an audience outside of the jazz cult. Substitutional harmony and rhythmic authority and elegance may not be what the average person wants to hear. The jazz audience dwindles: maybe the game is increasingly reserved for musicians, too rarified and insular for somebody looking for rhythm and a melody. Maybe the endless formal routine that most jazz adheres to, the head-solo-head format, has driven the audience away too: it's complacently framing just the game and leaving out the big gesture. Remember that every second of the day, jazz moves further away from an editing process forced on it when it was a practical music, music meant for a dancing audience.

Maybe the culture's geniuses have gone into video art or banking. With only the rules of the idiom to fool with, and basically only playing for an audience of other musicians, the average jazz musician, stumbling with the weight of a hundred years of genius, is just too concerned about making sure the grammar is correct. I can't quite figure out why I'm more interested in playing than listening to live music nowadays, but I am. Maybe those are some reasons.

A few days ago I was driving in my car, listening to a fairly new record by Donny McCaslin, a saxophonist who records for Arabesque. He's good. A friend of mine, Steve Armour, a trombonist and a promising writer about jazz, had passed me a review he had written about the album and, more to the point, he had told me how much he loves Ben Monder's playing; Monder's on the album. So I'm driving around, which is a good way to hear music and not take in telephone calls or the kids screaming, and it dawns on me that I've heard a truckload of CDs like his recently. Not like his exactly; God is in the details. But certainly records and shows where the harmony is not particularly based in traditional jazz harmony. To generalize, the stuff comes from Boston, from the lineage proposed by Berklee School of Music and its great teachers and players.

It made me wonder if maybe those records and bands and composers aren't the mainstream now, or on the way to becoming it, by dint of a majority shareholding in what is the jazz world. If maybe, quietly, the smoke slipped under the door and filled up the room while everybody was paying attention to Wynton. Let me reiterate: the music functions in virtually the same fashion most jazz has functioned in for a hundred years. It has harmony; people relate scales and arpeggios over the harmony. There are melodies. There is time, and as in most jazz it's pretty flexible, maybe more so than usual. But it sounds different, in the same way Joe Henderson and Wayne Shorter sounded different from Sonny Stitt and Sonny Rollins.

And to show how the mainstream is simply common majority practice, I propose that Arthur Blythe work with Reid Anderson. That Matt Wilson hire Johnny Griffin. That Kurt Rosenwinkle record duets with Mulgrew Miller. That Sonny Rollins share some of the juice that fuels the rhythm section of Nasheet Waits and Taurus Mateen. That Mark Turner and Lee Konitz form a band. That Etta Jones and Greg Osby delve into some ballads. That Danilo Perez use Oliver Lake for a solo or two. That the rhythm section of the Art Ensemble of Chicago record with Jackie McLean, Sam Newsome, and Abraham Burton, and that . . . well, the list goes on and on. No rehearsals—just great, common music. Music dictated not by style but by a shared way of thinking, by the reality of the present situation.

K. LEANDER WILLIAMS

The idea of a mainstream does indeed connote a shared way of thinking, but it seems to me that the key question at every stage of jazz's development has been, "Whose way of thinking?" In the mid-1940s, a musician had to decide whether to stick with the swing bands or follow Charlie Parker and Dizzy Gillespie. In the 1950s, the history books tell us, the choice was between East Coast "hard" and West Coast "cool," even though many musicians who still wanted to play swing and Dixieland did so and made good livings outside the spotlight, often via a circuit of parties, exclusive country clubs, cruise ships, and restaurants not unlike the places where Peter says the current mainstreamers hang out.

Is race an issue? I think it especially matters when we talk about the mainstream, because for much of jazz's history people of color have not only been outside that stream, they've also had a heck of a time getting compensated for the innovations they've contributed to it. Back in the teens, for example, trumpeter Freddie Keppard was reticent about recording because he was afraid that others would steal his licks, something that today may seem ridiculously paranoid and unrealistic, but it also stemmed from the knowledge that he had come up with something special on the trumpet and knew that the key to his survival as a black musician with limited employment opportunities was to allow that something to remain special. Jazz education, academicism, and a zillion other things have placed us *way* on the other side of that dilemma now, into a situation where the miracle of creation can be codified, duplicated, and mass-produced at just about the instant when uniqueness escapes the bell of someone's trumpet. I wonder what ramifications this has on who gets what gigs, who plays with whom, and how that impacts what everyone chooses to play.

One other thing. Since it is now pretty well known that the allegedly nonmainstream jazz avant-garde is forty years old, isn't it time that that the mainstream took on some of its values? Joe Lovano's work may provide the best example of this. Even though I don't necessarily think of him as avant-garde, I know some listeners do, and it's because his conception audibly embraces Dewey Redman, Eric Dolphy, and late-period John Coltrane as well as Sonny Stitt, Hank Mobley, and Sonny Rollins. And if we're going to look at the new mainstream as a perfect game system, it's probably worth remembering that in basketball, the behind-the-back dribble was a thing of the future until a hotdog named Bob Cousy made it into a staple in the early 1950s. Does anyone want to imagine one of today's games without that simple innovation?

TED GIOIA

When I was a boy, I often wasted long evenings playing various board games with family and friends—slowly ascending from Chutes and Ladders and Monopoly to, in later years, Stratego, Clue, and Risk, and finally embracing that mammoth time killer known as Diplomacy. But no matter what the game, I was always puzzled when reading the rules that came along with these diversions, which inevitably started by explaining the "object of the game." Heck, I already knew what the object was—to win, and win big! "Dispense with the bluster," I thought, "and tell me the rules."

Years later, studying the philosopher Wittgenstein, and followers of his such as Saul Kripke and Peter Winch, I learned that adults were no further evolved than my young schoolmates. These serious thinkers suggested that cultural practices can often be best understood as types of games. Participants follow the "rules" of the game, so to speak, seeking well-understood objectives and employing various tools and techniques along the way.

Peter Watrous applies this approach to mainstream jazz, where it provides a quasi-anthropological way of dealing with the subject. The rules of the jazz game, as it is most often played, include harmonic substitutions, scales, licks, rhythmic figures, even conventional ways of pacing a performance, dressing for a gig, or taking a break between sets.

This is a tempting approach. It casts an aura of objectivity and distance over our assessments. And some of the shared conventions of mainstream jazz—the joys of playing with a sense of swing, of mastering a new technique or song—are worth celebrating, as Watrous rightly points out. Players who have learned the rules and learned them well deserve our respect. I recall, when I was living overseas, saxophonist George Coleman coming to a local club where he demonstrated, among other things, his ability to play "I Can't Get Started" while modulating into a new key at the end of every eight bars. The local musicians took this seriously, even if the average fan was somewhat indifferent to the whole demonstration. Truly, George Coleman had learned the rules and could play the game.

But George Coleman is mostly forgotten in the jazz world, while the other saxophonists who played with Miles during the late 1950s and early '60s—such as Shorter, 'Trane, and Cannonball—have become legends. And understanding the difference between a George Coleman and a Wayne Shorter tells us why playing mainstream jazz must always be more than just mastering the rules of a game. Shorter put his own individual stamp on almost everything he played. Even when working through the most conventional material, as he often did with the Davis Quintet, Shorter never sounded conventional. He cultivated his own voice, and this often meant rejecting the standard phrases, scales, and cadences of the previous generation. Yet Shorter was also part of the jazz mainstream, managing somehow to balance his individuality with the dictates of a vast tradition that he had inherited.

This may seem like a small matter, but I believe it is a vital one. Yes, God is in the details! The great mainstream jazz players never sounded like players following a rulebook. Consider a handful of 1950s tenor players—I will toss out, as examples, Zoot Sims, Eddie "Lockjaw" Davis, Roland Kirk, and Warne Marsh—and marvel at how they could play the same songs at the same tempos, but each one could impart his own personal twist to the music. And what made these examples of mainstream playing laudable was precisely that element that could not be reduced to rules and game playing. The individuality stood out, even more than the mastery of the conventions. Sometimes this individuality required certain techniques not to be used. Style, recall, often depends on what is left out.

In short, if we reduce the mainstream to playing a game with set rules . . . well, we might as well pack it up now and put it back in the Milton Bradley box. We are no different from workmen assimilating an archaic craft. The beauty of the mainstream is the personal voice, the ability to find a place of one's own within the conventions without doing too much damage along the way. (Or maybe a little bit of damage is needed, too!) And this is what we should encourage, whether we are critics, educators, or performers. My philosophy now—turned topsy-turvy since my youth—is "dispense with the rules, and give me the bluster."

GREG TATE

Trumpeter Ahmed Abdullah once made the useful observation that the reason the jazz mainstream cats of the 1960s—i.e., those wading in the part of the stream most concerned with swinging and harmonic improvisation—were so kick-ass by comparison with today's group was the pressure the 1960s swingers were feeling from the outcats— i.e., those more concerned with timbral and tonal expressionism, and toe-tapping, finger-snapping music hardly at all. In those heady days, as we know, when Don Cherry and Archie Shepp might sit in with the Miles Davis Quintet and the class/social divide between established players was not as chasmic as today—meaning everybody, swinger and outré mug, lived in the same Brooklyn/Village neighborhoods and played at the same Brooklyn/Village spots, too—a lot more random cross-pollination seemed to have been the order of the day. In his *Bitches Brew* liner notes, Ralph J. Gleason made the point that electric Miles didn't make Ben Webster any less beautiful; but battle lines in jazz do tend to be drawn hard and fast when the subject is terrorism versus tradition.

What's especially ironic about the whole mainstream/avant-garde paradigm today, of course, is how the inside/outside thing breaks down along racial lines among musicians forty and under. Are there any African American musicians under thirty who are remotely interested in flying a post–free jazz banner? If not, then perhaps mainstream is the only stream that matters in the jazz context of today.

Per Abdullah I do believe that the mainstream jazz being played by the youngsters suffers from the lack of heat, friction, and tension that might result from having to answer the challenge of a prevailing counteresthetic from within its acoustic-virtuosic ranks. Saxophonist Mark Turner has spoken of injecting some "fire music" into his project, like it's simply a matter of making the right Promethean gesture. On the other hand, the master German painter Gerhard Richter (forgive the always problematic conjunction of the word *master* and anything German) has done a series of remarkable paintings using Abstract Expressionist forms as if they were just subject matter for some hyperrealistic still-life depictions. In the same way that I have been waiting for someone to push Jimi Hendrix's invention of harmonic/melodic feedback to its logical conclusion, and run bop changes with such noise at the fore, perhaps a new generation of players is attempting to solve this inside/outside problem in jazz even as we speak.

JOHN F. SZWED

"Even the little fish know when it's time to leave the school."
—Captain Beefheart to a Yale student audience

The history of the concept of a mainstream in jazz is one of exclusion and a critical means of escaping modernism in jazz. In its earliest form, I believe, it included swing and excluded bop and post-bop, as well as traditional jazz. By 1961 Stanley Dance began to call everything mainstream that rested between what he thought of as the reactionary backwaters and the excesses of the avant-garde. But as Peter uses it, mainstream would seem to mean the average, the majority practice— and by sheer numbers alone, he may well be right that it is made up of those educated in the usual jazz schools.

But is what they do only about rules? Lennie Tristano was as rule-governed and rule-demanding as anyone in jazz history. The models he presented to his students were from the pantheon of Louis, Duke, Lester, Tatum, et al., and his exercises involved learning to play these masters' solos by heart. Students were encouraged to stay within a small rhythmic compass and to create within conventional chords and progressions. And yet his students are among the most distinctly recognizable in the music, in part because of his insistence on melodic creativity. The AACM, also, demanded that its students know the conventional rules of music—Anthony Braxton, for one, has testified to how rigorously those demands for fundamentals could be enforced. But the AACM also insisted that every performer become a composer in the strictest sense of the term—and a composition was the first assignment given to a new student, one that was expected to be nonidiomatic and free of a doctrinaire vision of jazz. And speaking of Braxton, there is no performer or composer more rules-based or system-based than he. But they are his rules and his system. My point is that, in spite of their commitment to musical conventions, both of these "schools" have been denied a place not only in the mainstream, but also in some textbooks, some films on jazz history, and in one of our biggest concert halls.

STUART NICHOLSON

The jazz mainstream today is a very broad church. It's not like the 1950s, when the term was coined by Stanley Dance to accommodate the music of a group of displaced big-band musicians (mainly ex-Basie-ites) who continued to ply their craft within the conventions of the Swing Era, even though the musical climate around them had long since changed. Then a mainstream record could mean a pleasant diversion from the "real thing" that was going on elsewhere: an uncomplicated but engaging Buck Clayton jam session, a meeting between Ruby Braff and Ellis Larkins, or Vic Dickenson and Bobby Hackett fronting a band of engaging individual voices playing "Sugar" or "Struttin' with Some Barbecue."

Today, the mainstream is a very different place. To all intents and purposes, the mainstream is now "the real thing," and there isn't anything much going on elsewhere. If you're not in the mainstream, then to some you're not even playing jazz. Yes, there are still engaging individual voices of the elder statesmen, but they are almost drowned out by the competing clamor of younger voices playing in the adopted voices of jazz's older and sometimes posthumous heroes. These young musicians have received much attention in the press and in style magazines and so have raised the public profile of jazz, but it remains to be seen if they realize the deferred promise of their own artistic maturity. Lester Young once insisted a soloist tell a story. Well, these young musicians do tell a story: of practice rooms in Berklee, or North Texas State, or the New England Conservatory.

Too often young musicians have had record contracts thrust upon them in advance of artistic maturity. Listeners are invited to jump aboard their learning curve as they rummage around their assimilated influences for something that resembles an individual style. The problem is that so many musicians today support the same sources of stylistic inspiration, so they sound remarkably similar. As a kid I collected bubblegum cards. It's like the American jazz mainstream is today—I'll give you a Theodross Avery and a Javon Jackson for your Joshua Redman; OK, how about a Ravi Coltrane and a Don Braden for your James Carter? Everyone is interchangeable, and even if you don't have the full set, somehow you know you're not missing too much.

In a way, jazz has become ubiquitous. Jazz education is widely available and, as Peter Watrous has pointed out, there is no shortage of self-help books. And every town has several good instrumentalists who can bring on pre-college students and help hobbyists. To quote that well-known song, "Everybody's doing it!" And it has meant things have gotten a little boring of late.

For jazz to be taught, it has to be defined, and it has to be, as Mark Levine points out in *The Jazz Theory Book,* "Explainable, Analyzable, Categorizeable, Doable." The trouble is, so much in the jazz mainstream today *sounds* as if it is "Explainable, Analyzable, Categorizeable, Doable." By framing jazz in tried-and-tested methods of articulation, American jazz has become steeped in certainties that fail to acknowledge uncertainty as a precondition for adventure.

When Louis Armstrong recorded "West End Blues," Charlie Parker "Ko-ko," and John Coltrane "Giant Steps," these were, in the context of their time, stunning achievements. They went beyond the confines of what was thought possible. When Everest was conquered in 1953, this too went beyond what people thought was possible. Now mountaineers complain of litter as they make their way to the summit because so many people have repeated that triumph. In jazz we too are knee-deep in the litter of repeated triumphs. Only it's not known as that, it's known as "the tradition," which makes everything all right.

WILL FRIEDWALD

More than with brass instruments, there are a lot of giants of the saxophone not only still walking the Earth, but playing at peak level: Sonny Rollins, Lou Donaldson, James Moody, Jackie McLean, Kenny Davern, and Bob Wilber. All of these men have careers of upward of fifty years; they've all recorded prolifically and have gone through all the stages—from young lions, through long and productive middle years, to elder statesmen. Granted that major labels, for the last twenty years or so, have valued youth over experience; but most of these gentlemen have recorded consistently for major or semimajor concerns, and most of them can play the important New York clubs at least several times a year.

Except the last two, Wilber and Davern. It's not because they're white and the others are black—if Stan Getz were alive today he could name his own price—it's because the kind of jazz they play hasn't been current for a slightly longer period of time. At the millennium, the difference seems arcane: Rollins, Moody, and McLean learned their music from its originators, Parker, Gillespie, and Powell; and Davern and Wilber had firsthand playing and studying experience with such pioneers as Sidney Bechet and Jack Teagarden. More important, Wilber and Davern are remarkable musicians: each possesses a commanding tone, has an unbelievable repertoire not only of songs that they know and improvise on but an amazing storehouse of pet phrases and licks that they apply with aplomb, and each is an outstanding improviser. Yet because they play like Bechet or Johnny Dodds rather than like Parker, they are all but completely overlooked by the mainstream press and have never been courted by the major labels or the well-known clubs. The most they can manage is an annual appearance at George Wein's Kaye Playhouse series, which is a new and big step forward for a music that until recently had even less representation in the New York festivals.

If there is such a thing as a jazz mainstream, then the better swing and traditional players (whose younger ranks, sticking to reeds, include Ken Peplowski, Scott Robinson, Michael Hashim, and Dan Levinson) deserve to be part of it. It puts me in mind of an announcement that

Dick Wellstood made as he was about to tear into "Night in Tunisia" at a concert in the mid-1980s. "We call this modern jazz," said the late stride piano master, "because it's only forty years old."

JIM MACNIE

Peter's got two parallel ideas flowing in his piece, and each carries weight. Uno: yup, mainstream jazz works in a particular way, and if you're feeble when it comes to following the musical "rules," then you're likely to stand in the shadow of someone who ain't. I don't think anyone here is naïve enough to deem the music and its accompanying biz a meritocracy (and, in concurrence with Kelvin [K. Leander Williams], the first place I'd start to sniff around for a reason it's not is racism), but it's not hard to figure out that most aspects of life revolve around a large group of people participating in consensus thought, and that if you're intent on throwing the dominant "rules" out the window, you could find yourself a bit lonely. Commerce-wise that means a big share of the pie is going to the competition. Musical authority stems from a mix of expertise and emotion, or maybe I should say the process of communicating emotion, and sure, I'll throw emotional "rhetoric" in there too, if that's how Peter wants to phrase it. Jazz is best served when the subtleties of the improv are executed in a commanding way. I always doubted Denis Charles, didn't find him a competent enough mechanic to fully convince me of his craft or his sentiment. But all Roy Haynes has to do is fluff a brush down his ride cymbal to knock me out of my seat. Chops aren't everything, but in the large you've got to know what you're doing to make a dent. Technique enhances imagination. Rules, which are amended from generation to generation, don't set limits on the way jazz affects a listener, but they sure help focus an artist's articulation.

Watrous's idea numero dos is about what keeps the rules from becoming restrictions, and, fully agreeing with the "smoke under the door" notion, I really have to question John's notion of the mainstream being exclusionary. Coltrane was still a mainstream character when he stood next to Miles in Stockholm in 1960, erupting eloquently with shrieks, roars, and other locutions he found necessary to make his point. All of a sudden "On Green Dolphin Street" sounded pretty damn "modern." And lots of casual jazz fans heard bandleader David Murray play plenty progressive during gigs at mainstream clubs like Sweet Basil during the mid-1980s. At the time, his music pretty much awarded the same status to clamor as it did melody. So, to me, the mainstream is a fluid place. Spend an evening with Matt Wilson's quartet and you'll see how this generation deals. His yen for progress, learned at the hands of Dewey, McBee, and other characters we call prog veterans, doesn't deter him from blowing in a seductive, cogent, and mainstream manner. Dry cleaners from Des Moines usually have an easy time absorbing it. Indeed, I've seen several jazz innocents fall under its sway right in front of me.

This brings up another idea: audience reaction is significant when determining nomenclature. One definition of mainstream jazz is the kind of jazz most people are familiar with. Common musical elements, compellingly constructed, are going to win over the majority of listeners every time. Bandleaders who choose to do so can then get as "modern" as they prefer. And these days, many do. Flying a post–free jazz banner is what a sizable chunk of this era's mainstream leaders do every night, and I'm hoping Greg Tate gets out enough to hear how everyone from Dave Ballou to Jason Moran to Myron Walden to Ross Lossing updates ideas that I initially bumped my head on in shows by Cecil, the Art Ensemble, and yeah, Abdullah, too. "Heat, friction, and tension" is all I've ever gotten from them. A month ago at the Vanguard, Dave Douglas had patrons lined up outside the club hoping for a ticket. Inside, his quintet incorporated dissonance, funk, frenzy, and collectivism into its very swing-oriented, very melodically compelling tunes. Whether consciously or unconsciously, certain ways of playing—crashing over bar lines, sustaining tones way past their usual length, or shredding for shredding's sake—are part of the dominant lingo. The key word is *incorporate:* it's about usage. You don't write a paragraph in all caps, right? Too one-dimensional. But you do try to pepper an extended idea with a variety of sound strategies—that's called dynamics. One of my most frustrating professional moments in the last two years was listening to another critic chide the fully wild-assed intricacies of Marcus Roberts's last trio as "conservatism." It's just not so. Sherman Irby sometimes works a trio, and intermittently I've heard him preside over collective taffy pulls that echo the drama and design of stuff like "Keep Right on Playing Through the Mirror over the Water." As of a year ago, he had never heard of Air, and thought I was talking about the air we breathe when I referenced the mighty Threadgill/Hopkins/McCall troika during an interview. The stuff is part of jazz's extensive lingo, and it's out there being absorbed—that smoke under the door comes from a steadily refueled fire. For those who want to turn heads, the mastery of conventions is both a foregone conclusion and damn tough row to hoe. Maybe both god and devil are in the details.

And speaking of details, Stuart Nicholson's idea that Josh, Ravi, Don, Javon, and James sound similar enough to be interchangeable is perplexing. Yikes—he really needs to get to the clubs more often.

JOHN F. SZWED

I'm not sure what Jim means by saying that Coltrane was mainstream in 1960. Certainly audiences didn't think so. He mentions C. in Stockholm in 1960. I'll cite the night before at the Olympia in Paris, where the masses were booing and hissing and the press was reaching back to the premiere of *The Rite of Spring* for comparisons. But I was really thinking more of the exclusivity in the critical use of the concept of mainstream. Did Stanley Dance think Coltrane was mainstream in 1960? Don Gold? Whitney Balliett? Bob Dawborn? Ralph Ellison? Mimi Clar? John Tynan? ("Anti-jazz," anyone?) Or, for that matter, did the musicians think he was mainstream? Cannonball Adderley certainly didn't when he first had to play with him (see Miles's autobiography); for that matter, even Miles's brother Vernon told him, "You can't use that boy Coltrane. He don't resolve nothing!" Did C. ever become mainstream? Or were selected parts of what he did enshrined by those who wanted to rewrite history? (One thinks of the similar treatment Martin Luther King has received from the American mainstream.)

But I think the main problem with the concept of the mainstream is that it conceals much of what is most interesting about the developments of the last forty-plus years. Before the 1960s, jazz had developed a stable, comfortable position. People might not have been able to say exactly what jazz was, but they could usually distinguish it from classical and popular music. Jazz had an audience that had grown with it for almost half a century, and they knew what to expect from it. Even if the rules were not always easy to articulate, there was nonetheless a sense of what made for acceptable and successful jazz performances. When a group of musicians took the stage they already knew how to begin, where to go in the music, and how to end it. Put another way, they had fewer decisions to make. But post-1959/60 it didn't take a weatherman to know that jazz had entered a period of permanent diversity. A widely acceptable definition of jazz was no longer possible (or desirable, some would say). And the concept of a mainstream would henceforth signal either an antimodernist bias or a lack of awareness of what was happening.

JIM MACNIE

John, French audiences may have booed C. off the stage. They might have poured sugar in the gas tank of the cab that took him home. But that doesn't mean he wasn't a mainstream character. Travel the world with a string of very sizable gigs under your belt (including, I'd say, the Olympia), issue umpteen records for prominent labels (Prestige, Blue Note, Savoy, Atlantic), join one of the era's most recognizable and revered ensembles (Miles), you're far from being an underground character. C. largely worked in common formats through the 1950s: blues variations, standards, etc. So, yeah, in the autumn of 1960 I think he was a known, accepted quantity, playing known, accepted music—stuff I'd call "mainstream."

Vis-à-vis exclusivity and the mainstream: didn't know you meant the critics' perception of the term. Subjectivity being what it is, I'm sure you could find lots of folks—critics or not—who think a pear is a watermelon. Remember what Kelvin mentioned: some people believe

Lovano is "avant." And as far as the opinions of other musicians, Cannonball and such, well, no one said enlightenment was a de facto trait of those who do business on a bandstand. P.S.: Liked your MLK notion—you're dead on about that.

JOHN F. SZWED

Jim, given your criteria, who wasn't mainstream in 1960? Certainly Ornette would have been, with his five or six records, his work with a variety of bands, the Lenox School of Jazz gig, the forms he used, as well as the heavy media guns behind him; Cecil would have made the cut for much the same reasons, with extra credit for the West Indian dances he worked; ditto even Sun Ra, if you cut some slack for his own self-produced records. Is your point that virtually everyone is in the mainstream? If so, I admit I find it appealing.

STUART NICHOLSON

Although hardly new. T. S. Eliot pointed out that no artist can work outside the tradition because the tradition will stretch to accommodate anything artists do.

JIM MACNIE

Maybe Eliot's "stretch" is Watrous's "smoke."

K. LEANDER WILLIAMS

I'm not really sure that Jim's criteria would make Ornette or Cecil mainstream, John. But interestingly enough, I think that might be because Jim and I are about the same age. Being a late thirtysomething, when I came to the music in the 1980s it seemed like the struggles between boppers and swingers were to some extent over—at least sonically. John Coltrane still had quite a bit of straight-up boppish music ahead of him in 1960, and there's no denying that records like *Giant Steps* (1960), *My Favorite Things* (1961), and *Ballads* (1963) had much more in common with Duke Ellington than Ornette or Cecil. As a matter of fact, Ornette has actually described the music on those albums as "commercial." Consequently, it's quite possible that many of the folks in Peter's classification of the mainstream—maybe even Kenny Davern or Bob Wilber, for that matter—employ many things that Coltrane introduced during that period. I don't think Cecil's music has had the same influence.

BEN RATLIFF

The whole "mainstream"/"outside" duality in jazz fan circles is so gunked up with Rite-of-Springish, Dylan-at-Newportish ideas about aesthetic transgression and futurism that it may actually be beyond repair.

Right now, your average younger black jazz musician (to elaborate on Greg's idea about under-thirty black musicians not fattening the ranks of "out" jazz) is, in theory and in practice, beyond that duality entirely. Take the drummer Nasheet Waits, who's actually a little over thirty. His father played with Andrew Hill. He'd like to play with Andrew Hill. That's pride of lineage, and there are plenty of things to like about Andrew Hill. But he's interested in making a living, and he's interested in building a new sound with some other rhythm-section guys, and there's absolutely no reason for him to hang onto somebody else's preserved idea of what's against the grain and what's not. The stuff he plays is influenced by Tony Williams, who was the absolute king of far-out rhythmic concepts when he was eighteen and at the end of his life played in a pretty "mainstream" trio with Mulgrew Miller. So where does that put Nasheet on the spectrum? Because there is, in the mind of a whole lot of jazz fans, a spectrum—with, I don't know, Benny Green at one end and Charles Gayle at the other. My point is: abolish the scale. It will trip you up all the time. Benny Green, Mr. Mainstream, is a Horace Silver guy. Listen to the early Horace Silver albums and try to tell me they're stiff, or conservative, or right wing, or whatever.

About ten years ago, during the "conservatism" versus "liberal" wars in jazz—the back and forth involving Wynton and Stanley Crouch and Don Byron and Kevin Whitehead and so on—I became interested with players who played both sides of the fence, out and in. Like Hilliard Green, the bassist, who would play a soigné gig at Tavern on the Green in a tuxedo with Jimmy Scott, and then play down at the Knitting Factory in a dashiki with Charles Gayle.

Now, there are a sufficient number of people doing this (though generally in the same clothes from one gig to the next) that it almost ceases to matter. Wycliffe Gordon, the trombonist, who makes very traditional (and Wyntonesque) sounding records on his own, also plays in Ted Nash's band, Odeon, a Threadgillish mixture of chamber jazz and tango and time-no-changes and New Orleans. You've got Uri Caine, who can do hard, macho, East Coast piano trio stuff with Ralph Peterson and also records his own imaginative classical canon. (He seems to be modeling his career on Keith Jarrett, who was one of these types a long time ago.) Gerald Cleaver, the drummer. Tony Malaby, the saxophonist. Chris Lightcap, the bass player. Dafnis Prieto, the drummer.

The fact is that George Coleman plays split tones in circular breathing on a regular restaurant-club gig. Benny Golson and Steve Nelson can play some of the outest solos you'll ever hear. Marcus Roberts is in many ways as much of an oddball intellectual structuralist as Steve Coleman. Conversely, some of the models for the Gold Sparkle Band or Susie Ibarra are not only twenty to thirty-five years old, but rooted in their own time.

K. LEANDER WILLIAMS

Brad Mehldau, a pianist who is also in that age bracket, once told me that being a young musician in the 1990s was particularly overwhelming because at first he felt he should absorb all of the earlier jazz styles. He said he gave up on that approach when he realized it was creating "a sort of postmodern haze that turns [young musicians] into chameleons with no identity." Since Mehldau seems to be turning into an original, the fact that he recognized the dilemma may have helped him realize what Stuart called "the deferred promise of artistic maturity."

PETER MARGASAK

It seems difficult to argue against the fact that the scope of the mainstream constantly extends through accretion. Just as the blob metaphor sloppily applies to jazz history, so it does to the cumulative growth of what constitutes the mainstream. Of course, this assimilation isn't wholesale. As a whole the free jazz of the 1960s isn't part of today's mainstream, but many of its traits have been absorbed by the mainstream—the split tones, the circular breathing. But many of those sounds were flying out of the horns of the R&B bar-walkers many years before free jazz ever reared its head, which only underlines the difficulty, if not futility, of defining this glorious mess.

The prevalent mainstream sounds described in all of these replies ain't going away, but it seems more than likely—or, at least, I hope—that more and more players will nonchalantly work both ends of the conservative–radical spectrum, as Ben observes. It's happening all over here in Chicago, particularly with a wave of young musicians who arrived after Ken Vandermark and Rob Mazurek revived the city's scene in the 1990s. Those guys are too narrow to cover what seems to be happening with these young players. Musicians have never had so much information and ideas to draw from—and I don't mean the institutionalized stuff Peter is talking about—and it would be a shame if it were continually parsed to a consensus language. Let the music go multilingual.

2

BLACK AND WHITE AND TURNING GRAY

JAZZ AND RACE

BEN RATLIFF

There is no American popular music so well miscegenated as jazz, but I think we can still talk, in a very limited sense, and if we're careful, about black and white elements in it.

For example, Horace Silver's music from the 1950s and '60s—and the endless imitations it inspired—has obvious roots in black American identity. It uses percussiveness, vocalizations, call-and-response—the whole list of elements outlined by Olly Wilson in his essay "Black Music as an Art Form." There are younger musicians these days, too, who use elements of gospel and rhythm-and-blues oratory in their improvisations, like James Carter, Frank Lacy, Wycliffe Gordon, Antonio Hart, Eric Alexander, and Benny Green. These musicians—both black and white—use the shout in a controlled way, and their discourse depends on a visceral, transformative connection with the crowd.

On the other hand, the Boston/Berklee School musicians, from Gary Burton and Pat Metheny on through Kurt Rosenwinkel thirty years later, have used a heavily minor and nonblues mode of expression that accommodates a vastly greater number of white musicians than black musicians. I'm not sure of the ethnomusicological reasons for that, but it seems to be so.

Most jazz critics spend a lot of time trying not to say that a kind of music is "black" or "white," because those terms are severely limiting, as well as floppy, but also because a few critics have set up "white" and "black" as weaponlike notions to valorize what they like and ignore what they don't. In the past ten years—the post–Dinesh D'Souza era of cultural politics—some critics have come forward in print with their arguments that liberal historiography has strangulated the contributions of white musicians. On the opposite side, the ranks of critics who believe that jazz is black music and whites have a place there only by special invitation have winnowed to nearly nothing.

But let's leave that alone: I'm not particularly interested in who should get the credit for cool jazz, Dave Brubeck or Miles Davis. The fact is that race today means less and less—both in terms of the acceptability of a composer or musician to the "marketplace" of jazz, such as it is, and in terms of the music actually played. And as the music of Cuba, the Middle East, and Africa is incorporated with more accuracy and rigor into jazz, any divisions you might be able to crowbar between "black" and "white" jazz are looking more fraudulent.

What, racially speaking, is Brian Blade's music, for instance? It's made by a band that's roughly half-black and half-white. Blade is a black man from Shreveport, Louisiana, born in the early 1970s; his father was a minister in Shreveport's Zion Baptist church. In his teens he had to choose between tennis and music, both of which he excelled in. His literary tastes run to Sam Shepard and S. E. Hinton and Joni Mitchell. Miles Davis—who else?—opened him up aesthetically. There's some black gospel hymnody in Blade's music; there's some country music. There's a pedal steel guitar in the band, and a Boston-school jazz improviser, too. Yet the group is one of the best examples of the young jazz mainstream. It plays at the Village Vanguard; young musicians flock to see it.

This is not to say that jazz musicians live in a world beyond race. If you're a young black American musician playing jazz, chances are that you come from a supportive family, middle class or better, and that you have had a great deal of encouragement from your parents—to get you into magnet high schools, to send you to competitive colleges with music programs. It might well mean that you have a religious background, a "proper," goal-oriented way of looking at the world; jazz is not really a knockabout bohemian fantasy. For young white musicians—I am generalizing grandly—the picture is slightly different. Jazz, for whites, still packs some bohemian allure—complete with the idea that it's necessary to suffer and in doing so to adopt a new verbal language with the inflections of black Americans.

Perhaps the major lingering manifestation of this difference is the attitude toward getting in the van. Jazz has a tiny market, a tiny business support system. The best business model at the moment for keeping a band together comes from indie rock, the way R.E.M. and the Minutemen and now At the Drive-In have done it: living in a dented Econoline for twenty-three hours a day, booking yourself anyplace that will have you, coming out and trying to kill for one hour in a support-band slot. Medeski Martin and Wood did it this way: that's why the band has sold so many records. But it lives separated from the main line of jazz and operates within a mapped-out world of clubs and promoters for indie rock and jam bands. Most jazz groups don't. In addition, it seems to me that the average black American from the background that I've just outlined doesn't judge living in a van and playing divey college-town clubs an activity commensurate with the pride and propriety that his family has invested in him.

But if there's one truism about jazz, after all, it's that it allows for stereotypes to be defied. Think of Coleman Hawkins, the backbone of twentieth-century saxophone history. He was not a blues man, and his curiosity about altered harmony led him to make music that sounds like a precursor to academic-tinged modernism. Think of Lester Young and Lucky Thompson, who came up with new kinds of aesthetic virility in the tone and rhythm of their playing, neither of which are anybody's clichéd notion of blackness. Think of Teddy Wilson and Vernell Fournier—their styles were refinement itself, pared-down versions of virtuosity that left much to the imagination.

Race expresses itself most succinctly through vernacular culture, and jazz has almost left vernacular culture entirely; I love John Kouwenhoven's writings from the 1950s about how jazz takes a place next to comic strips, chewing gum, and skyscraper architecture, but these kinds of thoughts just aren't applicable anymore. The paradigm has shifted: in its lack of public support, its too-vaunted reputation, its recent character as a mostly educational entity, it's much closer to museum-vitrine culture than robust, mass-produced, nation-defining flotsam.

I often wish that that connection had not been lost. As indicators of a culture, rhythm is most powerful, then melody, and then harmony. Harmony has been on the ascendant in jazz since the 1970s; it's the area that, as plenty of musicians see it, hasn't been explored to death. Jazz harmony is science, and it isn't rooted in practical performance culture. It lifts us away from any basis in reality if we try to link it to race or cultural identity. And the rise of harmony as a priority in jazz composition is also, I think, the reason why jazz is so vastly unpopular now. A generation of jazz players is building a tradition of harmonically complicated music to be played for a negligible audience—forget about whether they're black or white.

The music itself of jazz, not only the bands, is well integrated. Many of the best bands of the last ten years have been racially mixed— including Dave Holland's, Greg Osby's (in certain versions), Leon Parker's, Branford Marsalis's, Dave Douglas's, and on and on; if these bands play in styles that you could call black music, they play in an equal number of styles that you couldn't. I doubt that in any of these cases the band-leaders are making conscious attempts to practice diversity in their hiring; they're just drawing from one mixed pool of jazz musicians who are all working on similar problems. That's impressive. It's enough to make you marvel at what a great country we have here.

Jazz's history of musical miscegenation was the thematic backbone of Ken Burns's recent *Jazz* series, where it probably got its best-ever popular retelling, despite its simplifications. Original Dixieland Jazz Band causes popular craze with noisy, caricatured approximation of black jazz: icky, shameful. Bix Beiderbecke and Louis Armstrong develop a mutual love for each other: wonderful. Young Dave Brubeck encounters old black man with slavery brand: a lifelong commitment to antiracism is born. Miles Davis hires Bill Evans, defends the right to play with musician of any race: the Defiant Ones! Burns's film stretched its thesis until the 1970s, at which point, in his version of events, the whole thing fell apart: the audience left, the joy left. What's really a shame is that he abandoned his racial theme, too: the film didn't get into today's race-crossing news in jazz. Jazz's future, it suggested, is high school kids reading freshly transcribed Ellington charts commissioned by Jazz at Lincoln Center. And that's part of it, no doubt. But I'm more interested in what will happen after those musicians have some ideas to rub together. At that level, the future of jazz is miscegenation.

Recently I've seen a popular American T-shirt that bears a list of racial denominations, vertically stacked and crossed out—white, black, Hispanic, Asian, et cetera. At the bottom, the only word that remains uncrossed is *human*. This sort of outlook—the most simpering expression of multiculturalism—ignores the fact that cultural differences do come from race. Race itself is a cultural construction, yes, OK. But what to make of the fact that white American teenagers, in their code of cool, speak in black American inflections? Are they speaking just as "people"? No: it's more specific than that. In Brazil, where I'm writing this, cultural origins are taken seriously. When a white musician appropriates something from Afro-Brazilian culture, it comes with specific cultural identification: Yoruban words and slogans of black consciousness are used. And these appropriations of blackness bring happiness: they're not oppositional postures, as Americans would understand them, attempts to put on a cloak of toughness or inscrutability.

I might wish for some improvement in the way white popular culture blacks itself up in America, but this is the way our miscegenation takes form; it's real, a part of our social history. Jazz, though, is a musical system of scales and chords and rhythm and increasingly built of wordless, theoretical subtlety. When a jazz musician appropriates a fraction of someone else's language—a Bud Powell, Charlie Parker, or Lennie Tristano line, a Paul Bley harmony, an Ornette Coleman melody or structure, a Keith Jarrett touch—it is rarely understood as a black or white thing.

To circle back to Brazil for a minute, I think that the reason its popular music still holds such incredible promise—and sometimes even delivers on it—is that smart musicians there are in love with the notion of laying vanguardist notions on top of regional music. America has vernacular culture, too: the blues, Gulf Coast R&B, gospel, country music, New York salsa, Sousa marches, the Mexican American music of the southwest. It is possible for jazz musicians to connect these with their own sense of high-art gamesmanship, and in the 1980s it happened a lot. So many musicians just cresting then had come through the tail end of the last live music era in America: they had played in R&B bands, like Henry Threadgill, Greg Osby, and Arthur Blythe; in gospel groups, like David Murray; in salsa, like Jerry Gonzales and the Fort Apache band. You could make a case that Wynton Marsalis is a product of the 1980s not because he was a glittery media phenomenon but in the same way that the aforementioned musicians were: his most consistent interest is in taking blues songs about trains and mutating them with arrangement effects.

In all these cases, it has been the transforming power of jazz to remake the vernacular culture of any race into vanguard culture. This is one of the major places where jazz and race intersect. Vanguard culture is for anyone (if not everyone), and jazz was the first American cultural expression to make this clear. So, to a certain extent, yes, the picture is rosy now: race doesn't matter in jazz; the jazz audience is enlightened; the battle is won.

But my major fear is that jazz will be overtaken by its most dangerous tendencies of conformity (and they've been there all along, despite what anyone may say about jazz being the language of freedom) and become a sort of deracinated monoculture: that there will evolve a standard of academic excellence in which you really can't tell what sort of background a musician is expressing. I think it's the fault of the growing jazz education sector, however perverse it may be to say so. The process of appreciating jazz and learning to play it can feel a bit like a public radio fund drive appeal: it is predicated on the notion that if you don't play it in the traditional way, and thus support its legitimacy, it will go away. But maybe to play it with the feeling that it may or may not go away—and with the feeling that it just doesn't matter—is to give it more credence as popular culture, to respect it more and believe in its longevity.

I long for jazz records that are as jolting as Garth Brooks's *Chris Gaines* experiment—a record that takes for granted that the audience knows the difference between the merest inflections of style in black and white styles of studio pop, and then twists them up together. That's hard to do in jazz, since jazz doesn't express itself much through majority styles. But when I hear certain musicians over seventy, like Von Freeman and Harold Ashby, with a regional and personal grain to their saxophone voices, I hear a sense of certitude that's missing among younger players. For these older players, jazz must still be a popular performing art in their minds—in the way that immigrants living in New York can still sometimes live in Managua or Hong Kong in their minds.

We do have polished oddball exceptions, like Cassandra Wilson and Bill Frisell. Wilson's *New Moon Daughter, Blue Light 'Til Dawn,* and *Traveling Miles* may not be jazz, by a strict definition, but they sound like black music. Frisell's albums—though they're often too precious for me—can use white American rural music ingeniously. Their albums of the last decade are prime examples of what the jazz record industry would like to turn jazz into. It's music that can be marketed via NPR and PBS, because it dovetails with a playful, refined, modernized sense of American culture. Nonesuch is the only label of sophisticated popular music for adults that has done well in the past decade, and jazz labels are reconfiguring themselves in its image, so we're going to see more artists like Wilson and Frisell, who make nearly nonidiomatic music with clear roots in jazz, blues, and country. In a sense, again, they are not jazz records. But they are jazz enough to ask you questions about what you value in jazz.

Is jazz dead when black people stop listening to it? I don't think so. But I do think that jazz is definitely moving away from its definition as a black art. This is impossible to quantify, but here are some observations from going to a few hundred jazz gigs a year: some of the best new jazz is coming out on labels like Fresh Sound and Palmetto that have almost no black musicians on their rosters. The black people you tend to see at clubs are middle-aged; very rarely are they under forty unless they're musicians themselves, supporting a friend or checking out the competition. In New York, the most fertile and adventurous small-club scenes for jazz—Smalls, the Cornelia Street Cafe, the Internet Cafe—are almost totally white. That's not to say they shun "black music": I once received an impassioned monologue by the proprietor of one of these places on the rightful dominance of the Negro rhythmic feel in jazz. It made you wonder why he didn't hire more black musicians, but that's a different issue entirely—it has more to do with personal relationships.

I have one other major barbell to unload: Latin music, inasmuch as it is making contributions to jazz, might be more of a life rope than we can even imagine, because when American jazz musicians come to it, it is already racially integrated in a different way than we're used to; and because, despite all its evolution, it has stronger ties to vernacular culture. Recent albums by Danilo Perez, Chick Corea, Avishai Cohen, Claudia Acuña, Papo Vasquez, David Sanchez, Los Hombres Calientes, and others are providing a framework, and they provoke a response in me that feels new: even when I don't particularly like the music, I think the cultural cross-fading within them comes right up front, strongly and admirably and suggestively.

Latin music evolved in Cuba and Brazil, among other places, as simultaneously an elite and a popular art form, which is the condition jazz always naturally aspired to. It obviously has roots both in dance and in religion; for these reasons it still has a sense of purpose, more so than jazz does. It has intertwining traditions of virtuosity and rural roughness, like jazz. And although jazz musicians, black and white, have been dipping into those traditions for an entire century—mostly Afro-Cuban and Brazilian—Latin music is neither black nor white. It represents a do-over: Americans can see it as free zone in which we can redefine what our race means or doesn't mean. The mestizo cultural ideal might pull along North American culture for a long time to come, and it makes sense that jazz, in spite of its tiny audience, will run at the front of the pack in this process.

TED GIOIA

Does any serious jazz musician really aim to sound "black" or "white"?

Frankly, I doubt it, although if one judged by what is written and said about the music, one would assume that this is a matter of obsessive concern to jazz players. I know that, during the course of many years of performing jazz, I have worried about many things—primarily harmony, melody, and rhythm. But fitting into some listener's racial stereotype has never been one of them.

Yes, I am certain that I rely on my "heritage" when I improvise, but that is a much different matter. The beauty of an art form—in contrast to our genetic pedigree—is that we can pick our parents, so to speak. Cal Tjader can choose Latin music as part of his heritage without identifying a drop of Latin blood in his veins. Andre Previn can claim an inheritance from Horace Silver. Stan Getz can select Lester Young as a father figure, who in turn finds his source of inspiration in Frankie Trumbauer. All this cuts across racial dividing lines. Hooray! Jazz stood out, at least for many decades, as one of the few arenas where some of us (maybe even most of us) could throw away the racial baggage that simmered throughout the rest of society and deal with each other through the unmediated channel of artistic collaboration.

Somehow we lost the thread. Instead of leading the rest of society, we have fallen far behind. The clamor of racial politics now resounds loudly in the jazz world. My advice to my colleagues: resist the temptation to fight in this battle, for both sides are losers.

I once met an Irish professor who spent a term teaching in Iowa. "What amazed me the most," he confided to me, "was what happened on Saint Patrick's Day. I was the only Irishman in this whole town, but everybody—absolutely everybody—was wearing green." Welcome to America—or, at least, America at its best—where every heritage is shared and every tradition is celebrated. Let the "racial identity police" worry about untangling the DNA strands. I prefer to focus on the festivities and green beer.

In the future, the jazz pedigrees will only grow more intertwined, more convoluted. Strong winds are blowing from Warsaw, Tokyo, Rio, Bombay, Dubai, Istanbul, Barcelona—everywhere and anywhere musicians congregate—and nothing encourages me more about the future of jazz than the cross-fertilization that this promises. Those of us stuck in the mind-set of "black" and "white" will miss the resulting rainbow that, in this instance, truly promises us a pot of gold.

K. LEANDER WILLIAMS

Once, when the Brazilian superstar Gilberto Gil was discussing the warm reception upper-class white Brazilians gave bossa nova, he was clear about the way "they claimed it, separated the parts, and took what [they felt] was cool enough and clean enough to be okay." But Gil didn't think it was proper to say Brazilian whites did this intentionally. "Cultural and social processes are always intricate and mysterious," he explained to Gene Santoro, "so [listeners] just reproduce the class concept or racial concept they've always known. They don't even have to be aware of it."

The paradigm Gil describes can easily be applied to jazz, even though it's hard to find anyone who writes about jazz's racial frissons in this way. Ben cites everything from racially motivated jazz critics to the differing perceptions black and white musicians might bring to rhythm, melody, and harmony, but as dead-on as much of this is, the key that would contextualize everything is still missing. Racial inequality and the persistent denial thereof generally govern the relationship between whites and non-whites all over the world; throughout jazz history, both real and perceived racial incongruities have been at the root of the gulf between musicians and audiences enamored of the same thing: hard blowing. For example, I'm sure it was easy for the young black musicians Ben spoke with to say that parental "pride and propriety" keeps them from getting in the van and touring like Medeski Martin and Wood, but as a young African American who has traversed some pretty hostile American byways, I'd be willing to wager that there are other reasons for their apprehension. Does anyone want to think about what three young black males in a beat-up Econoline—or even better, a brand spanking new one!—might encounter on the jazz trail across the good ol' U.S. of A.? Suffice it to say that they're probably better off with the racial profiling some critic hands them than the kind that comes from a jackbooted state trooper.

PETER MARGASAK

There are so many freely appropriated stylistic options available and at work now that matters of origin are fading away. In addition to what

Ben says about explorations of harmony representing the music's final frontier, I'd add the heightened interest in thoughtful hybridization. Jazz is itself a hybrid, of course, but it can go way further. Wilson and Frisell may make NPR-friendly blends, but I'm fairly convinced that such fusions offer vast and exciting possibilities. Everyone from Leon Parker to Chris Speed to Jeff Parker to Vijay Iyer to Danilo Perez has been vibrantly bridging disparate worlds, not to merely add some exotic melodic and harmonic ideas to the pot, but to create a new dish altogether. It's no longer about mixing black and white culture; every color is involved now. As Ben suggests, it may not be jazz, at least in the "mainstream" notion of it, but it sure seems to hold more excitement for me than another set of straight-up hard bop, no matter how well played or harmonically complex.

The most salient racial matter exists in the business end of things. With well-paid gigs and good recording contracts at a premium now more than ever, I think a perceived (and in some cases, real) racism is hard to escape. The have-nots will always search for motivations behind their deprivation, and I think race is a default choice. But as younger players increasingly ignore race lines—both stylistically and in whom they work with—perhaps this sort of insidious resentment will fade too, though few things speak louder than an empty wallet.

WILL FRIEDWALD

One thing that Ben's essay reminded me of was how much of what we think about in jazz as a racial issue is probably better described as a geographical issue—as Richard Sudhalter points out, jazz may be a primarily black music, but in the early 1920s, white musicians in New Orleans were playing with greater swing and jazz feeling than black musicians in New York. Race was not the issue: New Orleans musicians were just closer to the source. The New Orleans style is almost totally geographically defined—in that particular city, it isn't so much a question of black and white but black and Italian, as opposed to WASP or Jewish or any other variety of whiteness (or nonblackness). In fact, it's been said that Italians were lumped together in the same class as blacks and Creoles in turn-of-the-century New Orleans—they were regarded as having more in common with those races than with "ordinary" white people. When I listen to New Orleans jazz, I certainly don't think I could tell the difference between black and nonblack musicians other than because I recognize individual styles: I can tell Irving Fazola from Johnny Dodds just because I know what they sound like. (At some point, it might be fascinating to see if there's an Italian American strain of jazz and follow it up through more modern players such as Charlie Ventura and Flip Phillips.) But, ultimately, style is more a matter of experience (coming out of such factors as geography) than skin color.

K. LEANDER WILLIAMS

Will—if only you were right. I commend your loyalty to Sudhalter but, as usual, his comments betray a desire to continue his one-man war against what Ben has accurately described as liberal historiography. It seems to me that experience can be governed by skin color as much as by geography. I mean, you probably can't tell the difference between East Coast and West Coast rap, but I'll bet you think that both come out of experiences that have much to do with being black. You're right, of course.

Sure, some white bands started off in closer proximity to New Orleans than some black ones, but does that *really* mean anything? For obvious reasons, I'd just rather listen to Armstrong and Jelly Roll. Then, I wanna listen to Duke; then maybe Eddie Lang and Joe Venuti. It's like the difference between genius and commerce.

JIM MACNIE

I'm down with Kelvin's thought that African American improvisers barnstorming this here country in an Econoline is probably trouble waiting to happen. Hassles, be they physical or psychological, are one of the reasons to be judicious about your career path—even if you're a star of sorts. I remember a conversation with Josh Redman about getting the hairy eyeball in an antique store while killing time before a gig in a quaint (read: monied) Rhode Island town—that's town, not city. Meaning insulated, not integrated. The scene? Local arts center, fair amount of publicity for the gig, Redman and crew browsing some trinket house adjacent to the venue. All-white staff, well intentioned and surely wanting to move some of their alleged artifacts, sniffing around a foursome of young black men, suspicious of completely ordinary moves. Nothing vicious, just vibe, vibe, vibe. And when the guys came upon some "darkie" memorabilia? Well...I'll move along.

The next thought to squeeze through the synapses has to do with another of Ben's ideas—that the music's creators can be construed as foreign to their listeners because of jazz's "lack of public support, and character as a mostly educational entity." It's something I try to get to (a bit less articulately) in my jazz repertory piece [on page 87]. Now neutered as a vernacular art, jazz can't claim status as a common or familiar entity; it's highbrow, even though it allegedly invites all to participate in its wonder. That breach reduces the chance of racial interaction—call it a learning process if you want to get clinical—between blacks and whites and nurtures the kind of paranoia and stereotyping that Alice the Antiquer showed Redman and associates. Remove something from the daily language and you'll sustain misconceptions about its character. Gotta be in it to win it—or something close to that.

Last thought: I don't want jazz to be a "deracinated monoculture" (Ben again) either. Bring on the pan-Caribbean cadences, steel guitars, twin fiddles, Chadbournian plinks and plunks, or ECMish tidepool diddley doo—if someone can creatively integrate the stuff, I want a free copy in the mail. But when Peter Margasak reports about "matters of origin floating away," I feel blue. Jazz is a massive African American cultural achievement, and whether we're talking Toni Morrison's fiction or Max Roach's sense of rhythm, African American achievements deserve as much trumpeting as possible—the playing field ain't never been level in the U.S.A. Part of the reason I started to write about jazz was the fact that McCoy Tyner gigged in Providence back in the late 1970s and the daily paper didn't make a peep before or after. Yet the headlines around that time kept harping on a string of breaking-and-enterings in a low-income, predominantly black neighborhood. It's all advertising,

I thought, and the fuckers are in the curatorial seat. Let's not forget where the stuff came from.

JOHN F. SZWED

The mention of Sudhalter's *Lost Chords* gives me an opportunity to comment on the persistence of efforts to deny African and African American contributions to world culture. We are aware of the perniciousness of such projects when they surface as heavily publicized books from right-wing think tanks, but less likely to see their damage when they come from our own ranks. In academia, for example, there are those who would deny any recognition of the distinctive black contribution to jazz as a form of essentialist thinking, that is, allegedly, as an attribution of timeless and fixed characteristics to people of color. Some, looking to get past racism, tell us that this is a new age and nobody should think in racial terms any more. Others (Ken Burns, for example), touting a form of American exceptionalism, tell us that jazz is purely American and owes nothing to Africa. And then there are those who tell us that Europe provided the melody and harmony of jazz, and Africa the rhythm. Sudhalter seems to embody all of the above. His book is presented as a statement on the neglect of a distinctive and creative "white presence" in jazz. As such it's a real contribution (even if some of the musicians he discusses have never suffered from omission). But he conflates race ("color") and culture in order to portray anyone as a racist who makes a claim for black preeminence in jazz.

STUART NICHOLSON

It's surprising that Albert Murray's book *Stomping the Blues,* first published in 1976 and enormously influential in some jazz circles, has not been mentioned so far in this discussion. In many ways it sets the agenda for the debate over the current state and future direction of jazz, which amounts to a struggle over who "owns" jazz history because of the legitimacy this ownership confers.

In the book, Murray attempts to define jazz in terms of past verities. Crucial to his definition of jazz are a "blues" sensibility (a metaphor for *black*), "swing," and restoring jazz's primal relationship to dance, all of which become central tenets in deciding what is and what is not jazz. In addition, Murray asserts that white musicians "are not native to the idiom" of jazz.

Just how strongly Murray feels about this is exemplified by his comments on the famous photograph, displayed in the book, that became the subject of the Jean Bach film documentary *A Great Day in Harlem,* in which black and white musicians line up for a huge who's who–style photo in front of a Harlem brownstone. Murray identifies the black musicians as "first line"—a New Orleans phrase for musicians. A line of young black kids, doing what kids do and wanting to be a part of things, sit in the front. Murray refers to them as "second line"—New Orleans–speak for the followers of the band. White musicians (Gerry Mulligan, Gene Krupa, Pee Wee Russell, Bud Freeman, etc.) are referred to as "third line."

As is well known, writer Stanley Crouch is a Murray "disciple." According to the Ken Burns book tie-in to the documentary series *Jazz,* cowritten with Geoffrey Ward, trumpeter Wynton Marsalis, the most high-profile jazz musician of recent times, soaked up all the jazz history he could "with help from Albert Murray and Stanley Crouch."

On the one hand, Murray & Co.'s ambitions—to establish jazz as an art form with its own "cultural capital" of artistic tradition—are highly laudable. But on the other, in establishing that jazz had a long period of evolution analogous to that of Western art, they seem far from happy with jazz's European (white) connections.

Crouch's views support Murray's thesis. He considers the late Bill Evans, perhaps the most influential pianist in recent jazz history, as "all Debussy," and in his essay "Sketches of Pain" for *The New Republic* he famously lambasted white arranger Gil Evans's arrangements for Miles Davis's seminal albums *Miles Ahead, Porgy and Bess,* and *Sketches of Spain* as "high-level television music." As the writer Gene Lees pointed out in *Cats of Any Color,* the fact that any "white musician could have a major influence on jazz simply does not fit [their] political agenda," or indeed the kind of revisionism now underway.

Following the fragmentation of jazz into a number of subcultures from the 1950s on—"cool" or West Coast jazz, Third Stream (jazz and classical music), hard bop, modal jazz, free jazz, jazz-rock, and so on—defining "the real jazz" becomes a powerful weapon, and the way Murray achieves this is through exclusion, thus denying contemporary developments in the narrative of jazz history.

Murray's assertion is that if the word *jazz* means anything, then some central essence of its definition must remain constant throughout its development from its prehistory until today. For him and Crouch, Marsalis renews that link in the present. As a musician, Marsalis is a steadfast custodian of a jazz within clearly proscribed boundaries—boundaries identical to Murray's definition of jazz. Not for nothing was one of his band tours called *Sweet Swing Blues on the Road*.

No one would disagree with the central assertion that jazz began as a wonderful African American phenomenon and that all the great innovations were prompted by black initiative. It's just that Murray & Co. appear to be going that extra mile by implying that only African Americans can play the "real jazz"—a view that ignores jazz's actual history and does the music a disservice by asserting it has not grown beyond its roots.

If jazz is black America's gift to the world, then surely it is right to question a new orthodoxy in which a "third line" of participants is deemed to lack "idiomatic authenticity." Orthodoxies create insiders and outsiders, and the kind of orthodoxy that now seems to be looming looks likely to create more outsiders than insiders. Even worse, we are on dangerous ground indeed if jazz becomes a battleground to right the wrongs of racial injustices down the ages. The joy of jazz, surely, is that it is a truly democratic music; but what is in the wind seems anything but that.

GREG TATE

To paraphrase Art Blakey: no jazz, no America. Discussions of jazz and race tend to be over whether white people matter with respect to the artistic development of the art form. There are hardliners on both sides of the issue's racial divide—not surprising, considering how much race matters and will continue to matter in American society. As the cultural ground has shifted under the feet of jazz's pro-black advocates over the past couple of decades, the defense of jazz as a Black Thing has largely been quieted by the realization that, like rock 'n' roll, it is a black thing that few African Americans give a damn about. The fate of jazz has become so much the province of white scholars, critics, and fans as to drag the subject from the ironic to the sublimely ridiculous. A friend of mine is of the opinion that jazz died when black people stopped listening to it. Cornetist, composer, and conceptualist Graham Haynes believes that the jazz era, as defined by the generations who produced swing, bebop, and the avant-garde, is over. The last twenty years in jazz have produced a bevy of technically brilliant musicians—black, white, Asian, and European—who have not so much re-created the music in their own image as lent hope to the belief that intellectually fecund and musically sophisticated young people will continue to find in jazz an expressive and cognitive lodestone on which to sharpen their wits, wiles, and weltanschauung. The historical record— and Ken Burns—tells us jazz was predominantly nurtured and developed by the African American community and African American innovators. It also tells us that profound statements as to the nature of the jazz endeavor have been made by certain hip white cats on occasion, too.

The overriding question is whether American jazz has a vital, creative future if none of the next generation of inner-city African Americans are encouraged to bring the wit, ingenuity, and rhythmic acuity of their hip-hop surround into the fold.

K. LEANDER WILLIAMS

It's always a bit unnerving to me to hear folks go on about black people not caring about jazz. That's bullshit, plain and simple, but to deconstruct it you have to do some math. Statistically, jazz receives patronage from a higher percentage of the total African American population than it does from the total white one, but here's the rub:

although conservative polemicists would like us to believe that the lack of planned parenthood in the ghetto is helping change whites from majority to minority, there are still more white people in America than black people. *Way more.* That's why white rockers you've never heard of can pack stadiums on these package megatours—the now-defunct Lollapalooza thing was the blueprint—while black acts you've heard of can't. Factor in how little disposable income there is outside the non-athlete, non–arts biz black population, and it's easy to see why there are so few black faces at festivals and jazz concerts. It's probably true, though, that jazz booking policies would be quite different if the black turnout increased.

STUART NICHOLSON

Jazz as an art form, created by and evolving through the initiative and genius of African Americans, remains America's great gift to the world. It was, as Greg says, a black thing. But it has become so broad and diverse it can no longer be changed by the revelations of one great man, as it had in the past by an Armstrong, a Parker, a Coltrane, a Coleman, or a Miles Davis. With no single musician dominating the current era in the way these geniuses did in the past, the task of moving jazz into the twenty-first century has passed to diverse individual contributors. "I hear people everywhere saying the trouble with our times is that we have no great leaders anymore," wrote Laurens Van der Post. "If we look back we always had them. But it seems to me there is a very profound reason why there are no great leaders anymore. The message is clear...every man must be his own leader. He knows enough not to follow other people." Nowhere is this truer than in jazz, where jazz education—knowledge—proliferates. Every art form must grow beyond its roots to flourish. With the globalization of culture, change is happening at a bewildering pace at all levels of society, and this seems to highlight a dichotomy in American jazz between clinging to a paradigm of what it used to be (when social, cultural, and economic forces very different from today's may have provided the tensions that helped shape the music) or acknowledging an emerging worldview in which not only African American but American influence per se plays a lesser role in contributing to the music's destiny.

PETER WATROUS

The curious thing about race in jazz, as in certain personal relationships, is that it can be both everything and nothing. Race is the gigantic mountain one has to take on in both instances. And then, after moments of hard work, or the lightning strike of insight, race can be nothing: one is left with oneself, dealing with the hard problems of playing jazz or living with someone. Race disappears, replaced by, well, quotidian problems.

But then race comes back and, as anybody who has played jazz knows, there is a black approach to playing that one doesn't always hear in white musicians, or at least not so often. Music that comes out of the church, out of the blues—cultural areas that are harder to access for white people than black—has a distinct sound, perhaps an increasingly archaic one at that. Again, it has to be dealt with.

So by the time one is a mature musician, or person, one has come to some accommodation, both personal and cultural, about one's relationship to race. What I love about jazz, and the heinous golden triangle of the Americas—the mixture of indigenous, African, and European cultures—is that it is an experiment that hasn't come to a conclusion yet, though that quite possibly can't be said about much of jazz. In the rest of the musics of the Americas, the new is evident: mulattoism is the future. It's jazz's past, its present, but only maybe its future. As Ben optimistically points out, if jazz keeps moving with its assimilation and deepening knowledge of Afro-Cuban and Afro-Brazilian music, it too can keep its role as one of the important musics of the next century. I have my doubts, though. Sometimes even a cultural friction as central as racial tension can spend itself.

3

THE SONG OF THE BODY ELECTRIC

JAZZ-ROCK

STUART NICHOLSON

All self-respecting politicians in the Western world today, whether of the left or of the right, blame the 1960s for their nations' perceived moral decline. The decade when, according to Philip Larkin, "sexual intercourse began" is now held responsible for everything from graffiti to one-parent families. In jazz, however, the 1960s are held accountable for something far worse. This was the decade when jazz and rock got into bed and produced an illegitimate child called fusion, a creature every self-respecting jazz critic loves to hate. In fact, during the conservative 1980s and '90s it became distinctly fashionable to stop the clock in 1969, when electric jazz was ushered in by Miles Davis, start it again in 1982 with the arrival of that latter-day model of acoustic rectitude Wynton Marsalis, and pretend the fusion of jazz and rock never happened—not least because Marsalis, the highest profile jazz musician of recent times, saw things that way.

Yet jazz has always been a synthesis of many elements, something all histories of early jazz agree on. As Albert Murray has pointed out, in early jazz, "everything was turned into a dance beat," including "Gregorian chant, Christmas carols, Scotch [sic] highlanders' songs, German music, Italian, march music," to which might be added numerous vernacular musics including Negro spirituals, work and folk songs, ragtime, minstrel music, brass band music and blues—freely mixed with elements from hymns, popular songs, and popular classics of the day.

Jazz is a pluralistic music, and has eluded definition throughout its history because it has been in a state of becoming something else. Jazz is a story of adventurous exploration, a perpetual discovery and exploitation of new musical and expressive sources. Even as early as 1914, W. C. Handy's "St. Louis Blues" included an unambiguous *habanera* section, indicative of how omnivorously jazz consumed anything around it that might broaden its range. "We must acknowledge the fact that jazz music has always borrowed from other sources and changed the rules as it expanded and moved on," said drummer Jack DeJohnette in 1993.

This practice of appropriation is an important, if seldom commented on, feature of a music that already comprised a diversity of elements drawn from a variety of sources both from within and without the African Diaspora. The basic New Orleans repertoire was expanded by songs from Tin Pan Alley and Broadway in the 1920s and '30s, and this dialogue continued, albeit covertly, through the appropriation of chord sequences of popular tunes as a basis for many of the new bebop melodies in the 1940s, even though these new melodies consciously distanced the music from older "swing" styles and from a mass audience. By the mid-1960s jazz had appropriated Cuban rhythms, elements from classical music, modal principles, exotic scales from the Near East and India, and Brazilian rhythms.

This dialogue with other musical forms echoes the discourse between mass culture and modernist high culture since the mid-nineteenth century, with modernism appropriating whatever elements it needed for experiment and articulation. Jazz, an exemplary expression of the modernist impulse in American culture, merely continued this practice; yet when jazz turned to rock music in the mid-1960s to broaden its expressive base, it became the most controversial move in jazz history.

In all movements in the arts, it is usually the first flush of creativity that produces the greatest works, which are usually confined to just a few imaginative revolutionaries. So too in jazz-rock—only the revolutionaries were quickly buried by the foot soldiers. The shock announcing the new quickly ceased to be shocking as the music was mainstreamed from the margins and homogenized for the widest possible consumption by the record companies—precipitated by a rise of some 200 percent in recording costs, primarily through a shortage of polyvinyl chloride, a petroleum derivative known more commonly as vinyl. While spiraling costs were reducing company profitability, margins were being squeezed all the way down the line.

When it came to recording jazz, record producers became wary of fulfilling their commitment to the music unless it included some sort of "populist" slant. For example, Barney Kessel recorded *Hair*, Paul Desmond recorded "Bridge over Troubled Water," and both Duke Ellington and Count Basie recorded Beatles numbers. Gone were the free and easy days of the 1950s, when companies were more inclined to follow their instincts—now producers were less inclined to take chances, conscious of the marketing decisions behind every release. Consequently, many jazz musicians were forced to reassess their artistic directions along the lines of socioeconomic reality.

By 1975, the artistic promise held out by the eclecticism inherent in jazz-rock had surrendered to commercial homogenization. The dominant nonjazz elements of the jazz-rock equation no longer came from the creative side of rock, but from pop music with simple melodic hooks and currently fashionable dance beats. Similarly, a lot of musicians saw the opportunity for what they perceived as rock-style capital gains and leaped aboard a fast accelerating bandwagon following the commercial success of Herbie Hancock's *Headhunters* in 1973. What had begun as jazz-rock was now becoming known as jazz-rock fusion, or simply "fusion," and the ledger of major record-company signings from around this time is littered with names who ultimately failed to make their mark in any significant way: Dexter Wansel, Rodney Franklin, John Blair, Walt Bolden, Hilary and Janne Schaffer, and so on.

At this point I would like to draw a distinction between jazz-rock—the music of the early "revolutionaries" such as Fourth Way, Count's Rock Band, Miles Davis, The Tony Williams Lifetime, the first edition of the Mahavishnu Orchestra, and Weather Report—and "fusion," or instrumental pop-jazz, which followed around 1973. It is an important distinction to make, not least because many creative jazz musicians today—such as John Scofield, Pat Metheny, Bill Frisell, Wayne Krantz, and Mike Stern—seek to make it. These players say their music is empowered by the early jazz-rock experimenters and make a point of distancing themselves from the term *fusion*, which has now assumed pejorative associations.

Today fusion, often referred to in its present-day mutation as "smooth jazz" (variously marketed as quiet storm, lite jazz, hot-tub jazz, or yuppie jazz), has taken up residence on FM radio. Its place in the music marketplace has grown so large it fills the jazz viewfinder, blotting out jazz-rock and distorting its achievements. In responding to commercial logic, fusion all but turned an art form back into a commodity by allowing itself to be shaped by the requirements of commerce. Consequently jazz-rock has fallen into critical disfavor to such an extent that it has become fashionable to write off the whole genre—a classic case of throwing the baby out with the bathwater.

No one would consider evaluating the Swing Era in terms of Kay Kyser, Blue Barron, Jan Garber, Art Kassel, Tommy Tucker, Abe Lyman, Fred Waring, or Anson Weeks. Yet this is precisely the case with jazz-rock, which today is perceived in terms of Kenny G, Najee, The Yellowjackets, The Rippingtons, Kirk Whalum, and Spyro Gyra—at the expense of its true innovators.

Today the main thrust of jazz—that is to say, where major record company activity has centered, what "jazz radio" chooses to present, and the predominant style in most of New York's jazz clubs—is a kind of retro jazz that orbits the hard-bop style of the 1950s and early '60s. Given a considerable profile by Wynton Marsalis in the 1980s, it is now being perpetuated in a sort of pre-Nietzschean notion of eternal recurrence by young jazzers playing in the adopted voices of yesteryear's posthumous heroes.

It is as if the jazz clock has stopped. Jazz has become a museum of older styles and tried-and-tested methods of articulation. Walking into a New York jazz club in 2001 has become no different from what it was forty years before—"There were moments in his set when it seemed we were live at the Village Vanguard, circa 1961," recently enthused one well-known New York critic over a retro jazzer.

In contrast, jazz-rock renewed the cycle of change in jazz at the end of the 1960s and has continued to evolve through the 1980s and '90s and into the present day in a way that other areas of jazz, with the exception of the downtown experimenters, have not. (I have included the music of the downtown experimenters in this discussion since many of their experiments are empowered by the spirit of early jazz-rock—with their use of electric tone colors, non-"straight ahead" rhythms, and an inclusive approach to other musical genres.)

Perhaps the true potential for the future of jazz lies in the legacy of jazz-rock. Initially rock offered a new rhythmic backdrop whose cohesion was a fresh basis for jazz improvisation. In bop the cymbals had carried the basic rhythmic pulse, while in jazz-rock it went back to the drums since, at high volume levels, cymbals allowed little definition to the subdivisions of the beat, dissolving into a blanket of sound. Crossing this rhythmic Rubicon opened the way in quick succession to a new complexity indebted to James Brown (every instrument is a drum), world music influences, and a whole lot more. The rhythmic unit that had served jazz since its beginnings as a provincial Southern music was seen as dated, the sort of thing your parents listened to— "Hey, you hep cats, dig that c-r-a-z-y beat," cries one rock fan as he passes a jazz club, and his friends collapse to the pavement, crippled by mirth.

By the early 1970s jazz improvisation, enacted against the backdrop of the new electric tone colors ushered in by the rock age, suggested a future of considerable potential. As in the past, any sea change in jazz has been accompanied by a rhythmic revolution—but this time the revolution became a work in progress. Jazz-rock set in sway a hunt for new, interesting rhythms to invigorate compositional forms. And while much jazz-rock was based on simple musical structures such as vamps, ostinatos, and modes, musicians such as Wayne Shorter and Joe Zawinul were exploring ad hoc compositional forms of considerable sophistication—indeed, nowhere in contemporary jazz, for example, is there a corpus of work to equal theirs in breadth, imagination, and diversity.

Equally important, jazz-rock realigned jazz alongside popular culture, a position it has historically strayed from at its peril. It seems as
soon as jazz begins to desert its vernacular roots it is in danger of failing to interact with the social and musical environment that gives it its
relevance to a time and place in history. Jazz-rock set a new musical
agenda for change as free jazz was foundering on the discovery that
total freedom is in itself ultimately limiting. Like jazz itself, jazz-rock
was never a static genre with clearly defined boundaries, but a genre in
constant flux.

Examples of this in recent times include guitarist Pat Metheny, who
explores bold ad hoc compositional forms using a variety of rhythms
and electric tone colors on "The Roots of Coincidence" (from *Imagi-
nary Day,* 1997). Ingeniously appropriating rhythms from modern club
culture, he produces an impressive contemporary composition that
speaks of its time in a way that retro jazz does not. Medeski Martin
and Wood have pushed freeform composition to its limit with their
long, inspired rhythmic jams, yet are resolutely contemporary for
all that, claiming a huge audience on the jam-band circuit and showing that uncompromising improvisation (their 2001 album *The Dropper* incorporates free jazz inspired by Sun Ra) can be relevant to young
audiences when the music is of its time and not a re-creation of the
past.

One of the more impressive albums of recent years was Peter Apfelbaum's *Signs of Life,* which convincingly mixes world music and jazz
through the creative prism of his Hieroglyphics Ensemble. Using elements drawn from Yoruba praise singing, Gnawa music of Morocco,
Bambara music of Mali, reggae music, rock music, free jazz, and straight-
ahead jazz, the level of intrigue and logic of his compositions prompted
Phil Elwood to dub Apfelbaum "a genius." He may well be, but he is a
prophet unheard in his own land.

Since Michael Dorf opened the doors of the Knitting Factory in
New York in March 1987 and made it the main focus of the downtown
scene, many important musicians have emerged from it, not least John
Zorn, Bobby Previte, Bill Frisell, Don Byron, and Dave Douglas. They,
along with a host of other talented players, expropriate and transform
practices, fragments, and signifiers and relocate them within their own

highly individual expression. It is this appropriation of references decontextualized by juxtaposition that creates the "new." In particular, these musicians do not try to legitimize themselves by referring to the past like the somewhat self-righteous retro jazzers of the last decade or so. Yet for all its potential, the sheer stylistic diversity of the music bundled under the "downtown" catchall has meant its impact has been restricted to the recognition an individual player might receive, rather than the collective force of a community of similarly oriented and competing artists who have produced a single coherent style.

This contrasts with several emergent strands of European jazz beginning to spill across the Continent that are not only pleasing the critics but the public as well. The momentum for fresh innovation, the sine qua non of modernism, has become irresistible. With American jazz's preoccupation with its past has come a failure to acknowledge that the music is now so broad and diverse it has finally outgrown its country of birth, and that its stewardship is now no longer an exclusive American preserve.

In Europe there is a widespread belief that American jazz in the tradition of the great African American pioneers has now reached creative exhaustion. Many European jazz musicians have become disenchanted, even bored, with the sounds they hear from across the Atlantic. "I think American jazz somehow has really stopped, maybe in the late 1970s, early '80s," says the highly praised Norwegian pianist Bugge Wesseltoft. "I haven't heard one interesting American record in the last twenty years. It's like a museum, presenting stuff that's already been done."

Ever since the ragtime era, European jazz has largely marched in step to whatever developments were coming out of America, its musicians striving to keep abreast of successive shocks announcing the new. But with the American jazz scene pausing to explore its past, Europeans have increasingly been going their own way, seeing little value in following the Americans by performing in the adopted voices of jazz's posthumous heroes of the 1950s and early '60s.

"In Norway, once you reach a certain point, you are encouraged to find your own voice," Wesseltoft continues. "I was taught it is no good copying Bud Powell or Bill Evans, there are already hundreds of musicians in America who do that. We want to find our own voice, that speaks of where we come from. I haven't grown up in New York, so I see things differently. That's what it's all about. We go our own way and define our own styles."

Wesseltoft, together with fellow pianist Esbjorn Svensson and trumpeter Nils Petter Molvaer, are among several Euro jazz musicians (such as Eivind Aarset from Norway; Malik Mezzadri, Laurent de Wilde, Julien Lorau, and St. Germain from France; Britain's Courtney Pine and the Cinematic Orchestra; and Dutch group Michael Borstlap Meets Soulvation) producing critically acclaimed albums that are selling in the tens of thousands. These musicians are linked by an affinity with the sounds emerging from contemporary European underground club culture. "I like the minimalistic grooves of European House, very trancey, which you can easily relate to African music," says Molvaer. "I work with delays to make the rhythm float, so to speak. Some of the offbeats in rhythms like 7/8 and 9/16 have roots in an old tradition of ethnic musics, which I try and relate to the year 2001."

Combining contemporary rhythms with jazz improvisation is a step as obvious as Miles Davis appropriating the sounds and rhythms of rock in the 1960s and allowing change to evolve from that construct. Back then, Davis had no interest in competing with past achievements, which, in effect, is precisely what the jazz mainstream is now doing. Of course, there have been similar experiments combining jazz with rap and hip hop, but the results were generally indigestible and lacked any kind of subtlety, thus allowing the continued rise and rise of hard bop—to all intents and purposes the revivalist jazz of the twenty-first century.

Today, this new generation of young musicians is reflecting a twenty-first-century jazz, as inimical to its time as swing or bop was to theirs, with jazz musicians fulfilling the role they used to: making art from pop. It's not what jazz was, it's what it's now become, and suddenly it's sounding subversive, with young audiences queuing around the block to hear it—which may be a lot healthier for the future of the music than learning about it on PBS or in the classroom.

No one is suggesting this new European jazz is somehow better than American jazz, or that it is even somehow progress—indeed maybe the price of mixing artistic and technological media and breaking down boundaries between high and mass art styles means the artistic experiences of today will end up as the consumer products of tomorrow, as *innovative* and *new* replace the term *avant-garde*. Nevertheless, whatever this future does hold, Europe seems on course to capture it. "It has seemed like it was going to happen for years," says Svensson. "I think now it is. Europe is going to be the place for jazz. We're ready now. We like to sound different."

TED GIOIA

I share the belief that jazz critics have tended to be overly hostile toward attempts to fuse jazz and rock music. Jazz has always maintained an intimate relationship with popular music. Why should this change? Jazz listeners who want to take an elitist attitude should recall that only a few years ago our own cherished music was subject to derision from many highbrow critics. I feel strongly that the willingness of jazz musicians to beg, borrow, and steal from other styles and idioms is a great virtue, one that should be encouraged, not scorned.

On the other hand, I must admit that much of this fusion music falls short of its potential. I am fairly receptive to rock music in general—I may be one of the few jazz historians who is not ashamed to admit that the Beatles, Stevie Wonder, and Brian Wilson were as important in shaping my aesthetic tastes as were Coltrane, Dolphy, and Rollins. Yet only a small percentage of the fusion records I have heard have moved me. It is perhaps worth noting that I am usually more impressed by the rock players who have embraced jazz than by the jazz musicians who have tried to assimilate rock. This was true even during the supposed "great era" of jazz-rock fusion. Let me be honest about my own preferences: I would rather listen to Joni Mitchell than to Al Jarreau; I would favor Frank Zappa over Larry Coryell, Jimi Hendrix over Lee Ritenour; I would rather hear Blood, Sweat & Tears than the Yellowjackets; I would give the nod to Steely Dan over Spyro Gyra; I vote for Sting over Grover Washington. I would even pay cold cash to attend an ELP concert long before I would buy a ticket for the Rippingtons. If this is heresy for a jazz writer, so be it.

I suspect that my biases are due to an ineradicable suspicion that rock players have typically embraced jazz for artistic reasons, while jazz players have more often been tempted by the financial implications of rock music. Jazz, after all, is the "music of unemployment," in the words of Frank Zappa. No sane rock musician adds jazz to the mix in the hopes of making more money. In contrast, rock 'n' roll presents the jazz musician with a lucrative business proposition, and this has more often corrupted than inspired.

The upshot of this, in my opinion, is that jazz-rock fusion has not yet tapped its full potential. The jazz players who best succeed in achieving this will be those who forget crossing over and hitting the charts and focus instead on the artistic potential of this fusion. Also, it is possible, even likely, that rock musicians may take the lead in this process. This whole area of exploration strikes me as presenting an exciting prospect for the future, one every bit as promising today as when Miles launched the fusion revolution over a generation ago.

K. LEANDER WILLIAMS

Because it shares blues roots with jazz, rock has never been as distant a relative to swing and bop as some would have us believe. What's most interesting about the rift between the two musics is what it tells us about the line between the iconoclastic and the ordinary: it's not always where we think it is. The rock revolution led many people to proclaim jazz dead long before inventive musicians were through with it, and that frustration over perceived obsolescence led many jazz folk to cut themselves off from the future as it was expressed in rock. Too bad: if you let that frustration simmer a bit, you end up with Wynton Marsalis. Whenever I run into someone unwilling to accept the idea of the blues as an evolving continuum stretching from swing to hip-hop and beyond, I can't help remembering what

Sidney Bechet used to say: "You've got to be in the sun, to feel the sun."

Of course, even many jazzers who claim to embrace rock don't necessarily feel the sun, either. One thing that has hurt jazz as a whole—and jazz fusion in particular—is the kind of misguided emphasis on "sophistication" that generally leads jazzers to condescend to rock and other musics. Dance beats and rock rhythms are much more deceptive and mysterious than they seem, which is why it's just not enough to take some lackluster groove and run all kinds of "complex" chords and substitutions over it as so many jazzers do. The musicians who've made the most sense out of the mix—Miles, Hendrix, Steely Dan, Ornette/Blood Ulmer/Shannon Jackson, Fela Kuti, August Darnell, John Lurie, Sonny Sharrock—generally understood that true musical synthesis cannot be achieved if all the musics in play aren't respected.

JOHN F. SZWED

I've heard most of the Euro players you mention, Stuart, and find them interesting, though I admit I like them more for their eclecticism than for what they actually play. Incidentally, two names that seem to me progenitors of that music are Jon Hassell and Frank Zappa. (I know that you like the Zappa band with drummer Chad Wackerman, as do I, but I always felt that the band with Vinnie Colaiuta was even more persuasive—that floating beat-without-a-beat is still amazing to hear.) But as for those continuing the jazz-rock tradition, I'm drawn to some of the English drum and bass people, especially 4 Hero on *Parallel Universe* and Spring Hill Jack on *68 Million Shades.*

Incidentally, the problem with electronics is that it is hard to resist using the latest gear, which always seems so cool when you first use it but invariably becomes dated within five years by newer stuff. What's remarkable about the 1970s Miles Davis recordings is how fresh they still sound, in part because of his relatively restrained use of electronics.

BEN RATLIFF

Regarding the band that sounded like something from the Vanguard in 1961: there are real-world issues here. It's a given that if you see a lot of jazz, you see a lot of Vanguard-in-'61isms (especially if we're talking about Coltrane at the Vanguard in '61). Sometimes if the sound and conviction are in place, it's just not right for a critic to use the "you're not playing anything *new!*" sledgehammer.

Newness—as in music that has never been heard before—is a very tricky idea. I don't trust it much anymore. I think about what someone's trying to do, and whether he's achieving it with any measure of style; I also think about the originality of a personal voice, which sometimes results in newness, sometimes semi-newness, sometimes barely detectable newness. Talk about throwing the baby out with the bathwater: look, which of us would say that Charles Lloyd is useless because he owes something to John Coltrane? I've heard sets of his that owed the world to Coltrane, but this man has a sound. Has it been done before—in a very general sense? Of course. Is Charles Lloyd interchangeable with lots of other Coltrane enthusiasts? No, and that distinction is what listening to jazz is all about these days. (Nils Petter Molvaer, on the other hand, turns me off: I don't hear enough of a sound. It looks good on paper, but it seems flat in practice. I don't think, however, that I should be disqualifying Molvaer entirely because he reminds me a bit of electric Miles.)

Miles was so original that he didn't just create new-sounding techniques, harmonies, or instrumentation; he created whole templates for making jazz. To contradict myself again, I know that Greg Osby's small groups, when they play live, have a connection to the freer moments of Miles's 1960s quintet. But that doesn't bother me, because every member of that group has such a strong individual sound and relates to each other as an individual musician.

The problem with the "you're not playing anything *new!*" argument is that it's only half right. Yes, jazz has depended on lots of very individual voices to evolve it. But—in case we haven't noticed—it also has a delicious side to it that is about refinement of tradition. Any music, in its early years, rockets forward; it's not so universally codified. As it grows up it advances more slowly, with more of a reliance on the codifications. There are only so many Miles Davises out there; that's why he was so great. I even hear a lot of codified languages at the Knitting Factory these days, and I'm just as bored with not very dynamic Steve Coleman or Tim Berne knockoffs as I am with Herbie clones.

Wynton, at this point, is a special case; I don't think all the present woes of the jazz world can still be realistically heaped on him. You can complain that lots of his sidemen were signed up and hyped by dumb reflex, but most of them have been dropped already anyway. The main thrust of major label activity isn't still retro hard bop. I'm thinking about recent major label signings: Dave Douglas...Ravi Coltrane...Claudia Acuna...Kurt Rosenwinkel...Jason Moran...Soulive....When Bill Charlap, an excellent pianist but a total Mr. Old School, was signed by Blue Note, I found it kind of surprising.

One last thing that struck me funny: Stuart mentions the self-righteousness of retro jazzers, as if artists defending their adherence to a tradition was anything surprising. Has he ever noticed the self-righteousness of "futurists" in jazz? No surprise there, either. These are all guys defending what they do for a living.

Here I am caught up in something about newness and tradition, when what I meant to say was that the best fusion sounds a lot better to me today than it did in the 1980s or '90s. I'm glad, too, that some of the new American metal bands—which is the only current jazz-rock I spend much time listening to—are getting into Mahavishnu Orchestra: I promise to check out Aarset if Stuart checks out Candiria.

PETER MARGASAK

It seems necessary to raise the idea that musicians who've come around in the last ten to twenty years grew up with rock music (under which I'd include hip-hop, techno, etc.). You don't have to try to understand something that's in your blood. Jazz musicians have always been interested in other genres, but the industry has long frowned upon that kind of eclecticism because, for one, it makes things much harder to market. I'm confident that in the years to come stylistic boundaries will become more and more invisible.

There are loads of U.S. counterparts to the Norwegian musicians Stuart mentions, but by and large they're unwelcome in the New York jazz world. (In fact, I think there's been a tendency in these discussions, so far, to assume that if something doesn't happen in New York, then it doesn't really happen.) The way drummers like Jim Black have appropriated the frenetic rhythms of drum 'n' bass, to cite one example, is compelling; when he does that in Chris Speed's quartet it's clear that the musicians aren't dabbling, for marketability or any other reason. They understand this new sound and have adopted it for their own purposes. I hate to sound provincial, but what's happening in Chicago can't be easily dismissed, either. There's the whole Tortoise/Isotope 217/ Chicago Underground Trio axis, for which fusion, in myriad guises, is the collective's lingua franca. Tortoise isn't a jazz group—they may employ jazz voicings, yet there's not a lick of improv going on—but the flow of ideas and shared personnel between them and the CUT, for example, is something I find exciting. It's not about newness so much as wide-open possibility. Not everything these guys produce is good, but the way they constantly dissolve any stylistic hegemony is inspiring.

I'm surprised no one has mentioned the experiments of the M-Base crew. While a good chunk of their 1980s stuff failed, no one can deny that those early days were crucial to the highly original, style-bridging sounds Steve Coleman, Greg Osby, and, by extension, Jason Moran are currently churning out. Techno whiz Carl Craig's Innerzone Orchestra with pianist Craig Taborn and bassist Rodney Whittaker is very uneven but, again, it's a promising idea. The jazz guys aren't on board strictly for money; they have a deep connection and understanding of techno, a music they grew up with in Detroit.

There are lots of people reconsidering the good 1970s fusion stuff; the bad taste produced by Stuart's "foot soldiers" is dissipating and now we can hear how good those Miles records are, how they teem with possibilities that were never fully explored. Davis didn't fool around with clever little juxtapositions; he reached way out and swept everything into one glorious sound. I'd like to think that's about to happen again.

K. LEANDER WILLIAMS

I'd also like to think we're about to experience a creative windfall. But the music of Tortoise, Chicago Underground Duo/Trio, and Nils Petter Molvaer doesn't seem to be the right place to look. (And, for the record, that has absolutely nothing to do with where they live, either.) I actually like Molvaer's most recent disc and think the Chicago guys are, um, slick, but both sound much too indebted to Miles, the Art Ensemble, whomever to indicate promising new directions. Listening to even the good music I get the same feeling I do when I hear one of these amazingly proficient jam outfits that are currently so popular—Medeski Martin and Wood comes to mind: it seems like a bunch of nice guys who had to find something—anything?—to do with their extensive music educations. Sure, most of them grew up on rock, but it's their knowledge of jazzy chord subtleties and such that gives them "intellectual" or "bohemian" cachet.

JIM MACNIE

Ben did get away from the jazz/rock dichotomy in his notes to Stuart's essay, but addressing the notion of "new" is important, and since it's something several of us often debate during post-show sessions of sidewalk punditry, I'm glad he brought it up.

He says he doesn't trust the concept of newness anymore. I'll go a step further and say that it's been ages since I've heard anything that's truly new in any formal sense. You've seen that bumper sticker: codification happens (well, it's on the cars of musicians unloading instruments in front of the Knit and the Vanguard). But, in fairness, I'll tag that thought with the statement that I hear relatively new wrinkles on old moves—wait, make that impressive relatively new wrinkles on old moves—almost once a month. Usually, they excite me.

Those artists who stress that pluralistic nature Stuart speaks of probably do so because experimentation is a blast. But there are roots for Hagans and Belden, Ben Neill, and Nils Petter Molvaer, and yeah, those roots are Miles long. Davis was the first to decide to hitch jazz and rock (no, regardless of the profound improvisations he concocted, I don't think Hendrix ever truly had a thesis of integration in the front of his mind) and, as we here all basically concur, the first cut was the deepest.

So jazz and rock in cahoots? Nothing wrong in theory. But in practice it's been stew meat rather than filet, and while my general contempt for it has been steady over the years, I've never held either of the genres responsible. Music is as inventive or crude as its creators. *Hymn for the Seventh Galaxy* is pure wankery and *The Inner Mounting Flame* near genius. It's not jazz's fault, nor rock's. Ingenuity, passion, and in this particular case the full banishment of contrivance is what's necessary for the two genres to successfully stroll down the aisle. Unless we're talking James Blood Ulmer's *Freelancing* or Sonny Sharrock's *Monkey-Pockie-Boo* or Ronald Shannon Jackson's *Barbeque Dog* or the Mahavishnu Orchestra's "The Noonward Race" or Massacre's *Killing Time* or Funkadelic's *Cosmic Slop* or the MC5's *Kick out the Jams* or, for God's sake, Ornette Coleman's *Of Human Feelings* itself, there's not a hell of a lot to celebrate.

But even those ambitious templates haven't helped most of the intrepid souls trying to do the do of late. I give an ear to a fair amount of Isotope and Chicago Underground Duo and Squarepusher, but there are no true strides being made and therefore little to put faith into for the future. Even ultra-collaborationist Derek Bailey's drum 'n' bass disc was a hollow pastiche.

So I'm doubtful that I'll ever bet the farm on a future of jazz-rock, and here's why: there's something inherently graceless about it. The most compelling jazz has a natural eloquence, and I've long believed this eloquence is rhythmically derived (notice I'm not saying defined). That's what gives the music the exclusivity it has earned; that's what people buy when they buy jazz. From Lifetime to Last Exit, all but the best moments of jazz-rock have been somewhat ham-fisted. And though I don't think I've voiced it elsewhere, the post-1980 comeback version of Miles's groups—Stern, Sco, and the other guitar incarnations—pretty much reduced the gleam of *Bitches Brew* and the Davis-created music that came in that disc's immediate wake. To overgeneralize, rock beats just don't get the job done, 'cept in rock.

Interaction, meaning the kind of true group interaction acoustic jazz has been built on, is also what's missing from jazz-rock. The techno-noir of Molvaer is groovy background music, but I'm not hearing any advanced level of improvisation within his stuff. And regardless of Philip Elwood's opinion, Peter Apfelbaum, at least as represented on record and the shows I've seen, is no genius. I'm thinking the Minutemen's "Song for the Wind God" and the Allman Brothers' take on Donovan's existential nursery rhyme get the job done a lot better. Medeski Martin and Wood are adept at tossing the ball around to each other—I believe 'em to be true improvisers. But look what they've helped open the door to: the major label debuts by St. Germain, Soulive, and Karl Denson are much more pop than they are jazz. Deep improvisation is being shown the door again.

Can't say as if I addressed any of Stuart's main points. Synopsis? I'm pro-plurality (anyone here going to say they ain't?), but just haven't seen too many fruits of the union.

K. LEANDER WILLIAMS

Hear, hear, Jim; with one historical quibble. I'm not sure that Miles was the first to decide to hitch jazz and rock. Couldn't we also say that Milesian fusion was the culmination of ideas that had been floating around among the Blue Note soul jazzers since the late 1950s/early '60s? It's easy to sidestep, but I think it'd be a big mistake to overlook the R&B-flavored stuff that folks like Horace Silver, Lou Donaldson, and especially Cannonball Adderley were doing. I have to believe that Miles hired Joe Zawinul out of Cannonball's band as a result, and that, for similar reasons, the rock band Steely Dan considered it quite natural to appropriate—proto-sample?—Silver's "Song for My Father." And come to think of it—looking back to what Peter M. wrote earlier about rock being in the current jazz generation's blood—didn't many jazz musicians of the hard bop era get their start in R&B bands? John Coltrane and Ornette Coleman certainly did. Just something to think about.

PETER WATROUS

I think that the current and past critical obsession with valorizing the new comes from two poisoned fountains, one large and one small, and both aren't good. The large is this: the dopey idea that newness is somehow inherently good is the result of years of cultural pressure from commodity capitalism. It's an idea antithetical to individuality; that is, if one is castigated for liking last year's model it is because commercial pop culture wants turnover; critics that subscribe to that way of thinking, and they are legion, are saps.

The second thing is personal: I often find, when reading critics who run their spiel on the value of the new, that there is a separation between how they listen to music and how I do. I don't listen to music because it breaks boundaries, pushes envelopes, ruptures the social contract, etc. I listen to music that moves me, and usually there's some sort of rhetorical reason I'm moved. As a critic and a musician I've tried to find out what it is that I like, not the opposite. I started out by imposing an ideological cross on music, and seeing if the music survived. I repent, over and over. More power to the people who find lasting value in music that pushes envelopes; I'd just hate to be their lover or child.

As for the idea that European jazz is the future, I'd just say it's early to tell. This is how I see it: American audiences like American jazz, European audiences now apparently like European jazz. The chances that an American audience will embrace European jazz is slight (though it's happened in a small way before; think of the Jan Garbarek albums that were floating around a few decades ago). As long as American culture maintains its predominant position I'd guess that Europeans will be exposed and develop a taste for music that has the saltiness that blues culture has imparted to jazz. One can argue all one wants about the importance of the Nordic approach to jazz, but numbers argue in favor of American jazz retaining popularity: more people in the world have been exposed to it.

As for the original point: as Stuart notes, jazz-rock had its moments, and, frankly, I've rarely heard anybody badmouth the first experiments in fusion. But, as Stuart knows, the movement went mostly nowhere, which argues something about its original impulse. Oddly, fusion is much more important among musical intellectuals in other countries; Cuba, Brazil, and Argentina all like their fusion straight up, though I've always felt that fusion's predominance in the poorer parts of the world came from the marketing weight of the majors who sold the stuff oversees. Does one Matt Wilson CD exist in Havana? Kenny G surely has a pile, therefore is influential. That's how things work.

GREG TATE

I always feel that whenever an aging jazz critic's fancy turns to fusion that conversation stops at the Return to Forever/Mahavishnu gnat-note knockoffs and the magisterial Weather Report magi and never touches on the more musically successful ventures that bridged jazz and 1970s soul as can be heard in the recordings of Fela Ransome Kuti, Pharoah Sanders, Doug and Jean Carn, Norman Connors, Lonnie Liston Smith, Oneness of Juju, etc. These artists' works fueled my Washington, D.C., generation's notions of what a jazz-and-funk synthesis could be. On the other hand, fusion as we know it also inspired some of the most influential African American musicians of the late 1970s and '80s in the form of Bad Brains, Prince, Funkadelic, and Living Colour. Fusion inspired so many great black guitar players frozen out of the rock 'n' roll dream by an apartheid-oriented radio/recording industry. Gnat-note fusion was where these guys saw a guitar-shredding future that included string-playing instrumentalists of color. Once again race rears its pretty little head in the road taken in American music—the irony of white jazz fusionists like Holdsworth, DiMeola, and McLaughlin inspiring the next generation of African American soul and funk progressives shouldn't be lost on anyone. Nor should the impact jazz funksters like Herbie Hancock and George Duke had on the sound of 1970s and '80s mainstream R&B. As in quantum physics, there is a wave/particle paradox evident in jazz. This is to say, if we define as jazz that which operates squarely in the jazz tradition of harmonic improvisation and the hoary swing-to-bop repertoire, jazz is concretely understood as one thing artistically. On the other hand, if we define jazz as the exploration of sound, timbre, technology, and expressive musical effects, then the contributions of our funk and rock fusionists to the jazz and American musical lexicon are surely at least as attention-grabbing as the still-shocking sonorous contributions of a Bubber Miley or an Albert Ayler—less acoustic in orgin and perhaps less profound but a supremely jazz phenomenon nonetheless. Especially as heard in Miles's *Dark Magus,* which sums up a century's worth of black music and presages this century's as well.

WILL FRIEDWALD

I can't help but wonder: why a whole chapter on jazz and rock? I accept the basic notion that jazz itself, even in its purest form (whatever that may be) is a fusion; jazz was already a mixture of a million other musics even by the time it had left New Orleans. Yet surely jazz is not alone in this—nearly all the so-called "classical" composers, from Bartok to Liszt to Vaughan-Williams, were influenced by ethnic and folk music; country music draws on the blues; according to currently held beliefs, Irish music and Spanish music both owe much to African music; jazz musicians play show tunes while Broadway shows—for a time at least—tried to replicate the energy and syncopation of the jazz band. Bossa nova evolved in Brazil in a manner roughly analagous to the development of jazz in New Orleans, and the two musics have enjoyed a healthy give-and-take over the last forty years.

So why so much attention to jazz's relationship with rock? Admittedly I'm the wrong person to ask—I don't think I've listened to a rock record since roughly the last time I went to a basketball game, which would be around the time of the 1969 Knicks. (Unless you count the original Broadway cast album of *Bye Bye Birdie* as a rock album—or even Bill Potts and the Orchestra playing the jazz version of *Bye Bye Birdie.*) Personally, I can't tell any of those 1970s guitar gods (McLaughlin, Scofield, Coryell, Metheny) apart, and to me Return-to-Mahavishnu and Weather Report sound hopelessly dated in a way that Scott Hamilton records from the same period don't. (Both Hamilton and David Murray arrived in New York from California around the same time, and my father, who was a big jazz fan, and I never made a point of the way they played in different genres—to us, they were both just kick-ass tenor players.) I think the reason that jazz-rock is such a big deal—as opposed to jazz–bossa nova, jazz-calypso, jazz-klezmer, jazz-symphony, jazz-polka, or even jazz-jazz—is economic. Weather Report could easily be Financial Report. Jazz musicians added electrification to their bands for the same reason Carmen McRae started singing Simon and Garfunkel (because she wanted to sell records): expand not just to their musical horizons but their economic base.

Ironically, electrified jazzers may have been looking in the wrong place. Greener pastures were not necessarily in the fields of kiddie pop, they were out west on the lone prairie. Hillbilly music strikes me as a much more satisfying source of economic and cultural exchange—certainly it was up through the band era, when hillbilly superstars routinely used great jazz soloists on their discs and Bob Wills led one of the great swing bands (that it was western swing seems irrelevant). The country-jazz relationship has largely been overlooked since the premature death of Hank Garland, who might have been the first superstar of that crossover.

Or to put it another way: it's 1968. Miles Davis asks Clive Davis (no relation) what he can do to sell more records—Clive tells Miles that Hawaiian music is what's hot. Next thing we know, Miles is wearing a grass tuxedo, adding steel guitars to his band, and recording *Sketches of Honolulu*.

STUART NICHOLSON

I think Will's response indicates how jazz-rock still continues to be misunderstood, even at this distance. The point, surely, is that it was jazz that was relevant to its time, in a way so much jazz since then has not been, belonging to previous eras of the music. Today we are picking up the cost of all this, as the music heads inexorably toward high-art marginality.

4

COLLECTIVE PLAY

IMPROVISATION AND COMPOSITION

JOHN F. SZWED

Improvisation—the art of composing in the moment, in the act of performance, without a written score—has always been seen as what sets jazz apart from other musics. It may or may not be true that no other music counts so much on instant creativity, expecting every musician to rise to a certain level, but jazz musicians and their followers talk and act as though it is. They speak of going beyond the limitations of the precomposed, beyond the simply interpretive, to a more deeply inspired and more instantaneous creativity, to a level that may put the improviser much more in touch with his or her conscious and unconscious states. But truth be told, this discourse on improvisation is based on a false distinction between improvisation and composition, or, at the very least, a wildly exaggerated one.

Beginning even in its early years, there were some who defended jazz against the slander of classical musicians by arguing for the superiority of improvisation over composition, and by making claims for spontaneity that were difficult to support. However well intentioned, over the long run these characterizations have not been of much help: jazz musicians have often been kept away from teaching positions, awards, and gigs because they were thought to be operating on different musical principles. By the 1950s efforts were made to dissolve these distinctions, none more pointed than Gunther Schuller's and John Lewis's announcement in 1955 that musicians finally existed who, on the one hand, were well trained enough to be able to play complex forms of written music, and, on the other, could improvise like jazz players. Under the label of "third stream," a new music would arise to match their abilities. Whether this music was ever successfully realized is not the point here; but their manifesto may have had the odd consequence of reinforcing false distinctions all over again. (Were the musicians who read and improvised Duke Ellington's, Eddie Sauter's, or Bob Graettinger's scores not well trained?) A few years later, the AACM in Chicago also tried to minimize the distinction, requiring written compositions from everyone who worked with them under the assumption that if they could improvise, they were composers as well.

Yet even today, biases still exist against the sources and quality of improvisation, and no better example of this bias can be seen than in the resistance of many classical musicians and critics to call Giacinto Scelsi a composer because he improvised most of his compositions and then had them transcribed. Certainly there are those who still say that jazz improvisation means playing without thought, "intuitively," or "naturally"; that it involves no arrangements or plans for what will be played; or that there are no constraints on what is possible. Yet even where compositions are open and constraints minimized—as in a jam session—there are nonetheless agreed-upon principles as to what might be invented and how it relates to the whole, and at least some standards that determine whether improvisations will be successful or not. To varying degrees, the audience shares these standards as well.

But those who view improvisation positively also hold views that are burdensome for musicians. Jazz audiences expect that what they are hearing live on a particular occasion is different from what any other musician would play and—unlike pop audiences—different from what they have heard even on the performer's recordings. And if the same piece is played again later in the evening it, too, is expected to sound new. (The applause given each jazz solo—rather than just the tune itself, as in pop and classical music—rewards the fulfillment of this expectation, even if only as a formality.)

The level of creativity demanded here is incredibly high, and unrealistic: musicians are asked to sound different from all others, but also different from themselves. For a performer who manages to play several times a night for six nights a week for, say, thirty years, coming up with new ideas that nonetheless still sound like one's own poses a near-impossible task. In reality, even the most distinctive and creative improvisers (a Charlie Parker or a Sonny Rollins) play with personal stylistic elements (or "licks") that make them quickly susceptible to imitators. And even for these master players, there is always a fear of self-imitation, which can turn into self-parody over time.

The usual distinctions made between improvisation and composition (the improviser working within a group of musicians versus the solitary composer toiling alone, etc.) are not as clear-cut as they might seem. Both are forms of composition, and both are involved to varying degrees with performance. Some composers are able to communicate their compositions (which may or may not be written in a score) by singing them or playing them for the musicians who will perform them. And some compositions are at least in part developed during rehearsals. In any case, since the dawning of the tape recorder, the Synclavier, and other means of electronic storage and retrieval, distinctions such as this one make less and less sense.

It is also possible for a musician to play written music so that it sounds improvised, even play it physically so it looks improvised; and it is equally possible for a composer to write music that sounds improvised. In fact, there is great precedent in many arts for works to sound or look as if they were made in some other way than they appear to be. And some of jazz's most dedicated composers—Jelly Roll Morton, Duke Ellington, Tadd Dameron, Gil Evans, George Russell, and Anthony Braxton—have achieved just that.

Jazz grew up with recordings, and the role of the composer of written music in the beginnings of jazz was determined partly by technological limitations—the three-minute record—and partly by the location of jazz in the realm of commercial music. Though compositions could sometimes be as complex as Jelly Roll Morton's "Black

Bottom Stomp" with its four themes, most jazz compositions were made up of one or two themes at the most, with variations by soloists and the ensemble. But even after the development of the long-playing record with its potential for extending a composition for up to forty minutes, few jazz composers attempted longer works. Even Duke Ellington, jazz's greatest composer, either kept his compositions to about fifteen minutes or used a quasi-suite form to string together a series of short, somewhat loosely related pieces. (Though they have never billed what they do as suites, musicians like Julius Hemphill, Henry Threadgill, and John Carter have put together works in similar fashion.)

Some have seen the lack of long works in jazz as the failed result of integrating improvisers within compositions over long stretches of time. But this seems to be a red herring. The length of a musical work appears, rather, to be an artifact of a particular music's history. What's more, it is difficult to demonstrate that there is anything inherently superior about longer works (except that they are apparently the only means by which a jazz musician can win a Guggenheim or a Pulitzer Prize). Some, perhaps all, of the best jazz compositions are short, but they are gems of balance, detail, and shape, their beauty and power completely realized within a few minutes.

Besides, there have been enough longer compositions in jazz—John Lewis's *Comedy*, George Russell's *All About Rosie*, Ornette Coleman's *Free Jazz*, and John Coltrane's *Ascension*—to show that it is possible to achieve something original at length and still allow for improvisation. And Anthony Braxton, the Jazz Composers Orchestra, the Globe Unity Orchestra, and Barry Guy's London Improvisers Orchestra have all created compositions that call for the entire orchestra to improvise collectively over long stretches of time. On the other hand, the sheer prestige of producing long, expensive works seems to have been the source of some of jazz's most peculiar moments ("white elephants," Gary Giddins called them): Charles Mingus's *Epitaph*, Wynton Marsalis's *Blood on the Fields*, even Ellington's *Black, Brown and Beige*. (It goes without saying that uncontrolled length in classical music has produced far more anomalous works—Bernstein's *Mass* comes to mind.)

A further complication in the composer/improviser distinction is the importance of the arranger in jazz. An arrangement is a plan that musicians agree to abide by before they play, intended to give shape to their performance beyond melody, harmony, etc. An arrangement, then, may be as simple as an agreement to play the melody at a certain point, to solo in a certain order, and to stop at a particular moment. Arrangements can be written out, agreed upon just before the music begins, or even take shape as they are played ("head arrangements" are often developed collectively in the playing, made up night after night, with some parts being added as they go along, and others dropped). In small groups, an arrangement may provide riffs to be played behind a soloist, countermelodies to be used against the melody, or any number of small variations on routine. But in larger groups, especially, the arranger emerges as a more prominent figure, creating distinctive voicings for the harmony, changing the harmonic progressions, recomposing the existing melody by means of small variations, or writing full-blown variations of the melody. The best arrangers in jazz find ways to fit soloists into the orchestral frame, balancing the single voice against the whole. Duke Ellington, Gil Evans, Eddie Sauter, and George Russell, for example, made the groups they wrote for into the distinctive forces they became. As with great soloists and composers, the arranger's style is always recognizable, regardless of what material is being arranged. And in the best arrangements—the organic and unified ones—it's difficult for the hearer to separate the arranged parts from the composed and the improvised.

One of the great virtues of jazz is that it breaks with Western conventional thinking on these matters, denying the distinctions between composer and performer, creator and interpreter, composer and arranger, soloist and accompanist, artist and entertainer, long and short pieces, even soloist and group. In jazz, it is the activity itself that is as important as the result. It is a music that is learned in the doing, in collective play: it began as a social music, and some of the features of early African American performance and social organization are still evident in its execution. As such, it is a way of being as well as a way of doing. It is an emergent form, a social form, and as much an ethic as it is an aesthetic. No wonder, then, that many jazz musicians speak of their music in metaphysical or spiritual terms, or justify the music in terms of personal and collective survival.

How spontaneous is improvisation? How unplanned? Sometimes even the greatest musicians rehearse and plan a solo, playing the same solos year after year, making only small changes over time. One of Louis Armstrong's greatest "improvisations," his solo on his 1926 recording of "Cornet Chop Suey," had been worked out and written down at least two years before it was recorded. Sometimes an improvisation is partly written: Miles Davis wrote out the introductory and closing phrases of many of his improvised solos on the "Birth of the Cool" recordings so as to take maximum advantage of the short solo space allowed on 78 rpm records. Even Charlie Parker's acclaimed break on "Night in Tunisia" seems to have been preplanned, since he complained that he might not be able to get it right again when other takes were required. Some jazz composers did not trust their musicians to improvise the way they wanted, so some of the most interesting breaks and solos on Jelly Roll Morton's records were written out. On the other hand, some musicians have gone to extraordinary lengths to resist playing the same way twice. Derek Bailey's obsession with performing in different musical settings and combinations is his way of challenging himself. Ornette Coleman seems to have taken up the trumpet and violin in part to disrupt the conventional or formulaic figures he developed in his improvising on the saxophone.

How do musicians go about improvising? Is it possible to improvise melodies from scratch, working with nothing more than emotional and intellectual resources? Yes, but more often than not jazz musicians choose to improvise "off" something or "against" something. An astonishingly large number of sources and methods have been built up over the years for this purpose, and though few musicians ever use more than a fraction of them, they remain a reservoir of great artistic potential. Jazz musicians may work, for example, from a preexisting melody, a piece that all members of the musical group know from memory, or can read from a lead sheet—that is, a musical outline that contains the melody line, the harmonic structure, and perhaps the words of a song. They may alter the original melody in whole or in part, changing the phrasing, the intervals, the rhythm of the melody in various ways—by recombining, subtracting, adding, transposing, inverting, or playing it backward. For some improvisers it is enough to change only the phrasing of the melody, much as one would change the phrasing of speech, so that the internal organization of the melody is changed, with different points of emphasis or tension. Others prefer to paraphrase the original, or ornament the existing theme. This can be as simple a gesture as changing only a few notes or as complex as recomposing the whole melody. Still others (Jimmy Knepper, for example) may think in smaller units, by playing only a few notes, varying those, then varying the ones just played, and continuing the variation in sequence. Some take a small fragment or motive of the original melody and vary it throughout the solo; and some others may bring their own personal stock of formulas or clichés to the solo and link them together in creative ways. Whatever they play, improvisers strive to avoid what is called noodling, or aimless, shapeless playing.

Some musicians build their own melodies on the harmonic structure of a preexisting song, possibly never even alluding to the original melody. Or they may paraphrase or quote from another melody where it fits the existing harmonic structure. Players like Dexter Gordon and Nat King Cole were expert at quotation and could often construct witty narratives from parts of different songs. (Cole's piano solo at the Jazz at the Philharmonic on "Body and Soul," for example, is built almost entirely from bits of other pieces, from "Grand Canyon Suite" to "Humoresque.") Or they may play in what are called modes, but which may be nothing more than using only a scale or two for improvisation. Some even more minimalist improvisers choose to play on single chords, or single tones, drones, or vamps.

But this is only the beginning of the sources and means of improvisation: some musicians are drawn to improvise on songs with particularly interesting conjunctions between lyrics and melody (such as Jerome Kern's "The Song Is You," where the melody modulates upward just at the point where the lyrics ask a series of questions: the soloist is sent soaring upward by both a harmonic rise and the upturned pitch of the questions to a new place where the horn—like a voice—can sing). Some contemporary musicians look for new or older forms to play on;

others improvise from images, paintings, even colors and shapes. Still others make sheer virtuosity the basis of solo performance, using instruments in new ways, or using relatively newer techniques such as circular breathing and multiphonics. Throughout all of these, the improvisation's source can be intellectual, physical, emotional, or it can be spurred by "the spirit"—whether by trance associated with religious belief or in the subconscious spirit of Surrealism and Dadaism.

Many jazz musicians have justified their preoccupation with improvisation as a means of escaping the limitations on what can be written. There are, of course, limits as well on what can be improvised, but in many cases they are the same as those of the traditional composition: the degree of complexity of the form, the length a piece can be played, and the amount of time an audience can remain attentive to the development of the piece. Nonetheless, early jazz musicians (as well as free jazz musicians) developed remarkably complex collectively improvised polyphony. And the speed at which some players improvise is certainly much faster than composers can compose: Charlie Parker's 1945 recording of "Ko-ko," for example, generally agreed to be one of the greatest improvisations, is played at ten notes a second (meaning that Parker moved from idea to finger movement to key action, and breath to mouth and lips, at least ten times a second). Nor does length of improvisation seem a limitation: John Coltrane and Cecil Taylor have sustained improvisations of over an hour (longer than most symphonies), and saxophonist Evan Parker once gave a twenty-four-hour concert of continuous improvised music.

But what of mistakes? (Perhaps *mistakes* is too strong a word, since improvisers aim at innovation, and it's not always clear to the listener what was intended.) Errors do get made in improvisations—notes are missed, musicians run out of breath (or, worse, out of ideas), or lose the beat. But within the conventions of improvisation some degree of error is allowed and treated as part of the performance, especially where a musician is breaking new ground. And among the cognoscenti, mistakes may even be relished, as they offer access to the soloist's mental processes. The greater problem for the improviser is not to repeat him- or herself, or to become too comfortable with a certain level of expression. (Needless to say, mistakes get made in written composition as well, and often aren't corrected until performance—and sometimes not until a century or so later.)

Finally, composition has too often been considered to be creation in longer forms alone. Leaving aside whether or not there is merit in length, and whether or not that challenge has already been met by improvisers, the questions still remain: who will perform these long pieces, and who will listen to them in the twenty-first century? We now have several repertory orchestras in position to play such music if it is written, but, like classical orchestras, they, too, are shackled to the past in part because that's what their audiences know and will pay for, and in part because preparing new works for performance takes time and money. Most of the longer compositions of the last forty years (such as those by James Newton, Anthony Davis, Cecil Taylor, Anthony Braxton, and Roscoe Mitchell) have come from the underfunded, non-institutionalized margins and have been largely ignored by the classical establishment, treated superficially (and suspiciously) by the jazz community, and rewarded by being called not-jazz and not-classical. There is no reason to believe that this will not continue, with or without help and acknowledgment, in the future.

K. LEANDER WILLIAMS

It seems rather obvious to me that the compositional impulse is often sparked by the ingenuity of daring instrumentalists. For example, at least two musicians who worked alongside trumpeter Dave Douglas have told me that he went to the drawing board with something he'd heard them play in a rehearsal. That's also been the case with Jelly Roll, Ellington, Miles, and Gil, and many others, while on the other hand, folks like Charlie Parker, Thelonious Monk, and Henry Threadgill built extensive compositional vocabularies out of their own distinctive approaches to improvisation.

Recognition of the above has brought me to another conclusion, however. Whenever folks start discussing the distinction between composition and improvisation I always get the sneaking suspicion that they're actually talking about other things—like acceptance by the classical establishment or some form of legitimacy based upon creative guidelines established in the ivory tower. It's the classical world that actually set in motion the perceived schism between what is written and what is played, a circumstance that seems especially ridiculous once you realize that Bach, the mutha of us all, first improvised most of the music that is attributed to him as a composer.

If anything, the emphasis on composition as some type of sacred aspiration has only resulted in more rote and/or bad writing; basically, jazz musicians today often write using phrases that were becoming overused even two decades ago—and I'm talking about avant-gardists, too. One reason I think the music of a pianist like Tommy Flanagan truly sounds fresh right now is because he actually shows us the magic of bebop era composition by letting us hear it against all the wonderful harmonic things—and with Lewis Nash on drums, many of the rhythmic things—that have happened in the meantime. It helps that Flanagan was there near the beginning of the modern jazz movement because it gives him an understanding of the subtleties of feel in bop that a younger musician—i.e., someone who's *not* Bill Charlap—might only use as affectation. On the flip side, you have a composer-pianist like Rodney Kendrick, a guy whose understanding of the connection between the old and new is so acute that on his best records he infuses older jazz licks with what you might call a contemporary naturalness: they become danceable, edgy, nonchalant, and fun to listen to. And my guess is that if they're also fun to play, they probably inspire the kind of breathtaking solos that are a must for more great writing—by Kendrick or any futurist in earshot.

TED GIOIA

We tend to conceptualize composition in jazz as a process of putting black dots on pages. Many commentators make a further leap and assume that greatness in jazz composition will be achieved when we have lots of black dots on lots of pages. Under this scenario, one thick score of *Epitaph* by Charles Mingus is worth more than a dozen heads by Monk, Powell, or Tristano.

Yet jazz defies this senseless ambition to fill up reams of paper with notation. Jazz composition is primarily about creating an invigorating framework and fresh mental space for creativity. The breakthrough in modal composition signaled by *Kind of Blue* was not driven by putting lots of notes on a page, but by creating a new state of mind. Monk's greatness as a jazz composer drew from his ability to inspire musicians with a revitalized sense of how musical lines might fit together—and this was as much evident in the solos as in the performance of the written notes. I am suggesting that the success of a jazz composition can be best determined by what the players do at that point in the performance when there are no black dots to play. In essence, one listens to the quality of the improvisations as a way of judging the merits of a composition. If the soloist is not inspired, all the black dots in the world won't compensate for this deficiency. And if the soloist is inspired, just a few black dots—or none at all—will suffice. Even the jazz composers who wrote thick scores—such as Ellington or Mingus—recognized this.

From this viewpoint, jazz composers still have many untapped areas to explore. I am especially excited about the prospects of merging jazz with other musical genres that have developed their own unique methods of inspiring performers—from raga to calypso, tango to Gregorian chant, zydeco to klezmer. These styles are sometimes written down in formal musical scores but more often, like jazz, are a matter of sound and attitude. This is our future—one that no longer celebrates the ink, but rather changes how we think.

BEN RATLIFF

As for the future of composition and improvisation: being a newspaper critic, I get irritated about both, and I feel encouraged by both. In classical music they have the premiere, which is the magic word to boost a critic's column inches. It's also an event that makes people come out to feel connected to the arts, and there's nothing wrong with that. In jazz we don't have a lot of long written works, so we don't have many premieres, and when we do they're not particularly a big deal. The natural jazz equivalent of a premiere—the first performance of a new group, say—isn't particularly fetishized, and for good reason: there's an awfully high chance that it's not going to be very good, and will only get good once the band exercises itself on the road a little bit.

In jazz, we have premieres by composers who aren't necessarily trained (and by trained I mean experience more than I mean conservatory) to write long works, and they can be lousy. Take, for example, Wycliffe Gordon's recent piece *Body and Soul*. (Please.) It was written to accompany an Oscar Micheaux silent film and performed alongside it at Lincoln Center last fall. And it was No Big Deal: redolent of Wynton, filled with unarousing vamps and train-song clichés. But it was seen as the first long-form work by one of America's best jazz players, etc., so it sold tickets and got a lot of coverage. (Incredibly, the *Times* reviewed both the film and the music.)

Beautiful, concise blues themes by themselves—even the ones Milt Jackson wrote for the MJQ—barely count as "compositions" to the world outside of jazz lovers. But string them together into a suite and you've got reporters at your door. A lot of notes on paper really mean something. And sometimes for good reason: Ellington, both in themes and solos; that incredible Jimmy Giuffre–Bob Brookmeyer–Jim Hall trio, which had barely any improvisation; Gil Evans; and so forth. But usually they turn out to be little more than professional footholds to secure a gig, to get a grant, to sell tickets, to persuade the label to put out a new record. It's true: your basic top-level nightclub player—the kind of person who leads a great band but just doesn't find it within his breast to do large-concept albums as tributes to Italian film directors, French aphorists, or Dutch painters—doesn't get Guggenheims.

On the other hand, I can also feel frustrated by the absence of composition in a lot of run-of-the-mill nightclub jazz, because head-solos-head can grow wearyingly routine. The middle way is something like what Kelvin was pointing to: that elegant tradition of small-group arrangements like Tommy Flanagan's.

What I like about jazz groups at their most dynamic, though, is that they render material—who wrote the tune, what it is, what it refers to—fairly meaningless. The interaction of the improvisers, the relationship between them, trumps and works against the fetishization of the tune. As the musicologist Christopher Small likes to say, music is a verb, not a noun.

WILL FRIEDWALD

True confession: I like the written part of jazz. Not just with groups that were famous for their balance of composition and improvisation (like Duke Ellington's orchestra, or any of the great jazz big bands, or the Modern Jazz Quartet) but with virtually any band—even those modern jazz groups that supposedly stress improvisation above all other virtues. Not only do I like to recognize the tune, whether it's by George Gershwin or George Russell, but I like the sound of two or more horns playing together—the reed-section climax on the original "Cottontail," which is the aural equivalent of six lindy hoppers jumping in the air, appeals to me just as much as Ben Webster's celebrated solo improvisation. (It isn't entirely improvised either, but we won't deal with that here.) I've always been at least slightly ashamed of this— to admit that I get even more of a thrill from the opening minute—the melody—of Art Blakey's "Moanin'" than the eleven minutes of solos that follow. I think that's one reason that the so-called West Coast jazz of the 1950s appealed to me—the emphasis on the role of the arranger, the well-handled integration of the written and the improvised. I think that's even more attractive than the sound of the "cool" style itself. Sometimes I'm in the mood to hear chorus after blowing chorus of a marathon solo, but on the whole I think that 99 percent of jazzmen would be well advised to keep their statements down to, I don't know, three or four choruses. (Likewise, there are only a dozen or two singers since the beginning of time who I want to hear scat at any length— I'd rather hear scatting being used as atmosphere or window dressing for familiar words and music than as an end in itself.) None of this is a hard and fast rule—there's that great concert version of "My Funny Valentine" by Miles Davis, which has no overt melody statement and no ensemble playing whatever, just a series of solos, which is appropriate, because the improvisations all refer to the Rodgers melody in such a way that playing it outright would seem redundant. I think that's the tragedy of Davis's decision a few years later not to play standards anymore—other than his perceived economic incentive that there was more money in electronics and rock 'n' roll, he apparently genuinely felt that there was nothing else to do with the standard songbook. But his own work made a liar out of him—with a great jazzman, even the most familiar of melodies can say something new to us.

JIM MACNIE

I'm with Ted when it comes to the little black dots and the high-mindedness applied to those whose scores are overly rich in same. Yup, it takes a wondrous intellect to envision and effect pieces such as "A Tone Parallel to Harlem" (Duke Ellington) and "Comedy" (John Lewis). It's just that I'm not seeing any conceptual and compositional talents of that ilk on today's radar. I'd hoped that Anthony Davis was going to be the man to throw a lasso around the composed improvised dichotomy back when jewels such as *Variations in Dream Time* and *Hemispheres* arrived with such seductive eloquence in 1982 and 1983. But he began wearing turtlenecks and compounding the sophistication until it got the best of him. Grandeur, if not pomp, seems to be a central element of extended jazz works (and, yes, they help substantiate those column inches, as Ben rightly explains), which is why many individual "tunes" from *Blood on the Fields* speak to me more directly than the long-winded opera itself. And it took but one sitting through Wynton's *Big Train* to realize that a freightful of genial clichés could chug along quite well, even though it was on a track to nowhere.

The person who has always united score and solo for me is Henry Threadgill. From the gorgeous fog of Air's "Paille Street" to Sextett masterpieces like "Black Hands Bejewelled" and "Silver and Gold, Baby, Silver and Gold," Thread's always found a way to accommodate the collective as well as the individual (he's usually got an ear out for the audience's needs as well). As Kelvin points out, Dave Douglas has done fairly well in sustaining this trajectory as well.

I'm writing this a few days after hearing Derek Bailey and his latest version of Company in New York. The spontaneous lingo that has been the group's essence for decades—*en garde, you slave-driving black dots!*—still had its captivating moments, so I'm not ready to kiss the concept good-bye. But even the outcats like to quote Monk or Newk once in a while—it'll be a cold day at Tonic before we see the removal of reverence for "compositions" such as "Well You Needn't" and "Come, Gone." Perhaps we can lobby our magazine and newspaper editors to rectify Ben's dilemma, making a nightclub set of standards by Kenny Barron a genuine event. "Extra, extra, read all about it! Jazzbo invents alternative melody for 'Three Little Words.'" Get that Pulitzer ready.

STUART NICHOLSON

To me, John does not make clear the different functions composition and improvisation play in jazz, or that the tension between the two has often produced some of the finest jazz.

Compositions express a mood, a feeling, an emotional climate, but also set the tonality, harmonic infrastructure, rhythm, and tempo. John does point out that most of jazz's best compositions are to be found over shorter forms, these usually based on or variants of the American popular song. Through-composed song forms are still rare, although commonplace in classical music, and the one area in jazz composition that has yet to be convincingly mastered is thematic development. Perhaps here lies the challenge for the future of jazz composition.

To illustrate this, a 1956 record that passed unnoticed by the gatekeepers of jazz history revealed the kind of potential more advanced classical writing techniques might yield for jazz, and even now its devices have not yet been fully explored within the jazz idiom. Duane Tatro's *Jazz for Moderns* (Contemporary; rereleased on OJC) applies classical music forms (in particular those from the twentieth century) to jazz writing, and the smoothly flowing performances that result almost perversely emphasize the music's challenging ideas. Although Tatro used the standard thirty-two-bar chorus in all but one of his compositions, the whole point of the exercise was to remove cyclical chord progressions and let the developmental nature of the compositions dictate the underlying harmonies. Thus no key signature was indicated on the score, the tonality being indicated by accidentals along the way. For this reason, the soloists did not play off changes in the conventional sense but were given a guide to the underlying harmony(ies) or a scale from which to solo. Out of eleven brief tracks, "Easy Terms" was a polyphonic exercise where each voice had a destiny of its own; "Backlash" was a modal piece with trumpet and trombone moving in contrary motion; "Multiplicity" moved away from the tonic key to remote harmonies and back again through inspired part and developmental writing in miniature sonata form; "Turbulence" used a twelve-note tone row; "Folly" made extensive use of polychords. The album still remains a sourcebook of ideas for aspiring jazz writers.

Perhaps the most interesting composer and arranger in jazz today is Maria Schneider, who almost alone has successfully come to terms with thematic development and long-form composition in jazz and surely deserves mention here. Her debut album, *Evanescence* (1992), for example, includes the programmatic piece "Wyrgly," which deals with three subjects, contrasting meters, and tone rows; yet it flows as if guided by some unseen hand, the thematic material always appearing in a state of becoming, soloists fitting their statements into the overall structure of the work, which steadily builds to a brilliantly conceived climax. "Gush," in contrast, uses a simple AAB scheme based almost entirely on an F-sharp minor pedal, with the B section modulating to B minor; yet when the composition opens for solos, Schneider uses a CCDE structure that lends a feeling of spaciousness before returning to a recapitulation of the AAB theme. "Green Piece" takes a simple diatonic idea through dark Phrygian modes before returning the theme to a major-key tonal center. Schneider, a remarkable talent in her own right, has often been compared to Gil Evans, who gave her her start, although Evans was primarily an arranger rather than a composer, while Schneider is both.

When John comes to the techniques of improvisation, he overlooks one often employed by the contemporary improviser. An important distinction between swing and bop was that the harmonic rhythm (the rate at which one harmonic change follows another) was far more intense, and if it wasn't, beboppers inserted passing chords. The complexity of this new harmonic infrastructure was unlocked by musicians such as Sonny Stitt, who was extremely influential in negotiating a passage through bop's harmonic complexities through his use of *pattern running.*

To explain briefly, there are two methods of pattern running, or "sequencing," as it is sometimes known: "melodic sequencing" preserves the relationship of a group of notes through a new sequence of chords; in "rhythmic sequencing," the notes don't necessarily retain their melodic relationship to one another, but their rhythmic relationship is preserved. Either form of sequencing was hardly new to jazz at the time of bop—one of the best examples of melodic sequencing (and one of the oldest clichés in popular music) is moving a complete A section of an AABA popular song up a fourth to make the B section (as in Bob Haggart's "What's New?", Billy Strayhorn's "Take the A Train," and Victor Schertzinger's "I Remember You"). And in 1927, Louis Armstrong employed an amazingly modern-sounding nine bars of sequencing during his vocal on "Hotter than That."

However, the less predictable and rhythmically complex figures of bebop—exemplified by the playing of Charlie Parker—seemed at first beyond the ken of mere mortals. Stitt helped unravel such complexities by systematically applying patterns to negotiate his way through the complex, extended chord progressions of bebop, a methodology that became widely influential. Players such as Sonny Rollins, Dexter Gordon, Wardell Gray, Joe Henderson, George Coleman, and Frank Foster, for example, have all cited Stitt as an influence on their style in this respect. This method of improvisation would reach its apotheosis in John Coltrane's "Giant Steps," in which he used the scale fragment 1-2-3-5 approximately thirty-five times during his solo.

Patterns form an important part of an improviser's lexicon, and most solos can be broken down into patterns—imparted by countless study books ranging from David Baker's to Oliver Nelson's to the famous *Patterns for Jazz* by Jerry Coker, developed in practice, "borrowed" from this improviser or that or from the thematic material at

hand, or picked up on the spot from fellow performers during performance. They provide three functions: as a way of systematically getting
from A to B through a set of changes, as a back-up for the performer's
original ideas to lend continuity from one idea to the next, or as a
safety net while fresh ideas are organized. In most conventional contexts, the kind of total improvisation John alludes to in his opening is
quite rare—that is to say improvisation free of preconceived patterns.
Indeed, pattern running is often related to tempo: the faster the tempo,
the greater the recourse to patterns; slower tempos allow the mind to
consider a greater range of options creatively.

The use of patterns in jazz today is extremely prevalent: when I
wrote earlier that musicians like Theodross Avery, Joshua Redman
(the pattern king), Don Braden, Javon Jackson, etc., all "sounded" the
same, what I meant was—and I'm sure Bob Belden won't mind me
relating a discussion we had about precisely this point—not that they
all *literally* sound the same, but that the same ingredients went into
their manufacture—a pattern from Tina Brooks's *Back to the Tracks*,
one from Hank Mobley's *Roll Call*, one from Joe Henderson's *Mode for
Joe*, one from Dexter Gordon's *Doin' Alright*, and so on. Patterns are
one of the pillars on which the edifice of jazz education is built. While
once the sound of hard bop echoed the clubs and after-hours joints of
Harlem and Philadelphia, contemporary hard bop echoes the practice
rooms of Berklee and other music colleges. Too often young musicians are speaking to other young musicians, showing how they can
transpose technically difficult patterns through several keys, thus rob-
bing the music of its meaning.

Mechanical prolixity has replaced originality in the American mainstream: what guerrilla producer and bass player Bill Laswell calls "musical masturbation." This is precisely what free jazz was rebelling against
in the late 1950s. Yet there are alternatives. Jan Garbarek (whose sales,
incidentally, of the jazz-classical fusion *Officium* have now exceeded a
million—in an age when ten thousand album sales in jazz is regarded
as a hit) has pioneered an approach that can now be heard echoed in
the styles of U.K. saxophonists such as Tommy Smith and Andy Shepherd
and fellow Norwegian Bendik Hofseth (whom you might remember
from the group Steps Ahead). This less-is-more approach is steadily

gaining ground in Europe, where many critics and musicians regard mechanical prolixity as both old-fashioned and in bad taste. It is no coincidence that the most technically accomplished saxophonist of recent times, Michael Brecker, is currently looking closely at European improvisers who long ago rejected an overreliance on technique but who explore the expressive potential of the tonal properties of their instruments, an approach reflected in Brecker's 2001 album *Nearness of You: The Ballad Book*. In essence he is returning to earlier values of jazz, when a musician had to "say something" through his horn; a Johnny Hodges or a Ben Webster could invest a note with so much meaning that it seems that Garbarek has jumped back several generations for the inspiration of his style, rejecting the more combative blow-you-off-the-bandstand approach of post-Coltrane players.

JOHN F. SZWED

On the function of compositions versus improvisation: surely this is a matter of degree rather than kind. Can't mood, feeling, emotional climate, tonality, harmonic infrastructure, rhythm, and tempo be expressed without a composition? Doesn't, for example, the walking bass line that opens Miles's "Blue Haze" do all of that? One of the lessons of free jazz was how shared musical conventions can be activated by the slightest allusion.

PETER MARGASAK

As Jim wrote, the free improvisation of players like Derek Bailey still has something to offer, but the number of players who really do something new or push themselves in that area seems to shrinking. In the early 1990s Jim O'Rourke was participating in a recording by Swedish reedist Mats Gustafsson and angered some observers when he pulled out an accordion instead of his main instrument, which was—back then, at least—the guitar. Like Bailey, O'Rourke habitually challenges himself, and switching instruments, à la Ornette Coleman, is in itself an act of improvisation. But many free improvisers have fallen into using a language every bit as predictable as hard bop's.

I've seen more and more improvisers—Gustafsson, Chris Jonas, Assif Tsahar, Ken Vandermark, Fred Lonberg-Holm—work increasingly with composition, although I wouldn't call those pieces tunes. But organizational structures often serve the same function, directing the improvisations, giving them shape and concision, and forcing the participants into unfamiliar realms. Musicians won't stop improvising on tunes any time soon, but I think a good chunk of the real action in the future will see players delving deeper into this nexus of free improvisation and structure.

PETER WATROUS

Reading John's nice piece on the history and intricacies of improvisation and composition made me realize how little I care about the subject. For one, it's so freighted with cliché, reaction, and apology. Really, who cares? Shouldn't one just get on with the work of playing what one wants to play or hear? Those concerns of some fifty years ago seem so desiccated now. Some things work and some things don't, and whether they are improvised or composed is irrelevant to their function.

I'm more interested in a science of rhetoric, how combinations of notes produce sensuality or the subtleties of emotion. That's the science, the rhetorical ability to provoke. But then, having spent hours trying to transcribe and play parts of other peoples' solos, I'm consistently shocked at how improvisation is an issue of subtleties, that five notes written down and played are often so radically different in their emotional intent and immediacy than those same five notes nailed down deep in the battle of improvisation.

Or that the same lick played by one player sounds profoundly distinct from the same lick played by others. That is, what Miles Davis played is, at times in his career, musically simple; the notes are easy to find and put in the context of common jazz practice. But what he played is impossible to reproduce; one can know the notes, find them on your instrument, understand their relationship to the underlying harmony of the tune, and still fail to even come close to reproducing the rhetorical charge that incites, that fires the emotion. Harmony, rhythm, sound: all of it can be irrelevant, since all jazz is now retrievable, and everything can be figured out. Except what makes Miles Davis special, the nuances, the combination of elements that make his imitators unlistenable and keep him sublime.

GREG TATE

Because improvisation is where the magic quotient of jazz is kept, it often blinds some romantic commentators to the fact that there is any scored material in the mix at all. Most of the jazz musicians we find memorable were either exceptional interpreters of melodies or interesting theme writers, if not full-blown arrangers. If the last twenty years have proved nothing else, it's how lacking the 1980s generation was in memorable theme writers. This is of course in keeping with how few of that generation are recognizable stylists as well—how few are players of that Albert/B. B. King variety, recognizable after one note. Some of the greatest jazz musicians write in immediately recognizable ways as well—Monk, Mingus, George Russell, Parker, 'Trane, Wayne, Joe Henderson, McCoy Tyner, Herbie Hancock, Roscoe Mitchell are all distinguishable from others in their camp by their melodic, rhythmic, timbral, and harmonic formations.

What often gets lost in these discussions of composition and improvisation is the importance of individual tonality and rhythmic sensibility as crucial elements in the creation of a riveting jazz performance. Whether someone like Dexter Gordon was composing original material in his solos or interpreting a favored melody, his sound and swing was what kept you spellbound. Ditto for Rollins, Miles, Shorter, or any number of pianists I could think of. In the avant-garde, both Ornette Coleman and the Art Ensemble of Chicago originated group sounds and group rhythmic approaches that were as engaging as their bracing, bristling melodic content. Great jazz demands great interpreters of the jazz sensibility, no matter where the material comes from—a composer's hand or the ether.

5

CANON FODDER

JAZZ REPERTORY

JIM MACNIE

White napkins, neatly folded. Pleasantries whispered by the genial robots who bank on tips while delivering million-dollar hamburgers. The hush of an American performance art being given the respect it deserves. There can be a fair amount of formality in jazz clubs—ostensibly aural art galleries that live and die on providing short-term comfort and a palpable sense of community.

Early in 2001, Manhattan's Jazz Standard was performing these tasks nicely, the room crowded with listeners taken with the septet on stage. Maybe the patrons realized they were getting something offered nowhere else: the band was performing a tune called "In Honor of Garner." It's a piece by Herbie Nichols, and in the hands of this group, it was a joy. Itchy and wry, it nonetheless boasted a certain urbanity, like it wanted to be the life of the party while sustaining its dapper demeanor. And even though the band stretched the melody—pianist Frank Kimbrough bouncing his hands across the keyboard while building a string of parallel themes, and saxophonists Ted Nash and Michael Blake intersecting each other with a variety of dissimilar notions—"Garner" sounded familiar.

It shouldn't have. Nichols never recorded the tune, and few musicians if any have previously played it. One of jazz's more compelling also-rans, Nichols was a bandleader and composer who worked without fanfare in the 1940s and '50s. Though a prolific composer (he allegedly wrote 170 pieces during his forty-four years), fewer than forty-five were recorded. Disappointing, because his work is wonderfully clever and easily enjoyed; the pianist claimed Chopin and Villa-Lobos as inspirations while delivering a somewhat rounded take on the sound of Thelonious Monk's piano trios. The Nichols tunes that did make it to records—terrific stuff like "2300 Skidoo," "Applejackin'," and "Cro-Magnon Nights"—are usually considered treasures by those who have heard them.

More than treasures to the band onstage. Kimbrough and cohorts call themselves the Herbie Nichols Project, and they regularly convene to interpret the pianist's work. They've recorded two discs of his material, *Love Is Proximity* and *Dr. Cyclops' Dream;* as I write, they're beginning work on their third. Fully smitten with Nichols's canon, they have taken it upon themselves to convey both his talents and their appreciation.

Although each member of the group is a bandleader and composer on his own (indeed they're part of the Jazz Composers Collective, an organized aggregate fully dedicated to writing new material), there's an unflagging consensus about sustaining the Project, a sense of dedication to go with the preservation. Like if Nichols's music doesn't receive proper attention, maybe their own work has no shot at having a historical impact.

In a formal sense, playing the pieces of a bygone era should be considered jazz repertory. But the members of the Project don't have the luxury of knowing how Nichols meant "Garner" to sound. With help from producer Michael Cuscuna they discovered the tune at the Library of Congress. Using the melody line from the lead sheet (a musical sketch rather than a full-fledged score) they collectively arranged their take during a rehearsal. No original indications of tempo, dynamics, or chord voicings are available. This is literally imaginative stuff.

"We don't have any idea how Herbie would have done some of these pieces," says the group's coleader Ben Allison. "But we feel we can take it in any direction. And though we love it, we probably wouldn't deal with it if we couldn't bring our own sensibilities to bear."

Sitting at the celestial Steinway, Nichols must be cackling. His music was recorded in trio form only: piano, bass, and drums. He never got to hear horns applied to his charts. So later in the septet's set, when trombonist Wycliffe Gordon joins Blake, Nash, and trumpeter Ron Horton (bassist Allison and drummer Matt Wilson supply the rhythmic oomph) for a few swoops around "Ina," I jot the term *living legacy* in my notebook. If there was ever a case to be made for the thrill of jazz repertory, this was it, million-dollar hamburgers and all.

Of course, that's not always how jazz repertory works. Usually, rep ensembles are formed to promote the accomplishments and boost the resonance of a highly celebrated composer's oeuvre. Over the last fifteen years, the music's big guns—Morton, Armstrong, Ellington, Mingus, and Monk—have been accorded such treatment. At powerful cultural bastions such as Lincoln Center and Carnegie Hall, at festivals in America and around the world, in underground bars and alternative art spaces, plenty of tickets have been sold in the name of classic jazz. It's a search-and-rescue mission of a sort, and participants include those proud of their progressive status as well those who have been branded conservatives. How broad-based is the zeitgeist these days? Just type the phrase *jazz repertory* into Google.com and go pour yourself a tall beer. You might be there awhile.

Myriad examples of jazz rep have emerged during the last two decades. In Boston a reeds-only group called Your Neighborhood Saxophone Quartet transcribes and arranges the music of Sun Ra. Melodies sometimes lost in the Arkestra's din are placed front and center, and the band receives kudos for its creative retooling. In New York John Zorn and Tim Berne unite to slam the hell out of Ornette Coleman's songbook on a program called Spy vs. Spy. Their maniacal interpretations are defended by the claim that they want "Chippie" and "Ecars" to be considered in a fresh light. In 1997 Chick Corea spends the entire summer reupholstering Bud Powell's songbook with a star-studded band that includes Roy Haynes, Joshua Redman, and Christian McBride. Many of the shows sell out. And in the fall of 2000, Joe Lovano releases a gorgeous record called *52nd Street Themes*. It's built on bop-era blowing staples like "Sippin' at Bells" and "Tadd's Delight" and uses plush orchestrations for nonet. A Grammy lands on the saxophonist's doorstep.

As jazz fans know, there have been questions regarding the value of such retrospectives. To wit: does a healthy art need to promote its yesteryear glories? And what happens when those glories compete with, if not overwhelm, the music's contemporary practitioners? Are the golden oldies golden or old?

Depends on who's doing the listening. Most of those pondering the issues are insiders: jazz critics, booking agents, academics, historians, and the musicians themselves. But it's a big world out there, and jazz doesn't cast much of a shadow in the larger pop sphere. UPS drivers, mafia dons, and middle-management dudes at Betty Crocker might not be familiar with "Django," "Ko-ko," or "Doin' the Voom Voom." So when such jewels are spilled before them, epiphanies aren't out of the question.

In a practical sense, repertory is about edification. "Art does not reflect society, environment and consciousness so much as it tells us what society, environment and consciousness do not know," says Martin Williams. In discussing the future of interpreting venerable works, it's proper to stress the need to learn something in the process. For musicians, just the act of playing the tunes can be revelatory. Negotiating the nooks and crannies of "East St. Louis Toodle-oo" or "I Let a Song Go Out of My Heart" is a lesson in luminous chord voicings and disarming melodies. In an improviser's hands, repertory becomes a chance to scrutinize from within and examine the imagination that went into creating timeless architecture. Sonny Rollins has said that he became a better composer after deciphering Monk mazes like "Friday the 13th." Scores are blueprints of beauty, and transcriptions are done in hopes of capturing the emotional verities that the tunes so eloquently offered when they were initially introduced. Musicians work through them to be literate.

It can be different for an audience. One listener's brave new world is another's memory lane. When I'm sitting at a repertory show, I usually feel a certain amount of nostalgia in the air, regardless of how unique the update. But I seldom mind. To some degree I'm there because I believe these pieces will bring me enjoyment, or at least have their emotional vitality revealed. Now and again at a gig, saxophonist Michael Blake will glide through Coleman Hawkins's "Maria." He plays it straight, and the theme flutters away from the bandstand. It's unlike much of Blake's own stuff, and somehow it never fails to make me swoon. Formally it could be called anachronistic, its old-fashioned ways representing sublime cultural totems often devalued in modern discussions about what's new and important. But this tune and others like it are nuggets, and even when they're not played straight, their virtues are fairly obvious.

The brave-new-world side of the coin is obvious. For skilled listeners, jazz rep is a chance to hear what a particular group of musicians can bring to a brand name. Modernism is a perpetual work in progress, and the slants that have been put on classics over the last couple decades have not only removed mystery, but added to the profundity of some pieces. Inserting curious vernaculars, inverting durable frameworks— if a tune can be substantially sculpted and still sustain its musical gravity, there's a flag to be raised somewhere. And there in row 32, seat 6, incisive questions can trump prescribed emotions. Like, is the regard accorded this composer truly merited? Like, what kind of insights are the musicians bringing to bear? Like, shouldn't they dump the drummer? For those on the receiving side of the bandstand, repertory can unlock as much as it secures.

One of my first experiences with jazz in New York was the 1981 Interpretations of Monk show put on by producer Verna Gillis. A novice at the time, I nonetheless thought I had a pretty good fix on the music at hand: my pop rearing primed me for the composer's catchiness, and I was utterly taken with way the tunes simultaneously offered depth and whimsy. But when pianist Anthony Davis went into "Monk's Mood" at Columbia University's Wollman Auditorium, his playing led to an unexpected place. In Monk's hands the piece presented blue thoughts that somehow offered a promise of a less turbulent tomorrow. Davis wasn't so sure about that sunrise. His take was comparatively forlorn. The emotions I had gleaned from Monk's discs were rerouted. It was twenty years ago, but I can still remember feeling juiced about having a fresh view of the tune.

The modern rep movement got its start almost a decade earlier. The New York Jazz Repertory Company was born in 1974. Its George Wein–produced Carnegie Hall shows were under the guidance of four dedicated codirectors: Sy Oliver, Stanley Cowell, Dr. Billy Taylor, and Gil Evans. Although it sustained itself only a year or so, it pretty much birthed the activity that resounds today. And it formalized an esthetic that had been floating through many peoples' minds: the jewels of the past are valuable enough to be worn with contemporary fashions.

Those up on their history know that the floodgates opened soon after. *Village Voice* critic Gary Giddins convinced the brass at New York's famed Cooper Union to underwrite a program that would create and support a new entity, the American Jazz Orchestra. A band of pros under the baton of John Lewis, the AJO tipped its hat to Gillespie, Fletcher Henderson, Basie, Ellington, and others. The goal was simple: spotlight, savor, and study jazz's back pages.

"I think the past is truly, truly important, and a lot of the criticism directed toward repertory bands has been a little bit unjust," says Jon Faddis. The trumpeter is the music director of the Carnegie Hall Jazz Orchestra. Though not a formal repertory band (Faddis defines reps as ensembles that transcribe original charts and re-create original solos), they've performed Wein-produced concerts in the name of great composers and classic jazz works since 1992, paralleling similar strides made ten blocks north at Lincoln Center by Wynton Marsalis and the Lincoln Center Jazz Orchestra. Expert at creating novel contemporary pieces out of bonafide antiques, over the past decade the CHJO has had Jim McNeely, Slide Hampton, and others provide kaleidoscopic reconfigurations of tunes as different as "In the Mood" and "Giant Steps." "We try to strike a balance," Faddis explains. "We've got great arrangers who put their own stamp on the pieces, and I think that's crucial to moving the music ahead."

When done correctly, repertory unlocks new perspectives as it secures a position for its subject. Just because you play older pieces doesn't mean you're not going to make new music. Perhaps the artist who's struck the best creative balance with the repertory question is Dave Douglas. The trumpeter has cut three discs of music of other composers' work. With each, he's included his own tunes, written under the inspiration of the composer at hand. *In Our Lifetime,* a nod to Booker Little, contained five originals and three Little pieces. It's much the same for *Stargazer* and *Soul on Soul,* dates that celebrate Wayne Shorter and Mary Lou Williams, respectively. Douglas deliberates on his subject's structural tendencies, factors in their creative aura, and comes up with a two-sided repertory statement, one that gives the honorer as much dap as the honoree.

Repertory also works because young adepts often need something meaty to sink their teeth into. Combing the archives is a task to savor. Imagine fledgling horn players in Tampa and Tucson. Their progress is bolstered by a wealth of musical information that comes in the form of an established paradigm: deal with "Body and Soul," deal with "Anthropology," deal with "Giant Steps." In any given year, jazz sees the arrival of more advanced improvisers than it does advanced composers. Consider James Carter's initial salutation. In 1993 the precocious twenty-three-year-old had chops galore. But his album debut featured Ellington, Byas, and Ra nuggets alongside three rudimentary blues tunes of his own devising; that balance foreshadowed the title of his covers-only sophomore date: *Jurassic Classics.* He may have been a tomorrow man, but he needed to access yesterday to make his point.

If programs built around classic canons do sustain themselves in the future, in part it will be because repertory moves have become career boosters. Monk's talent was appreciated by a wider public after he tipped the hat to his most obvious forebear on 1955's *Plays Duke Ellington.* The modern era finds Joe Henderson as a prime example of classicism's clout. In 1985 Stanley Crouch reminded us of the then-forty-eight-year-old tenor saxophonist's vitality, producing a live recording at the Village Vanguard with the help of Michael Cuscuna. Jazz insiders were reminded of Henderson's skills, but the tenor player remained a rara avis until he found a nifty portal for his work by cutting *Lush Life,* the sublime 1991 nod to Billy Strayhorn. Mainstream magazine articles on historic reclamation for both musicians and material followed. So did better paying gigs. In an essay about the World Saxophone Quartet, Martin Williams weighed in on such a turn of events: "Artistic retrenchment is not stagnation; it may be a necessary, even healthy state of affairs."

Securing a future for repertory bands has an extra musical value as well. Defending any particular art from oblivion is a hero's undertaking, and while many hands have shaped jazz during the course of the century, it's primarily a product of African American minds. But rust never sleeps, and before outfits like the LCJO and CHJO got on the case, there were whole slabs of black cultural achievement decaying in the shadows of history.

"Milt Jackson felt that jazz had never really got its due because it's a black music," says Faddis. "Whether or not that's true, I think that there is a discrimination about our music in this country. So it's important to understand exactly how much it's worth."

Art's impact is enhanced when its value becomes part of a larger discourse. The work that lies ahead for jazz rep is defending its spot in the great American narrative—an overwhelming conversation when you consider how the floodgates opened in the mid-1980s with the arrival of compact discs and the archive liberation they engendered. Some musicians feel that assuring a position for repertory is equivalent to fortifying black identity, a way of balancing the cultural scales.

"Fifty years from now, who's going to care what you played?" queries pianist Marcus Roberts. "I mean if we don't protect Monk, how we going to protect the modern guys? Who draws the line in terms of establishing at what point what's being called 'new' right now has value seven years from now?"

One thing is certain: it's crucial for those touting repertory to avoid the eau de mothball. The listeners who find current repertory gambits too precious sometimes grouse about the venues in which they're presented. There's something antiseptic about huge halls. I've had less than stellar experiences at Carnegie Hall and Lincoln Center affairs, even when the bands were doing their job just fine. Large ensembles are about dynamics, and while the expansive rooms signal significance, they have a tendency to rob the music of impact.

The coziness of lower Manhattan's Fez club is part of the draw for the Mingus Big Band shows that take place there every Wednesday night. The composer's music—rhythmic rumbles, sprays of melodies and countermelodies, that joyous mania—bounces off the walls of the oft-packed house. Mingus's push 'n' shove esthetic is in full blossom when "Moanin'" or the like is careening around the room. Ditto for the way that Ballin' the Jack or Steve Bernstein's Millennial Territory Orchestra dominate their comparatively tiny environments at the Knitting Factory and Tonic. Though elaborate and sophisticated, this music was originally written for social situations. Plopped into low-rent hangouts, it takes on a buddy-buddy vibe that eludes it in more posh locales.

When heard in context, it picks up a more visceral tone. Charts initially written to get dancers out on the floor need to have their punch be purposeful. The Lincoln Center Jazz Orchestra learned that lesson when it began its "For Dancers Only" events. The band is a different kind of creature when it swings and stomps for a ballroom full of couples in motion. Whether it's tickling a summertime crowd on the Lincoln Center patio at dusk or driving a crowded dance floor nuts in some St. Petersburg, Florida, theater, the music makes a deeper impression. Artistic Director Marsalis says he's been excited by "the communal aspect of it." The thrills become more palpable as the informality grows.

But perhaps the best reason repertory has a future is that it's deepening its own definition. These days, a wider scope of historic figures is getting the treatment. The Jazz Composers Collective wasn't the first group to herald Herbie Nichols. A pair of Dutch musicians, pianist Misha Mengelberg and drummer Han Bennink, hooked up with trombonist Roswell Rudd and saxophonist Steve Lacy to flitter through Nichols's tunes on 1983's *Regeneration*. Chicago's Witches and Devils ensemble is out to examine Albert Ayler's tornado of sound. New York's Prima Materia makes hay with Ayler, too—though it was created to almost exclusively address late-period Coltrane. A few days ago I ran into French horn player Tom Varner. He said he'd just cut a record that interprets Don Cherry's *Complete Communion*. Evidently mainstreamers aren't the only ones to feel the grasp of beloved canons.

"The success or failure of the American Jazz Orchestra may ultimately be measured not only by the quality of its own performances but also by the number and tenacity of other ensembles that take the plunge," said Giddins about his baby way back when. On both large and small scales, that number is rising.

Recording-wise, some the best discs of the last thirty years have been made in the name of repertory. Jazz would be a lesser place without

Lambert, Hendricks & Ross's *Sing a Song of Basie,* Louis Armstrong's *Satch Plays Fats* (Waller), *Air Lore* (Morton, Joplin), Arthur Blythe's *Light Blue* (Monk), World Saxophone Quartet's *Plays Duke Ellington,* Paul Motian's *Bill Evans,* Jerome Harris's *Hidden in Plain View* (Dolphy), Fred Hersch's *Passion Flower* (Billy Strayhorn), Uri Caine's *Toys* (Herbie Hancock), Kenny Garrett's *Pursuance* (Coltrane), Danilo Perez's *Panamonk,* and the *News for Lulu* hard bop project concocted by John Zorn, Bill Frisell, and George Lewis. Who knows what kind of results will come from further investigations into ancient songbooks?

Remember Ornette's declaration: Tomorrow is the question. He's dead on, completely correct. But those golden oldies are golden, and a glance over the shoulder should never be enough to hobble a true forward stride. I've got five bucks that says right now, as you're reading, "The Stevedore's Serenade" is being played in Kentucky, "The Pearls" is being banged out in Louisiana, and, somewhere in South Dakota, "Hackensack" is wafting through the Black Hills. That's the kind of geography I like. Here's to 20/20 vision and a 360-degree vista.

JOHN F. SZWED

What strikes me about those in the high-profile jazz repertory movement is that they forget (or never knew) that for years there have been musicians out there doing what they are now doing, and often doing it far better in terms of scholarship, musicianship, and sheer excitement of results. More often than not they are in the provinces, unfunded and unsung. One such older group (apparently no longer active) was the New McKinney's Cotton-Pickers, a Detroit band, I believe, which devoted itself to the old McK's. C.-P. book and recorded it for Bountiful Records. Other musicians have gone abroad to find sympathetic souls to help carry out their work—Bob Wilber, for example, who went to France to get Fletcher Henderson's unrecorded arrangements for Benny Goodman recorded for Arbors Jazz. Or they have come from abroad, like Marty Grosz, whose *Unsaturated Fats* put unrecorded Fats Waller songs on record. Another one is C. W. Jacobi's Bottomland Orchestra, whose Clarence Williams re-creations for Stomp Off seem definitive. James Dapogny of Chicago, on the other hand, has painstakingly orchestrated some of Jelly Roll Morton's piano works in the style of the Red Hot Peppers. Meanwhile, other musicians, like Vince Giordano's Nighthawks, have become specialists in learning the styles of entire eras.

I might add that jazz scholars have also been amiss on this subject, since few of them have ever taken revivalists seriously, instead treating them as the moldiest of figs. Long before there were repertory groups per se, there were clusters of musicians who were pursuing the same goals by reviving New Orleans jazz (in the early 1940s, and twice again in the late '40s and the '60s) and boogie-woogie (in the '40s). And what those musicians accomplished back then has helped make what we know about those musics today as complete as it is.

TED GIOIA

I take a guilty pleasure in hearing old jazz music resurrected by repertory bands. I am almost ashamed to admit it. I know that the fixation on re-creating the past is not a healthy sign for an art form. I realize that our music should be looking ahead, not behind. I even admit that I should be listening more to new music by unknown (to me) players from distant lands, rather than hearing "Ko-ko" and "Mabel's Dream" for the umpteenth time. But I can't help it. Give me a band of young turks playing like they were Hot Peppers on Jelly Roll Morton's payroll, or even Jazz Messengers under Art Blakey's tutelage, and I go gaga.

And let me be honest: I listen to music for enjoyment. This may seem like a platitude to many people reading these words, but they would be horrified if they knew what was really going on in the jazz scene. After years laboring as a jazz scribe, I know the sad truth. Many critics—perhaps even most of them—don't give a hoot about listening pleasure. So many reviews are written with odd agendas—the writer wants to impress readers with how hip he is, how progressive, how "out there" he goes. He wants to show off his inside knowledge, his macho aesthetic, his cool attitude. In many instances, the jazz record review is merely a pose, not an honest emotional response to the music.

If I could wave a magic wand and make one change to the world of jazz criticism, I would cause all these posers and their contrived attitudes to disappear. Only real responses to the music would be allowed in print. My advice to aspiring critics: if you want to act a part, then pursue a career on the stage and leave jazz writing to people who deeply care about the music.

So, on closer reflection, I don't feel quite so guilty about my enjoyment of jazz repertory efforts. At least it's an honest attitude. And the pleasure I take in this music is testimony to the vitality of jazz. How many other cultural artifacts from the 1920s hold up as well as "Mabel's Dream" or "Sidewalk Blues"? Very few, in my opinion. This legacy deserves to be preserved, studied, shared, and enjoyed.

And repertory efforts aren't always incompatible with creating something fresh and new. When John Zorn takes on Sonny Clark or Ornette Coleman, the cold chill of the mausoleum is nowhere evident. Jazz musicians are tough cusses—even if you tried to get them to play the old stuff in the old way, they will still find a loophole in the deal, some way of making the old become new. I suspect that this ingrained hostility to the formulaic will prevent jazz from ever becoming as stale as most other repertory arts.

Remember, too, that everything is a matter of degree and balance. Repertory efforts are far too prevalent in the classical music world, where they flourish almost to the total exclusion of new works. Just last week I saw a headline in the newspaper—it read, "What's New in Classical Music? Not Much." I would not want to see this happen in jazz. But for all the fussin' and fightin' about jazz repertory, it still accounts for only a small percentage of the music being performed and recorded. So don't worry, be happy. For my part, I plan to enjoy the old classics until I find a good reason to stop.

K. LEANDER WILLIAMS

Not to sound like a Johnny One-Note, but I tend to view talk of jazz repertory with the same suspicion that I do the composition-as-sacred-endeavor discussion. Isn't it sort of much ado about nothing? The reason we even have a jazz "canon" is because musicians and listeners have elected to return to, rediscover, unearth, and anoint those compositions that have charmed us and left some sort of imprint on our psyches. This has *always* been the case. As I see it—and as it is underlined in the pieces Gary Giddins wrote as he was starting the American Jazz Orchestra—the jazz rep movement seems like yet another attempt to lend jazz a legitimacy, protocol, and subsidy generally reserved for classical music. That may be why sometimes at Lincoln Center it almost seems as if *where* the music is being presented is more important than the quality of the music itself.

Basically, I just feel like if the composition is great and the musicians tackling it are sufficiently inventive—Tommy Flanagan comes to mind again, as do the Mingus Big Band, David Murray, and some Don Byron—therein lies the value. If there happen to be a few folded napkins and tuxes in the vicinity, well, so be it.

WILL FRIEDWALD

I usually agree with my friend, the saxophonist, bandleader, composer, and scholar Bill Kirchner (whose best line might well have been about the Manhattan Transfer, which he described as "the kind of music that gives white people a bad name"—I wish I'd said that!), but when he announced that there should be a moratorium on tribute records, I couldn't disagree more. Jim Macnie wisely locates the heart of the repertory music not necessarily with the late American Jazz Orchestra or Lincoln Center, but with those dozens of grassroots groups formed by musicians to celebrate certain specific forebears, most notably the Nichols Project (Herbie, not Red). I'm also fascinated by the way these new takes on the old sometimes become matters of ethnic or gender pride—Latin American trombonist and composer Steve Turre reinterpreting the music of Latin American trombonist and composer Juan Tizol, John Zorn making a claim for Burt Bacharach as Jewish Jazz (and though the all-female big band Diva doesn't exclusively play the music of jazz women, they usually open with Mary Lou Williams's "Roll 'Em" and include an Ella Fitzgerald medley).

By that definition, virtually all jazz incorporates some of jazz repertory. Your average instrumental jazz album these days generally consists of three types of material: original tunes, which is to say new compositions by the leader or members of the group; popular standards (works not generally written for jazz purposes, but which were usually introduced in shows and films before becoming part of the jazz tradition); and jazz standards, which 90 percent of the time means something by Ellington or Monk. We could even take it to an extreme and posit that, in all cases when musicians play tunes other than their own originals, they are in fact participating in some loose definition of jazz repertory.

Perhaps the term *repertory jazz* could then be applied to those musicians who play in premodern styles—they generally hate the word *Dixieland*, while *traditional jazz* isn't too exciting and *New Orleans Jazz* isn't always accurate. Still, these modern jazz rep groups, which perhaps began with Steve Lacy's all-Monk-all-the-time band circa 1960, were directly inspired by what had long been going on in the traditional jazz world, such as Louis Armstrong's salutes to Fats Waller and W. C. Handy (produced, by George Avakian, around the same time as Ella Fitzgerald's salutes to Cole Porter, Rodgers and Hart, et al.). Even earlier there was Bunny Berigan's suite-style tribute to Bix and the Bob Crosby big band's glorious reinterpretations of the New Orleans repertoire. In jazz rep, the distinction isn't necessarily classic versus modern (in fact, such a distinction could even be considered counterproductive) but large scale and institutional (Lincoln Center) versus independent (Dan Levinson's brilliant re-creations of the Original Dixieland Jazz Band and other very early "fabulous five" type units), and, most important, between those groups that strictly re-create the old as if it were Mozart or Haydn, which is indeed a worthwhile pursuit, and those that reinterpret through a personal sensitivity (i.e., Dave Douglas has so far not done a tribute album to Kenny Dorham, but if he did, it would sound very different from Don Sickler's series of tributes to Kenny Dorham at the Jazz Standard, which feature new improvisations in the style of KD's bands but re-create the ensembles fastidiously).

The trouble with jazz rep is, in the end, not a trouble with jazz rep at all—it's that other areas of jazz may not be as well organized. Now in the jazz world, as in the classical world, there's attention being paid to the past, but, unlike in traditional European art music, there are few support systems that commission and underwrite new jazz composition. The same way that contemporary classical composers have to compete with Bach and Mozart, contemporary jazzmen have to contend with the entire history of jazz as a gauntlet thrown before them.

BEN RATLIFF

Jazz is definitely a cumulative art form: it gathers momentum gradually, when various composers and bandleaders add bits and pieces to what already exists. So repertory jazz sort of helps the process, stimulating high-quality transcriptions of old pieces, and even making a difference in the jazz scene at large. The Herbie Nichols revival—starting with Rudd, Lacy, and Mengelberg, continuing through Mosaic's Nichols box set, and reaching its highest moment yet in the work of the Jazz Composers Collective—has definitely spread the word about Nichols. I hear him loud and clear in some of today's interesting players, from Ethan Iverson to Andy Biskin to Anthony Coleman. And the massive Ellington reconsideration has probably had some sort of impact, if mostly on academics, critics, and certain musicians within Jazz at Lincoln Center's sphere of influence (I think most jazz musicians ready to produce interesting work already have their own take on Ellington and aren't among those shelling out to hear the LCJO homages).

Repertory can also pose arguments and question favoritism. Jazz critics, and the prevailing notion that jazz without some root in Afro-Americana is not quite jazz, have buried Stan Kenton, for example. But I recently heard the Chicago Jazz Ensemble, directed by Bill Russo, play a mighty impressive set of 1940s-to-1970s Stan Kenton music. In the past, just thinking about him made me feel sort of tired. But there I was suddenly admiring the music's energy, its otherworldliness, and the composer's crazily dogged belief that works of jazz need readily graspable "concepts." Russo's face looked strained with a mixture of humility and evangelism. "People used to love this music," he said to the audience. "Today they love it a lot less, because it is loud, and pretentious, and muscular. But there is great quality here, and I ask you to listen for it." It was at Birdland, and I think the house was packed with hard-core Kentonites—that is to say, I didn't recognize anyone—but Russo's mission worked for me.

On the other hand, even Wynton Marsalis says he hates the word *repertory*—because it intimates something refrigerated—and I know how he feels. The idea is that reevaluating old minds should stimulate new minds. But I don't see it happening nearly as much as it should. What I do see, for sure, is the use of old, familiar names selling tickets and propping up an ailing jazz business. When I talk to nonjazz friends about what I'm going to see and hear, they don't quite get the emphasis on tributes and reworkings of. They feel rightly suspicious that a purportedly living art form should have so much abiding interest in its glorious past. In most respects, America is not a country that revels in its own cultural traditions. And jazz is looking more like a strangely isolated island.

PETER MARGASAK

I don't buy the notion of preservation for jazz rep. The music of Monk, Ellington, and Mingus has endured thanks to its own virtues, not because of a repertory band. But, of course, those three wrote such gripping, multifaceted tunes that it's natural and perfectly legit for musicians to explore them over and over again. Jazz musicians have a rich history to loot and I don't know anyone who would object to players running wild through such riches. When it comes to overlooked composers like Nichols or John Kirby, it's not so much preservation as it is about discovery. I love listening to the Herbie Nichols Project recordings because it lets me hear tunes that I'd never encounter otherwise. On the other hand, the Lincoln Center Jazz Orchestra's take on Ellington sounds stiff to me; give me the readily available original stuff every time. Good tunes will survive, even if they fade from view. Eventually someone will uncover lost gems. The CD reissue market is currently doing an amazing job of digging up such treasures.

I guess my itchiness about jazz rep occurs when it becomes institutionalized. It gets nicely packaged, but it usually sounds stale. It seems to me that such offerings are more useful for attracting subscribers to a concert series than for delivering the musical goods. I know that Nicholas Payton took plenty of artistic liberties with his recent Louis Armstrong homage, but they all seemed fairly cosmetic and dull to me; funking up Satch—how risqué! But the concept made for a fine lure to the festival circuit and the formal concert hall subscription series.

STUART NICHOLSON

All forms of contemporary culture at the moment strive for what is perceived as "authenticity"—the difference between, for example, Duke Ellington's *Blanton/Webster* CD set and Wynton Marsalis and Jazz at Lincoln Center's recording of Ellington tunes. It is here that lies the problem with the current repertory movement, exemplified by Marsalis's recording of Jelly Roll Morton's "Tom Cat Blues" using the old acoustic recording technology at the Edison Studios in West Orange, New Jersey. Compare this sort of revivalism to the creativity of Gil Evans's version of Morton's "King Porter Stomp" from *New Bottles, Old Wine* or Charles Mingus's version of "Wolverine Blues" from *Epitaph*.

Repertory re-creations, unlike classical music, are in competition with original recordings made without preconception or purist obsession. Tex Beneke was the first to re-create the Glenn Miller band, and subsequent leaders included Ray McKinley and Buddy DeFranco, who churned out Miller's hits for nostalgia buffs. Warren Covington directed the Tommy Dorsey Orchestra and even had a hit with "Tea for Two Cha Cha"; Lee Castle directed the Jimmy Dorsey band; and currently Woody Herman's orchestra is directed by Frank Tiberi. These used to be known as ghost bands, and jazz repertory is in considerable danger of straying into this territory.

Today, with the need to get funding like ballet or classical, the mission seems to be to prove that jazz has a canon of masterpieces that bear constant performance. Thus Jazz at Lincoln Center is not a ghost band, but serious art, jazz-as-America's-classical-music. Yet the notion of playing compositions from the jazz repertoire is hardly new. Max Harrison has pointed out in *The Essential Jazz Records Vol. 2: Modernism to Postmodernism* that "jazz has been in too much of a hurry, rushing through its resources, failing properly to explore avenues of potential major growth." He was talking about John Zorn's *News for Lulu*, where Zorn and his musicians perform a series of originals by the likes of Kenny Dorham, Sonny Clark, Hank Mobley, and Freddie Redd: "Improvised with much greater variety of expression than might have been thought possible from the earlier rather dour hard bop presentations." This kind of approach clearly represents an important way ahead for jazz, but it should not be the only way.

We are getting rather a lot of repertory and reiterations of renascent styles lately, and not much adventure. Players play in the adopted styles of jazz's posthumous heroes and give no indication that anything has happened in jazz in fifty years. If this represents the way ahead, then jazz is well and truly dead and repertory is a safe haven. It's almost as if the jazz tradition weighs so heavily over the present that everybody is scared to move out of its shadow "in case it's not called jazz." With the cachet jazz has now acquired, nobody wants to be caught outside the tent.

One of the problems of jazz entering academia and jazz-as-America's-classical-music—of which repertory is integral—is that in exchange for breathing such rarefied air, the gatekeepers of culture want to know what jazz is. In the past, anybody rash enough to offer a definition of the music could be pretty sure that, within months, somebody would come along with a style that would blow that definition out of the water. Today, the shutters are coming down. With the proliferation of jazz education, the obvious by-product of streamlining an art form is conformity. Jazz is in danger of becoming an art within clearly prescribed limits, which is beginning to stifle the music's promise of growth.

I was recently talking to the veteran French bass player Henri Texier, who played with Bud Powell and Dexter Gordon as a young man on the Paris jazz scene. He currently leads a forward-looking band in the same scene and was reflecting on jazz today. "I was a kid, but all these great musicians I was playing with in Paris—it was the Blue Note, famous place. When I was playing with Dexter Gordon and Arthur Taylor on drums, the MJQ was in town and John Lewis and Milt Jackson came down and they started to speak together. I started listening and they were speaking about originality. That was the main word, *originality*. Somehow this is staying in my mind and I think if you want to be original you have to be adventurous too. And now we are in a period that is kind of strange from the young generation of the American artists; it's not very easy to be adventurous but to be accepted it's much more easy to play something academic, much more easy."

As the American saxophonist and educator Dave Liebman observed, "I go to Europe once or twice a month to teach and play. The European musicians are definitely not tied to the bebop tradition. They have respect for it, but it doesn't mean anything to them. Some of them do it better than others, but it's not something that's part of their repertoire by necessity, which it is here, of course. So they have much more original music, much more combinations of the new. So there's a lot more mixture going on there and in my eyes, much more risk taking and adventurous music than you would hear with the standard thing in America. America you get pretty much up and down the line. It's wonderful jazz playing but not that creative to my mind. Europe is a great scene, there's a lot of musicians there who have a particular way of playing that is unique." The jazz party is not yet over, it is simply moving to a new address.

GREG TATE

Sonically speaking, all current American jazz, barring that of the surviving masters like Roach, Rollins, and Ornette, is repertory jazz, because it all sounds vaguely like what somebody else did on some record released sometime between the 1920s and the 1980s. "What does your soul look like?" asks the trip-hop artist DJ Shadow. This question could easily be put to the copycat cast of characters now inhabiting the jazz uniform in all camps. Dave Douglas, Jason Moran, Bill Frisell, and Mathew Shipp deserve to be excluded from this indictment, I think—

all four are immediately distinguishable from their peers and predecessors. All are also dedicated to expanding our notion of what a jazz performance, a jazz composition, and a jazz repertoire can be—and *will* be, if they have any say about it.

PETER WATROUS

One can argue all one wants about repertory jazz, but here are three things I consider facts:

One: All jazz musicians are repertory musicians in that the act of learning how to play usually involves a long period of adoration, adulation, fixation, imitation, etc., where the younger musician absorbs an older musician's style. Clearly to leave it at that isn't particularly interesting, except as a parlor trick. But lurking in there is a deep love for something older.

Two: The official, upper-middle-class repertory movement has virtually nothing to do with jazz practice. That is, what happens at Lincoln Center doesn't affect what happens at the Knitting Factory. Jazz is so big that the east and west sides of it hardly know they're part of the same continent.

Three: That arguing about it is pretty much a waste of time; repertory/not repertory is all part of the same jazz mess; what exactly was Sun Ra playing when he performed "Space Is the Place" late in his career, and who cares as long as it functioned for the audience and the performers.

OK, my personal experience is that hearing Ellington played by Lincoln Center is an extraordinarily sensual experience, that the sumptuousness of the music can best be felt in the presence of an orchestra, that recordings, literally accurate, don't compare. And that the grassroots repertory movement often produces something that can't usually be heard in clubs. Remember that average jazz practice, for all sorts of different reasons, is usually improvised music with not so much planning. The repertory movement has often provided the exception, one welcomed. And finally, that moment of reproducing, or reviving, or meddling with the past, is often temporary; for every Ben Allison–driven

Herbie Nichols show (if they irritate somebody conceptually), there are Allison's exceptional recordings.

STUART NICHOLSON

Yes, sitting in front of a big band is indeed a powerful experience, and at a subjective level can indeed be sensual and sumptuous. But this still leaves the matter of "authenticity" in repertory moot. There are any number of big bands all over the world that play the music of Ellington, but, like the Lincoln Center Orchestra, usually fall down in a number of key areas. Well before the "repertory" movement was given a name, Bob Wilber achieved an equal measure of success and notoriety for his re-creations of Benny Goodman's orchestra. He was even whistled up as music consultant for the Francis Ford Coppola film *Cotton Club* back in 1984. But in both instances the rhythm sections were unable to master the conventions, or indeed sound, of the 1920s and '30s, and solos often betrayed an allegiance to contemporary times. This is also true of the Lincoln Center Orchestra.

I am very sympathetic with the movement in classical music that insists that the only "authentic" way to hear the music is as the composer intended, with the instruments of the time and—as far as possible from musicological research—obeying the composer's original instructions for expression, use of ornaments, dynamics, and tempi (so avoiding the wide variations between Solti, Bernstein, and Rattle). Here a viola or violin made as "late" as 1841 is deemed entirely unsuitable for Mozart's music, since he died fifty years earlier. This raises a very germane problem that the repertory movement has not yet solved: what, precisely, are we listening to?

A group of halfway decent sight-reading musicians can work their way through a Basie or Ellington chart and make it work, but is that art or merely craft? I submit it is the latter. I have played in and led big bands through this type of material, and I would never have claimed it was "art." For a repertory performance of Ellington, Goodman, Lunceford, et al., there has to be a real, concerted effort to get into the musical nomenclature of the period from which it comes. I think the "art" comes in getting into the heads of the musicians who originally performed this stuff, the stylistic and rhythmic nuances, the vibrato, the precise tonal qualities of each instrument and the internal balance of these bands (which only used a limited public address system, if any). I think if this trend is to have any value it must replicate the past exactly, so the audience gets a feel for how the music actually sounded in its time—so the past reaches out into the present. I also think that re-creating original solos or, as Loren Schoenberg has shown, performing solos in the spirit of Ben Webster or Paul Gonsalves (after years of study and a deep understanding of the style) is highly apposite.

Such re-creations enable us to experience at first hand, or in modern fidelity, the dynamic range of this music and the impact it might have made upon those who first heard it. The Dutch group the Beau Hunks use period instruments and the original scores on albums such as *The Modern American Music of Ferde Grofé* (1998) that bring to life "symphonic jazz" pieces he wrote for Paul Whiteman between 1924 and 1931 that have not been performed for almost seventy years. As early as 1975, on the album *Runnin' Wild*, the New Paul Whiteman Orchestra showed that "authenticity" can be achieved in re-creation. With period instruments, original scores, and a rhythm section that understood and honored the conventions of the 1920s, one got a sense, through modern fidelity, just why Whiteman enjoyed the phenomenal success he did.

The other route, as I have indicated in an earlier post, is to completely reimagine the work of an Ellington or an Armstrong. The issue of whether we are listening to art or craft is no longer an issue with highly imaginative recastings of the repertoire. Take albums such as Martial Solal's *Plays Ellington*, the NDR Big Band's *Ellingtonia*, the Vienna Art Orchestra's *Duke Ellington's Sound of Love*, or the French Caratini Jazz Ensemble's masterful tribute to Armstrong, *Darling Nellie Grey*. Far from "meddling with the past" whose effect "is often temporary," these are serious interpretations that will be listened to as long as people seek out the best of jazz, from whatever era. This is repertory looking forward, and here perhaps lies the future of the genre, making it relevant to today's ears at the same time as making you want to refer back to the original recordings.

6

LOW-BUDGET CAREERS

THE BUSINESS OF JAZZ

PETER MARGASAK

Art and commerce are always uneasy partners, but it's an especially troubled team when you're talking about jazz—which, at least according to the cliché, is a music of freedom and unpredictability. Art, here, is all about surprise, while commerce seeks to eliminate it. In theory, at least, jazz transforms itself into something new before ever becoming formulaic, while business identifies something as a form and attempts to develop a hard and fast definition; it's easier to sell something that's solid than something that's amorphous. Since jazz inherently tries to avoid such pigeonholing, certain strategies have slowly emerged to make it viable commercially; nearly all of the tacks described here require the artist's vigilance and participation in business affairs.

The business of jazz has always been a dicey proposition, especially since the music began to fall from popular favor in the 1940s. By 2000, jazz garnered less than 3 percent of U.S. record sales (that figure also includes smooth jazz sales). Amid ruthlessly efficient corporate consolidation, the general atmosphere of business today involves little goodwill toward art unless it generates attractive returns. Stockholders are the new arbiters of taste. Leaving aside jazz—a term applied here with great looseness—produced for strictly commercial purposes (the Kenny Gs and the Najees), the major label system has developed a relationship with creative music that is by and large adversarial.

The jazz business, like any business, isn't monolithic. Countless models of production and distribution are at work within countless artistic scenes and subscenes. The music's regular stylistic shifts serve to propel the business; swing, bebop, free jazz, and fusion captured the public imagination and generated widespread media attention. The last big movement to attract that kind of broad notice was the neoconservative Young Lion explosion of the 1980s spearheaded by Wynton Marsalis. Since this movement, which is more about creative regression than progression, gained ascendancy almost twenty years ago, there have been no developments to galvanize the music in the same way. If anything defines the jazz world now, it's its sprawling diversity and relentless stratification; there's repertoire jazz, neo-bop, neo-swing, free jazz, jam bands, and fusions of every stripe—funk, rock, electronica, world music styles. For each pocket of activity there is a specialized, obsessive audience to go along with it.

Too often jazz recordings released by the major labels serve as barometers for the health of the music. The major labels spend the most money on advertising, receive the most record-store shelf space, and garner the most press; to the general public, the major labels *are* the record industry. According to that model, jazz would seem to be in sorry shape. Back in the 1970s and '80s each of the six major distribution companies handled a number of self-contained, independently operated jazz labels, but in the last few years the landscape has been altered greatly. There are now five companies following the merger of UNI and Polygram—a similar merger between EMI and BMG threatens to reduce that number to four—and they now exert a much greater control over a radically reduced number of jazz labels. Such consolidation is a cost-cutting measure, and it follows that jazz departments at each label undergo the same downsizing process. The UNI–Polygram merger found the former's jazz department, GRP, combining with the latter's, Verve. To enhance economic efficiency both staff and roster were reduced. In addition to such shrinking opportunities for jazz at major labels, the stakes have also changed dramatically.

With an ongoing short list of exceptions—singers Cassandra Wilson and Diana Krall are recent examples—it's been a long time since jazz sold records on a pop music level. Despite this, the major labels apply pop's bottom-line mentality to jazz sales. Whereas the labels once respected their jazz departments as high-art loss leaders, now media conglomerates expect jazz to generate significant profits. "I have seen larger companies swallow up smaller companies before, but now they're strictly about commerce," says veteran producer Steve Backer, a man who has long reflected the music's diversity. In the 1970s he produced commercial acts like Gil Scott-Heron and the Brecker Brothers along with envelope pushers like Air and Anthony Braxton. Backer says the autonomy of the jazz departments has been eroded by the short-term profit-grabbing and expense-shrinking methods of corporate boards. Jazz records rarely sell large amounts when they're released, but accrue sales over decades, like *Kind of Blue* by Miles Davis— the 1997 rerelease alone has sold 1.5 million copies. These days, however, the major labels rarely have the patience to let that happen. Labels cut out most titles long before they get the chance to demonstrate that kind of consistency.

In those rare instances when major labels have retained young jazz artists, their development is frequently stunted by the heavy hands of producers. The synergistic savvy of getting New Orleans trumpeter Nicholas Payton to cut an album that pays homage to his brilliant Crescent City ancestor Louis Armstrong during the latter's 100th anniversary makes plenty of sense from a marketing standpoint. The project has celebrity, history, geography, and lineage on its side—all superb factors in generating media coverage and record-store shelf space. But the actual music seems like something of an afterthought. The majority of such concept albums, as well as inappropriate songbook collections and well-placed cameos by big, cross-pollinated stars, would seem to be born of marketing meetings.

The reality of marketing isn't lost on newer generations of musicians. "A lot of what the business is about, as far as I'm concerned, is putting a name to something," says bassist and composer Ben Allison, an inside-out player who's made all of his recordings for independent labels. "What better way to keep your own thing going than to create your own category?" In 1992 Allison cofounded the Jazz Composers Collective in New York with a handful of like-minded musicians who believed that they were lost in the growing crack between the uptown neo-boppers and downtown dilettantes. By forming a nonprofit organ-ization and promoting their own concerts the members succeeded in obtaining grant money—a relatively new but significant variable in the jazz economy—scoring record contracts with good independent labels, generating press, touring Europe, and getting into New York's most prestigious clubs. The key factor to the JCC's success was its members' willingness to double as musicians and businessmen in order to develop their own brand. Allison admits, "I don't find it depressing. What is depressing is when people don't take an active role in defining what they do, and some other loser does it for them. The beauty of it is that we define it on a daily basis."

Although jazz musicians have been involved in selling themselves to a certain extent for as long as the music has existed, Allison feels that most younger musicians understand the need for a savvy, hands-on approach, where creativity in presenting and selling oneself is analo-gous to the approach taken to the music itself. "It's a hard nut to crack to figure out how to be successful, but still maintain your identity," he says. "This is a tough world for that. To me that's the struggle, but it's also the great adventure."

Allison and his cohorts—pianist Frank Kimbrough, saxophonist Ted Nash, and trumpeter Ron Horton—all record for scrappy independent labels like Palmetto, Arabesque, and Omnitone, which give their artists great creative latitude. As the majors turn their backs on jazz there's been a staggering proliferation of independent labels, long the backbone of the music. In many cases such imprints are labors of love that owners operate as backbreaking hobbies; the owners of labels like Okka Disk in Chicago, Wobbly Rail in Chapel Hill, and AUM Fidelity in New York all support themselves via other means. Even for labels that provide full-time employment to a small, devoted staff, presenting the music is a constant struggle; generating press, airplay, store shelf space, and distri-bution are chronic problems for independents without the muscle of the media giants. Many of these labels engage in a sort of entrepreneurial improvisation, finding new ways to promote and sell records.

Jazz has a long history of artist-run imprints, from Debut (Charles Mingus) to Survival (Rashied Ali) to Screwgun (Tim Berne). The emergence of digital recording and design technology has made it easier than ever for artists to release their own music. The downside to this process is that too many records are being made; there's a glut of music on the market, bombarding consumers with choices and making the already competitive routine of getting albums into shops that much more difficult. But it's now possible for musicians to record their music directly on their computers, where it can also be edited and mixed. With recordable CD technology it's possible to manufacture limited-run releases with very little up-front money. Of course, CD-Rs are, at best, a convenient creative outlet. Most record stores demand a more professional, finished package. Yet even album packaging is something that more and more musicians are involved in. European stalwarts like Peter Brötzmann and Han Bennink usually make the artwork for their albums, and Allison not only does graphic design for his own recordings, but he's begun to earn income by doing the same for other musicians.

The rapid advancement and affordability of technology is radically altering the landscape of the jazz business. The Internet certainly isn't the solution to jazz's commercial marginalization, but it may be part of it. Web sites and Internet mailing lists work as cheap and efficient promotion machines, providing information on recordings and concert appearances that jazz fans once had great difficulty nailing down. MP3s allow artists to offer samples of their music as an inducement to consumers to purchase a finished product. In addition, many labels now sell their catalog online, potentially getting their products into far more homes and at a much greater profit margin than with traditional methods of distribution, which involve record stores and distributors each taking their cut of the sale price. While the decline of brick-and-mortar record stores has been exaggerated, online distribution has provided a significant sales supplement, particularly for the music's most passionate consumers.

When sales of a thousand copies of an album frequently represents a success in jazz, it's hardly surprising that recordings are rarely the primary source of income for a musician. But without recordings it's often impossible for a musician to land gigs, particularly out-of-town ones, and out-of-town gigs often help to precipitate press and record sales. Saxophonist Ken Vandermark—the recipient of a valuable Mac-Arthur fellowship in 1999—says he frequently prefers to be remunerated for a recording with product rather than cash; selling his own releases at gigs generates significant revenue, sometimes more than he gets for actually performing. He's also one of many younger musicians who isn't shy about taking his act on the road, touring the country like a rock band, playing night after night in venues not typically associated with jazz, from churches to rock clubs, with cover charges usually less than ten bucks. "Take the music to the people," he says. "Bring it to where they want to go and where they feel comfortable hanging out." It's certainly paid off for Medeski Martin and Wood, who for years lugged all of their equipment—including a hefty Hammond B-3 and a Leslie speaker—around in a van to relentlessly tour rock clubs. Over time the record sales soared—they went from the indie Gramavision to vaunted major Blue Note—and the venues grew in size, in some cases, from 300 seats to 3,000. Unfortunately, they also dumbed their music down for jam band hordes, but they unquestionably made a passionate, physical connection with big groups of people, a bona fide community.

Playing in rock clubs isn't merely an example of creative thinking on the part of the musician. Those musicians, record labels, and promoters who don't recognize that today's as well as tomorrow's rock audience ostensibly is the new jazz audience are hopelessly stuck in the past. Musicians who found their voice in the 1980s and '90s are something new; most of them grew up with parents who grew up with rock as the everyday style of choice. So why wouldn't music fans of the same era be the same way? Record companies like Thirsty Ear (Matthew Shipp, Tim Berne, Charles Gayle, Mat Maneri) and Atavistic (Vandermark, Nels Cline, the reissue imprint Unheard Music Series) began as rock labels, and it's no fluke that people like Sonic Youth's Thurston Moore are playing with improvised music heavies from Cecil Taylor to Mats Gustafsson. It may just be a replay of the heady days of Filmore West, when Charles Lloyd was a big star, but I'm convinced that something different is happening now.

It's one of jazz's most debated topics: how to bring new audiences to the music. Presenting musicians in high-priced clubs with drink minimums isn't an effective way to attract younger fans with limited resources. Concert halls also tend to be expensive and sometimes steep the music in a rarefied air that can be off-putting to the novice listener. Jazzers have been operating outside of the club circuit for years; the AACM used churches, Ornette Coleman rented New York's Town Hall in the 1960s, and Sam Rivers opened up his New York loft spaces to concerts in the 1970s. Vandermark is doing it now, curating concert series in café basements. His approach to touring isn't lucrative, and it requires that his bands accept rustic accommodations, long drives, and cheap meals, but he views the effort as an investment in the future. "You get a hundred people at a gig, maybe ten of them will leave hearing something they've never heard before that they'll want to hear again," he says. "If you didn't do that gig that number would be zero."

It's hard to imagine anything changing jazz's status as fringe music, but without an increased degree of autonomy on the part of musicians, many of them will slide into a punishing irrelevancy. In an ideal world, perhaps, musicians could focus exclusively on their music, but if anything is certain about the future of jazz, in a business sense, it's that such myopia will lead nowhere. The business model of high-priced jazz clubs is becoming extinct, as is the notion of purity that comes with it. Jazz has always absorbed new musical currents, but in the future jazz's hegemonic reign could well dissolve into a wide-open pluralism. Those players who snooze will surely lose.

JOHN F. SZWED

Accepting scraps from the table, being left out of the party, playing the frog prince—this is all old news to jazz and its players and devoted followers, and, frankly, part of the consequences of being devoted to an African American art form in this society. But being passed up by the forces of commerce is also part of the music's strength. (If it were a different time, one would here quote Mao on how those who know they are weak will win because they know their weaknesses, etc.) The view from the bottom, after all, gives a special perspective from which one comes to know what's false and what's worth having. In any case, it's difficult to imagine jazz as we know it being bought by the pre-teens who feed the coffers of the record industry, or being funded by the captains of industry.

What we might practically be concerned with is the shallow attention that jazz gets, and the level to which jazz criticism has fallen. If it's now axiomatic that one can't walk into a record store and receive guidance on what's interesting and important, things are almost as bad in the press. It's worth remembering that distinguished magazines like *The Jazz Review* ran on something smaller than a shoestring, edited by people who were themselves scuffling journalists, and no one was paid for their work. Jazz discography is the best discography there is, written by self-taught scholars, and no one ever receives enough to cover their efforts. Jazz history, likewise, is largely the product of amateurs, written in the fever of fandom. The important writing may never ever be paid for and never be fully rewarded in any form, but that is no excuse for it not to exist...and it is the writers on jazz who should be leading the way toward creating new means of communicating what we know.

Though folks may not know it—to paraphrase W. C. Williams—there are people out there dying for the want of this music....

TED GIOIA

I don't see why jazz and commerce need to be in conflict. The conventional wisdom tells us that capitalists have exploited jazz musicians—that club owners and record producers are greedy parasites who take advantage of struggling artists in order to maximize profits and lead lavish lifestyles. I beg to differ. While conducting research for my book on the history of West Coast jazz from 1945 and 1960, I compiled a database of jazz nightclubs that operated in California during this era. I found that all of them, without exception, had either gone out of business or stopped featuring jazz by the 1990s. I pose the question: if running a jazz nightclub is so profitable, why do they all fail? If running an independent jazz label is so lucrative, why do most of them disappear after a few years?

The truth is far different from the conventional wisdom. The greedy may indeed inherit the earth, but they won't do it by running jazz clubs or starting indie labels. Jazz capitalists are our friends, not our foes, and most of them are beset by the same financial pressures as the artists themselves. Of course, we have all heard horror stories about promoters or producers who have resorted to duplicity to further their financial interests, but read the biographies of various jazz stars and you will find that the musicians were also capable of underhanded dealings. No one in the jazz world has a monopoly on virtue (no, Virginia, not even the critics!). Until the socioeconomic structure of capitalist society disappears—and I'm not holding onto my circular breathing waiting for this to happen—artists and capitalists will need to work together to further their common interests.

The encouraging sign, from my perspective, is the growth of disintermediation technologies that allow the artist to reach out directly to listeners—via the Internet, or MP3 files, or other previously unknown modes of communication and distribution. The jazz musician can now take on much of the role formerly filled by the capitalist. (Mao would not have approved, but he didn't know the changes to "Confirmation" either, so I don't look to him for guidance on how jazz artists should operate in the new millennium.)

These technologies will slowly change the economics of jazz. By my calculation, an artist who sells compact discs or downloadable music files directly to fans can live quite comfortably with an audience of less than 20,000 serious listeners. And a "low-budget" career can be sustained on an audience of perhaps half that size or less. The bottom line: all commercial aspects of a performing career—from booking gigs to publishing lead sheets—are becoming easier and more manageable through new technologies.

Of course, musicians can continue to ignore or criticize the dictates of commerce, but they will do so at their own loss.

WILL FRIEDWALD

As someone who's actually worked in the record industry, I have a slightly different perspective on the business of jazz—it isn't about who gets recorded and who doesn't, or who's on a major label and who's on an independent label or even self-produces his own product. It's not even about promotion or getting airplay (Peter didn't mention radio and it is a crucial issue). God knows all those things are factors, but the real issue is distribution. I don't have the statistics in front of me, but it seems that 90 percent of records are retailed through chain stores in malls that have precious little shelf space for jazz, and those give considerably more attention to some established smooth jazz star—if they have a jazz section at all. You won't find more than a title or two in the Miles Davis or Sonny Rollins sections and all of a sudden you will understand why companies like Verve devote so many resources to one new series of compilations after another—because mall chain retailers are much more likely to stock *The Best of Charles Mingus* than they are *The Clown*. (Retailer tip #1: any album called *The Best of So-and-So* or *So-and-So's Greatest Hits* will sell significantly more than any other album by So-and-So.) What gets into the stores? It doesn't depend on ink or airplay, it depends entirely on how hip the buyer is. In that respect, Cliff Preiss is one of the most powerful men in jazz, not because he's a distinguished journalist, broadcaster, and producer, but because he's the jazz buyer for all the stores in one of the larger chains in the largest city in the country, Virgin Records in New York. Thanks to Cliff, Virgin has just about the most comprehensive coverage of the total jazz scene I've ever seen. If every store had a Cliff Preiss, someone with the dedication and knowledge to put the right stuff in there, jazz would be a much healthier music. But it isn't; it doesn't matter if the *Times* rave reviews some hot new trumpeter or you hear something sensational on WBGO if by the time you get to Coconuts the record isn't in the racks and probably never will be. Obviously, the majors have an advantage over the minors, but there are B-level releases with the conglomerates that probably get less attention all the way down the line than, say, Chick Corea on his Stretch imprint distributed by Concord Jazz. As good as the rest of the jazz support system is or isn't, the whole thing collapses at the distribution level. That's why I welcome all alternatives to traditional record distribution. Selling records at gigs can only get you so far (although Paula West, certainly one of my tip-top fave jazz and/or cabaret singers, does so well self-producing and -selling largely on gigs that she doesn't even bother to solicit labels), but it's a start; so is the Internet, whether that means that the music itself is delivered via factory-produced CDs through the mail or sent over the wires in MP3s and other hard-drive formats. These are only the beginning. For jazz to experience a true reversal of fortune, something—I don't know what—has got to come along to totally supplant traditional retail distribution. A certain part of me hopes it will put it out of business entirely. Virtually everyone I've ever met in the music industry would agree that it couldn't happen to a more deserving bunch of fellows.

BEN RATLIFF

The upper-level jazz record business seems to stay afloat mostly with corporate shakedowns and constant new arrivals of executives who want to prove that they're loyal to jazz. Some gestures are made, some cash is spread around, and then it becomes clear yet again that jazz doesn't really sell. And the musicians go back to their little indie labels or whatever. So many jazz albums—the vast majority, I think—are basically souvenirs of a live performance. Jazz needs its context to be understood; it needs the clubs, the small but deep listenership, the obsessive conversations. If you go see, for example, the Andrew Cyrille–Mark Dresser–Marty Ehrlich trio, you'll probably want their album, *C/D/E*. If you haven't, there may be little reason why you'd want to buy it.

But then again, one of the patterns of jazz record buyers—no matter whether they're at Tower, at gigs with an extra twenty dollars to spend, or looking at MP3s—is that they climb these backward rope ladders: if they liked Charlie Haden's new solo albums, they might want to check out Ornette Coleman, which might make them want to check out Cecil Taylor's *Unit Structures*, which might get them interested in Andrew Cyrille, which would lead them to *C/D/E*. And if the Internet makes these branches, or leaf veins, or family trees, or whatever, easier to navigate, it will be that much easier for prospective record buyers to pull the trigger.

Basically, though, I think we're still talking about a live medium. The best jazz record sales come from artists who are really persuasive in concert—whether on the Diana Krall level or on the Los Hombres Calientes level.

K. LEANDER WILLIAMS

It's all about expectations. I think it'd be nice if the musicians I dig could get rich off the music, but in the absence of that trip down Easy Street, I'd settle for the assurance that, at the very least, they can make good livings off their labor. Unfortunately, the commodification and subsequent corporatization of everything has placed us in a Darwinist climate that links basic existence to numbers: "Can't guarantee an audience of half a million? So what do you expect from us, a free ride?" At this point we probably shouldn't make record sales an indicator of the idiom's health because quite a few people who don't purchase large numbers of jazz records are not averse to going out and hearing the music live.

As Peter M. points out, the thing about jazz is that no true business model has ever existed for the music's sale. It seems like there might have been one during the Swing Era until you talk to someone like Artie Shaw, a bona fide icon whose love-hate relationship with the business actually drove him to hang up his clarinet for good back in the 1950s. Every so often in jazz history a "Take Five" or "Poinciana" or "The Sidewinder" or "Hello Dolly" strikes a chord with larger audiences, but every one of these has proven an isolated incident. "How High the Moon" was being recorded by just about everyone at a certain point in time, but only Les Paul and Mary Ford's bare-bones version with Paul's proto-overdubbing scored a hit. Paul would be the first to suggest that no one has figured out how to guarantee a whopping return on a jazz investment.

On the flip side, however, as limited as the major label/retail distribution apparatus is for jazz these days, the DIY aesthetic Peter M. is describing also has its share of drawbacks—the biggest of which is its propensity for flooding the market with vanity products. I'm sure every writer in this book has received a ton of self-produced discs that, for any number of reasons, just aren't worth listening to. ("Audible spam" is the phrase Gene Santoro used to describe them.) Then there are the records that kind of sound like some earlier jazz breakthrough but are served up with some small, usually technological or technical gesture that's supposed to suggest contemporaneity. I could be wrong, but that's the way I hear many of the records by the folks in the Jazz Composers Collective. It's almost like the idea of jazz as a private game system that Peter W. was advancing earlier, which may be why those discs don't seem to resonate much beyond heads in that circle. There's no denying the musicianship, but I think what jazzers really need to do is stop talking among themselves.

JIM MACNIE

After spending a few years at *Billboard*, framing most of my pieces around the way the music is treated as commerce, I hadn't thought of the business of jazz for a while, and reading through the responses to Peter's piece has thoroughly depressed me. John's got a point: in general African American art music ain't worth diddly in the U.S. of A. (though I stress the art part over the blackness part—obviously D'Angelo and Dr. Dre ain't feeling no money crunch). And Will's correct, too. Mom-and-pop stores buy CDs for eleven or twelve bucks and sell them for sixteen, seventeen. That's not much of a markup over the initial investment, so no wonder they have to go with the hits packages and super-obvious titles. The travails of distribution and product placement are a nightmare that begets a vicious cycle of can't-sell-if-you-don't-have/can't-order-if-you-don't-sell. If you're not servicing a hip population, your store is unlikely to be hip. And don't forget: if a shop or a chain doesn't have an impressive inventory of titles, its management looks like half-stepping fools. Frustrating for retailer, consumer, and artist alike.

Future-wise, if anything is going to level the playing field, it's e-commerce. I'm not talking Amazon and Barnes & Noble and the rest, though the breadth of their stock has no doubt thrilled fans of online shopping. But at this point it's so easy for an artist to have his or her own simple Web page that it should not only enhance the presence of indies, but also really, really, really indies. It's unlikely that rural parts of the country are dotted with stores that keep the Nagel-Heyer or AUM Fidelity stuff in stock. So if the jazz buffs on North Carolina's Outer Banks want to get Eric Reed's *Happiness* or Joe Morris's *A Cloud of Black Birds,* they're only going to have to Google around until they find their hero's site (which will likely connect them to the product) or the label sites (which will surely connect them to the product). Moving product can now take place with a mouse click or two, and though the Internet revolution isn't here yet, the broadband future is inevitable. Coconuts won't talk to Eremite? No problem, the customer will. Those people dying for want of the music, as John says? By uniting them through their myriad interests, giving them a forum for exchanging viewpoints (be it know-nothing bluster or insightful scholarship), and broadening the power of their niche, I'm thinking they'll die a little less often.

GREG TATE

The only thing I know about the business of jazz is that if I go to Tower Records' jazz section I can find a recording of some obscure New Orleans trumpet player whose masters owner is still getting paid for the work of this fella, probably in his grave for decades. Which is to say that over time jazz is making hell-a-money for somebodies other than those who play it. Jazz being a part of the criminally unchecked American recording industry, we can't be surprised by the disparity between living musicians' incomes and the fortunes their work will provide for nonplayers (and player haters) and their great-grandchildren. Stolen legacy indeed. Flautist James Newton once told me he records music that will never be released in his lifetime so that his progeny might profit from it after he's gone. As an end run around corrupt record company accounting practices it seems a stroke of genius.

PETER WATROUS

Yeah, yeah, yeah, big business is bad, indies are good; now if that isn't as simplistic and cliché-laden a posture as the one used by last year's swing revivalists, I don't know what is. Here's my personal experience: big business record companies are big business, and they don't owe us (musicians, critics, fans) anything. Would that they did, but they don't. But even so, they at times put out historically important music. That Blue Note records the Greg Osby spectrum and loses piles of money doing it suggests that even within major labels there is a conscience. Miles Davis recorded for the Devil, Columbia Records, changing the world. And they kept recording him, even after his music became diffi-cult and lost money. While the market, and capitalism at large, dictates much of what goes on in the jazz recording industry, there are wrin-kles, shadings that often are a product of an individual's conviction within the system. Steve Backer and Bruce Lundvall (both entrenched in major labels) will be lauded a hundred years hence for their deftness in recording good music, and lots of it, against the short-term best interests of the companies for whom they worked.

Under this discussion runs a thought: American music, along with many of the greatest moments in American cultural production, has been formed by the pressures of audiences pushing against the expres-sive needs of the artist. That is, to speak to Kelvin's point, the less insu-lar the music is, the more of an audience it gains. Duke Ellington and Louis Armstrong figured out a third way between art and commerce, producing an audience for their creations. Large record companies helped them do it. There's one of the distinctions of American culture: that genius can come in an artist's ability to reconcile what seem like oppositional impulses.

Finally, two points. I'd like to suggest that endless monologues against bad guys—in this case big business—be backed up with either some facts and figures or a little bit of research; otherwise it just sounds like weird howling. How about calling the record companies and get them to explain why X was dropped, and why Y, even though he or she sells twelve copies a year, is kept on. And second: how does race play into the periodic convulsions of the record industry? Who suffers first, and why?

STUART NICHOLSON

I liked Peter M.'s piece. It said so much that needed to be said, and the responses fill in the blanks. The business of jazz is certainly a depressing subject. Will mentioned Virgin Records, but walk into their jazz department and all the records that are displayed above or at the ends of racks mean a record company somewhere has paid for that privilege (end-of-rack deals being the most expensive). Look up at the so-called "best selling chart" in Virgin (or HMV or whatever the big record chain store near you), and, again, some record company had to pay for the record's position there, even if the deal often includes limited advertising in the press.

In the U.K., for a jazz release to go on the listening posts at Tower costs around £600 (almost $900), and even with limited advertising thrown into the deal, what small independent can compete? Shopping space is at a premium, particularly in prime sites in big cities, so record chains have to work out if they can actually afford to rack jazz releases— in other words, a jazz release has to pay its way. Chain stores are not in the business of displaying stock and leaving the rest to fate; if it doesn't sell, and quick, it's out. And most deals with record companies are done on a sale-or-return basis, so don't even blink when some releases hit the racks—so quickly will they be pulled by computer stock-keeping methods if they fail to sell. But, as several record company insiders have often assured me, if you think that's bad, in Japan a *Swing Journal* "Seal of Approval" allegedly costs $5,000.

Then try to get a new jazz album played on jazz radio. In order to do this, the music has to conform to certain requirements: it must be acoustic first and foremost, it must "swing," and its overall characteristics must not venture too far "outside." The only alternative—on the radio, at least—is the smooth jazz stations, who also make specific demands: strong melodic hook, simple catchy melody, bright and breezy themes, a contagious backbeat, no more than four minutes in length, and so on. Both are hardly incentives to innovation.

Jazz clubs and concert halls can be expensive—no, are an expensive way to consume jazz. That's why I like jazz festivals. People go there as much to hear jazz as to consume the atmosphere, whether it's a big field site or in a complex like North Sea. You can try this concert, that concert, and, if you don't like it, try somewhere else, since most of these festivals have several bandstands—in Montreal's and Vancouver's outdoor concerts, jazz becomes a part of the community, and it works.

But, ultimately, jazz artists have got to get out there, tour their product, and build up an audience base. Back in the 1970s, when Pat Metheny was engaged in tireless low-budget touring, he didn't have the Internet to help him. But, as he told me, all he needs is an audience base of 250,000 people worldwide, and if half buy his releases he's in business. This is the reality: building up an audience base from ground zero, and now there's the Internet to help.

We all moan about how hard it is, yet when artists do make it (viz. Medeski Martin and Wood), there are always moans about "selling out," "diluting the product," "dumbing down," and so on. So MM&W have "dumbed their music down for jam band hordes," have they? Yet their releases don't bear this out. The major label releases *The Tonic* or *The Dropper* are far more interesting than the indie *Shack Man*. In London this year they had a non-jam band audience (we don't have that phenom here) eating out of the palm of their hands, and in the European fests I saw them play last year, and the year before with John Scofield, the response was equally ecstatic. Good for them. It does seem we still want our heroes to endure a respectable degree of penury.

I think in our discussions we have tended to hope that jazz as we now know it can reach beyond the congregation of its true believers; that independents, the Internet, and MP3s can somehow gain new converts to the music. I don't see things happening this way at all. I think the music has got to change with the times. Jazz has always been inextricably linked to the social fabric from which it emerged. It is significant that in the last ten years this link has become estranged, as has jazz's arm's-length relationship to popular culture, and jazz has drifted further away from public consciousness. I think these elements have got to change.

Why do MM&W connect with young audiences? Because there are young and not-so-young pop fans who can see through the sham of the pop record business and want something a little more adventurous and challenging. The question is, how does jazz reach this audience? I am convinced Wynton is right about one thing: jazz is a dance music, a social music. But while it worked in the Swing Era, Wynton is trying to re-create the golden past, and that's a sham, too.

It's equally unrealistic to believe that jazz will regain its audiences in terms of the old "swinging" rhythms of the past, the pianist comping like Bud Powell, the bassist playing four to the bar, the drummer accenting the two and four with his high hat while playing ride rhythms on his twenty-two-inch Zildjian.

I've been across Europe and have seen young crowds queuing around the block for a new breed of jazz artists who mix club-culture rhythms and jazz in Oslo, Stockholm, Copenhagen, Amiens, Paris, and Cologne. These guys are touring their music, getting out there and building up an audience base. Their rhythms and sampling resonate with the familiar musical landscape of European club culture, but, best of all, the improvisation fascinates them. Many are unaware that this sort of thing is jazz, but they are dancing to the music, transfixed by improv. What's more, when these guys have played in Turkey or India, the audience response has been the same. They must be doing something right.

Here is an entry point into a puzzling, forbidding music. And I'm sure, having seen how keen these audiences are for the music, that once they've got their bearings they'll be off. Yes, it may be back catalog that gets the initial benefit—Miles (as usual), then Coltrane—but then things open up. It's a sure sign jazz is alive and kicking and doing business on its own terms. It feels right. I'm getting fed up with this musical necrophilia that passes as jazz: players who are in eternal competition with jazz's great past because they opt to play in the style of masters. Don't they know it's been done better years ago?

I always remember Peter Apfelbaum and Pat Metheny at different times telling what amounts to the same story. They both said, in their own way, that when they see a band acting as if the Beatles never happened, they have this urge to go up to them and say, "Hey, didn't you know, there've been all these changes since that music was first played." This jazz of the new millennium is unmistakably jazz of now. No one is saying it's better than what has gone before, or that it is even somehow "progress." But people are voting with their feet to hear it, and they are buying new albums of the music in the thousands. Maybe this is the future of jazz. If not, maybe it's pointing in the right direction. Loosen up. Enjoy the ride.

PETER MARGASAK

Writing about the business of jazz could easily constitute a full book itself—a reality that obligated me to focus on a few specifics if I wanted to offer anything more than lame generalities. Yes, as Will pointed out, I totally neglected radio, partly for the reason I just cited, and partly because jazz on the radio seems to have less and less of a future. What we hear on NPR stations keeps shrinking in terms of both hours programmed and stylistic breadth; marketing research and professional consultation is killing jazz on the radio. College radio will continue to feature the music, and a few bastions within public radio and AM will still play jazz. But aside from the rare specialty show, jazz's presence on the radio seems certain to be negligible at best. Internet radio stations may offer some hope to hard-core fans, but I don't think it will produce many converts.

Will mentions promotion, but few labels beyond the majors can afford to do this in any meaningful way. Marketing jazz has always had a cheesecake factor, but I see it increasing. I encounter pictures of Diana Krall's legs more than I hear her music. I agree with Kelvin that the music's health should not be confused with its sales, and I also agree with him that as recording technology becomes more affordable and accessible we'll be stuck with a lot more crap; the idea of anyone being able to make a CD is great, but the reality usually means more mediocrity.

Stuart shares my enthusiasm for musicians creating their own micro-businesses using this technology, but I find his Pat Metheny example to be a poor choice: "all he needs is an audience of 250,000 people world-wide...." Hell, if most jazz musicians had a worldwide audience of 2,500, let alone 25,000, they'd be pigs in shit.

I object strongly to Peter W.'s characterization of the piece as "big business is bad, indies are good." The fact is, major labels are the face of jazz to the general public; they can afford to advertise the most, they get the best positioning in record stores, generate the most press, and get the most airplay. Clearly some of these things are directly related to the music's quality, but they're undeniably linked to finances, too. Yes, labels like Blue Note have stood by artists like Osby and Moran as long as they've been in business, but I'd say these are exceptions. Indies are not all good, but in most cases the artists are more involved in the decision-making. In a recent *Down Beat* article pianist D. D. Jackson chronicles his depressing experience with RCA; when the company downsized in 2000 he spent months trying to figure out if he was still on the label. He's thrilled to be back with an indie—Justin Time—that's willing to give him a straight answer. Sour grapes, perhaps, but I think there's more to it than that.

Technology has exerted a profound effect on business in a very short time, so I hesitate to prognosticate too much. But, again, I assert that musicians who don't bone up on these matters will only undercut themselves in the future.

7

ORIGINAL RECIPE VS. EXTRA CRISPY

JAZZ VOCALS

WILL FRIEDWALD

It might be a minority opinion, but it seems to me that the millennium marks the most productive era in jazz singing since the 1950s. CDs (many of them self-subsidized) by new singers cross my doorstep almost daily, and New York features several clubs that spotlight emerging vocal talent. It's certainly the richest period that I've experienced firsthand.

How well I remember the loft scene of the 1970s: an occasional vocalist would make an appearance, but her talent would be limited to marathon, free-association scatting (not even following the chords) and mangling the melody to "Lush Life." Any time Mel Tormé or Sarah Vaughan was on one of the talk shows, they were singing something by Stevie Wonder.

In the 1980s and early '90s audiences realized anew that they loved the Great American Songbook. These were prime years for established talent—with the exception of those who died tragically young, virtually every major singer of note was alive and at peak form. Then, in the mid and late 1990s, a new crop of jazz singers began to attract attention, and by the turn of the new century not only are the artists of a half-decade ago maturing rapidly, but even newer talents are coming out of the woodwork.

It's tempting to divide all contemporary (and, presumably, future) jazz singers into two very broad categories: original recipe and extra crispy. Original recipe singers are those who come more out of the jazz-and-standards tradition, who use the Great American Songbook and familiar jazz instrumentation. Extra-crispy singers are those who venture beyond the cutting edge, doing things that, for instance, you can't imagine Carmen McRae doing in a million years.

This observation is not meant to cast either of these camps in a pejorative light. In the first group, there are some contemporary retro princesses who are little more than a faint echo of the great ones on jazz singing's Mount Rushmore. To come up with a new style, a sound all one's own, while remaining faithful to tradition and without resorting to futuristic flakiness, is indeed a worthy goal. Sometimes tearing off on an avant-garde tangent can be just a way to hide an ignorance of the basics of singing in tune or in time. However, many of those who travel beyond the radar of tradition are winding up in some fascinating places indeed.

To a large extent, the future of jazz singing will be about the rediscovery of great ones who have long been long hidden in plain sight. The 1990s saw the passing of Ella Fitzgerald, Sarah Vaughan, Carmen McRae, Billy Eckstine, Joe Williams, Mel Tormé, Betty Carter, Frank Sinatra, and many others. Their places were filled not only by newcomers, but by veterans who had been around the block a few times but never fully appreciated: Shirley Horn, Abbey Lincoln, Freddy Cole, Andy Bey, Mary Stallings, (no longer Little) Jimmy Scott, and, briefly, Teri Thornton. (There are some who consider Tony Bennett a 1990s rediscovery—it's true that he found a whole new audience in this decade, but by any reasonable standard the remarkable Mr. Bennett has never been away.) Two of the finest singers of experience who seem due for immediate rediscovery are both middle-aged white women named Carol—Sloane and Fredette. But most in need of proper presentation is the amazing Bill Henderson, who existed only on the peripheries not of jazz but of jazz consciousness, and only made a handful of albums over a forty-year period. The way he sings now—

with his raspy, soulful voice, somewhere between Ray Charles and Johnny Hartman, and his sure-footed command of blues and ballads—sounds better than any of his vintage recordings, outstanding as they are. And when will it be time for the likes of Ernestine Anderson, Jackie Paris, and Etta Jones to receive the acclaim due them? Nancy Wilson could mop the floor with any singer, old or new, if only just once she would take a break from those zillions of jazzless, "adult-contempo" quiet-storm-type albums she insists on turning out year after year and merely do an album of standards with an acoustic rhythm section.

The veteran artist who, as of this writing, seems to have the most impact on the present and future of the art form may well be Mark Murphy, both as a vocalist himself and as a teacher. Murphy is that great rarity, a hipster with heart, himself a student of the entire history of the form who has mastered every technique from scatting to vocalese, from the blues to bossa nova; moreover, he is a superlative balladeer. Murphy performs and teaches all over the world, and, speaking from a New York perspective at least, a goodly portion of the more worthwhile new talents have found themselves at one time or another in his workshops: Barbara Sfraga, Mary Pearson, Tessa Souter, Kurt Elling, Diane Hubka, Kendra Shank, Andrea Wolper, Catherine Dupuis, Joan Bender.

The Marsalis thing turned everything around in the 1980s—now, apart from living legends such as Rosemary Clooney and Bennett, most of the big names are young. Even though it seemed scatting (and "Lush Life") was overdone in the loft era, it continues to be a useful technique, one much employed by younger singers (that is, those born in the 1950s or later). Saving Diana Krall and Jane Monheit for later, it seems to me that the three biggest names in jazz singing in terms of popularity and critical consensus are, in order of appearance, Dee Dee Bridgewater, Cassandra Wilson, and Dianne Reeves. They are virtually the only younger singers to have achieved true diva status (somehow the word doesn't apply to Krall or Monheit), and all three are original recipe part of the time and extra crispy at other times. All three use wordless improvisation—although in Wilson's case it might not best be labeled "scatting." Traditionally, extended vocal improvisations are a sure bet for testing the patience of an audience—the only two singers who could unfailingly hold your attention during long scat episodes were Fitzgerald and Tormé. (Louis Armstrong all but invented scat, but you hardly ever heard him do it for a whole chorus.) Yet when Bridgewater or Reeves start scatting, crowds just eat it up. In Sarah Vaughan's day, singers used scat and melodic variations merely to embellish a standard—Reeves, on the other hand, spins elaborate, extended webs of wordless improvisation that only briefly detour through the familiar words and music. This should be taken as further proof that Bridgewater and Reeves are like catnip to audiences: they can virtually do no wrong in a concert hall or a nightclub.

Cassandra Wilson is considerably more introverted than Reeves or Bridgewater. Indeed, in the earlier phase of her career (the years surrounding her association with Steve Coleman and the Brooklyn-centric M-Base group), she seemed determine to bury herself in her ensembles, as if she were afraid to let audiences see or hear her. She still seems inner-directed, even in as large a space as Carnegie Hall, only now she's figured out how to let the rest of us in as well. Yet while she will probably never be as outgoing as Reeves, the two ladies have one major point in common: the influence of Nina Simone. Reeves, in fact, once said to me that she couldn't understand why Simone wasn't as revered as the major ladies in the pantheon, such as Vaughan, Fitzgerald, and Washington. To be honest, I myself had never fully appreciated Simone until this discussion (likewise, it was Nancy Wilson who first got me to understand Little Jimmy Scott).

Tonally, it's easier to hear the derivation of Simone's husky monotone in Cassandra Wilson's dry voice, but Reeves was talking about more than vocal quality. Simone was probably the first major vocalist to grow up in gospel and blues, then establish herself in the jazz world, next add liberal elements of "traditional" (American) folk music, then bring "world beat" (i.e. international folk music, often related to the lands of the African diaspora) to the mix, and ultimately wind up a pop icon. Obviously, most jazz fans prefer those performances (such as "My Baby Just Cares for Me") that are based in jazz and standards, but it's easy to see how this eclectic range of options could be a major influence on the contemporary generation, in much the same fashion as the more firmly jazz-rooted eclecticism of Betty Carter and Mark Murphy. Yet it wasn't just influences that Simone passed on, it was attitude. Simone was a deeply political artist, and without even considering the content of her original compositions (such as "Mississippi Goddam," inspired by the death of Medgar Evers), you could get a sense of her hardly suppressed Afro-militancy. Simone's antisocial stance can barely be detected in the user-friendly Reeves, but something of that monotone remains in Wilson's well-applied drone.

Those folk influences can also be traced back to Abbey Lincoln, although, unlike Simone, Lincoln is a jazz artist through and through. Her art was more explicitly political at one point, but in recent decades it seems more philosophical, that is, more concerned with man's relationship with God and the universe than the practices of injustice among men or even the boy-girl thing that most songs concern themselves with. Lincoln's primary message to the younger jazz vocalist is the importance of writing one's own material. This is entirely a mixed blessing. Lincoln's own songs, which are personal yet open to a variety of interpretations by diverse artists such as Kendra Shank, Joan Bender, Freddy Cole, and Baby Jane Dexter, are indeed one of the great joys of contemporary music, and each time a new Lincoln CD is released, the thing I look forward to most is hearing what new pieces she's written.

But Lincoln is an exception, not the rule. Most singers, even the talented ones, simply should not be encouraged to write their own songs. With a new CD by a younger singer, it becomes tiresome to slog one's way through original after uninspired original. Cassandra Wilson does compose much of her own material, perhaps a third to half of every album, but her originals are at least sublimely suited to Wilson's own style, even if I can't imagine anyone else singing "Little Warm Death." (The same thing could be said of Betty Carter classics like "Tight," which more than worked for Carter but indeed was so tight that there was no room for any other artist to open it up and reinterpret it.)

Which isn't to say that doing strictly standards, or even doing them well, guarantees an interesting performance. Most of us who listen to too many CDs by too many new singers feel that an overdone standard is just as bad as an undercooked original. Just as "Lush Life" was over-done in the twenty years following John Coltrane–Johnny Hartman, by 2001 I feel like if I ever hear "Never Never Land" again I'm going to jump off the second star to the right. (The same goes for "Peel Me a Grape.") Most original songs by young singers seem anemic, yet most standards seem like overworked soil, so depleted of nutrients that noth-ing else will grow. Yet there are eight zillion worthy songs from the 1920s on that have hardly been touched in the CD era. (If anyone is taking notes, how about "More than Likely," "Oh Yes, Take Another Guess," "Strange," and for that matter almost anything by the late Mar-vin Fisher.) What's more, veteran professionals like Lew Spence and Ervin Drake continue to turn out words and music of the highest cal-iber. My fondness for the 1940s and '50s notwithstanding, talented vocal-ists find material in the most unlikely places: the Afro-British Tessa Souter has resurrected the Pharaoh Sanders–Leon Thomas "The Cre-ator Has a Master Plan" and found the well-crafted song at its center, while on *Traveling Miles,* Cassandra Wilson has taken pieces from Miles Davis's least melodic period and made them work in song form.

In recent decades, singers have increasingly found material not just in the traditions of American jazz and pop but from Brazil. There are a number of younger, pan-American singers who can be described as equal parts bossa and bebop. The inundation of Brazilian beats is a largely positive trend, but with some caveats. In the 1940s and '50s, your average jazz singer, it seems to me, would spend a token portion of her time addressing the blues. Now the twelve-bar blues is barely part of the picture anymore and the bossa nova has become the fall-back position, the default parameter as it were, for jazz-and-standards singers. (There are exceptions, such as Laurie Krauz, and the largely black, largely female group of artists like LaVern Butler, Carla Cook, and Renee Marie, who come out of Dinah Washington and early Aretha Franklin and who record for the Maxjazz label.)

I've got nothing against Brazilian music (although sometimes my mind races back to xenophobic anti-Latin airs of the 1940s, such as "South America Take It Away" and Peggy Lee's "Caramba! It's the Samba," with the line, "There must be a million / Songs that aren't Brazilian") but I think I've already heard enough of it to last a lifetime, from American jazzers anyhow. Surely there must be other pan-American rhythms worthy of our attention. Why has no vocalist addressed calypso music in the same spirit as Sonny Rollins? Or found a way to blend jazz and reggae à la Monty Alexander? And why do only Latin-born singers try to use Cuban forms such as the mambo? (No one has done it since Perry Como's "Papa Loves Mambo"; Rosemary Clooney's inspired meeting with Perez Prado, *A Touch of Tabasco;* and Peggy Lee's *Latin ala Lee*).

Speaking of unusual rhythms, the retro-swing movement of recent years produced surprisingly few vocalists of note, although Ingrid Lucia of the Flying Neutrinos, Lavay Smith of the Red Hot Skillet Lickers, and Quinn Lemley are all worth hearing. It's also rather surprising that few singing instrumentalists other than pianists have come along and captured our imagination. The fine, Nat Cole–inspired guitarist John Pizzarelli may well be the best known, but Kermit Ruffins and Byron Stripling are two contemporary trumpeter-singers (based in New Orleans and New York, respectively) in the tradition of Louis Armstrong. So is Jim Ferguson, a bassist and singer based in Nashville, whose day job is playing and singing backup vocals behind country star Crystal Gayle, but whose own recordings are undisputedly jazz, sung in a dry, woody tone that extends the legacy of Mose Allison and Bob Dorough and the understated humor of Jay Leonhart.

If Bridgewater, Wilson, and Reeves are the industry leaders by one measure, no one could argue that Diana Krall and, more recently, Jane Monheit have moved a lot of product. They don't scat or try the patience of their audiences in any way: everything they do is like a younger version of a traditional jazz-pop chanteuse, with far less authority and authenticity. The worst charge that can be leveled against Krall, who has an effectively sultry voice and somewhat less skill as a keyboardist (you wouldn't want to hear her do an all-instrumental album), is that she sounds cold—when she re-created the repertoire of the King Cole Trio (on the 1996 *All for You*), she lacked warmth and wit, two factors that were at the very heart of that great group. (Obviously somebody disagrees, as the record sold a hundred thousand units before you could say "Hit That Jive, Jack.") The idea seemed to be coolness at all costs, and showing any kind of emotion simply was not cool. (Then along came the pianist and singer Patricia Barber, truly the Ice Queen from Hell—or Chicago, at any rate, who makes Krall look like Doris Day by comparison.) But Krall's humorless cool seems to have been a phase that she thankfully passed through: her 1999 *When I Look in Your Eyes,* with arranger Johnny Mandel, and her 2000 tour with Tony Bennett offer ample evidence that the thaw has begun. As for Monheit, who certainly seems to know what she's doing better than most of us do at twenty-three, it's too early to make any judgments—other than that her success seems to indicate that a lot of people want to hear the familiar repertoire done in a familiar way. Her second album tried too hard to be dark and sultry—much of it seemed artificial and forced. What I like best about Joan Bender, on the other hand, is how she embodies the joy of jazz and lets her cockeyed optimism and sunny disposition come through. Like I say, you don't necessarily need to do anything outrageous or experimental, but if you're going to work in a traditional vein and you know you're going to be compared to the Dinah Washingtons and Peggy Lees of the canon, you had better be pretty darn good.

If Monheit and Krall represent the more conservative element in jazz singing, there are those who work in those peculiar New York venues—where pop standards are heard with cover charges and drink minimums—that are not considered jazz clubs at all, but cabaret rooms. And a lot of good jazz singing goes on here, often more innovative than what you'll hear at the jazz joints. The mind races to Paula West, who performs at the Algonquin in New York and the Plush Room in San Francisco, not exactly havens of hot harmony. But stylistically she could be equally at home at Birdland. West has a style and a sound all her own, a way of leaning on vowels, of holding certain notes, of shading meanings and finding new colors both tonally and lyrically. She takes the classic songs, including quite a few that haven't been heard to death, and makes us feel them all over again.

There are other, surprising developments of the very recent past that will be a part of the future of jazz singing. For one thing: dudes. The years from the 1960s to the '80s produced hardly any new male singers of note. (Al Jarreau and Bobby McFerrin both acted as if they wanted to be jazz singers for a hot minute, and then changed their minds.) Yet by the end of the Clinton era, the men's room was full. There has yet to be a male who's achieved the same level of runaway success as Krall or Wilson, but at least two jazz guys have made it to major label status: Kevin Mahogany, who, more than all the other artists I've discussed, keeps alive the connection to the blues, and Kurt Elling. The latter is a committed eclectic, even eccentric, in the Mark Murphy tradition, who uses a broad range of techniques—he may be the last major practitioner of the (often justifiably) neglected art of vocalese. Elling's work is marked by two traits: a distinctly spiritual orientation in his many original works, which reflects his background as a theology student, and a tendency toward relentless experimentation, often balanced by a crowd-pleasing side. Elling can jump off on a tangent that will leave an audience yawning and then grab them back with a simple, direct, and swinging piece like "Never Say Goodbye." He seems almost conservative, however, compared to Miles Griffith, whose extended improvisations are more purely sonic than verbal. Other male singers worth following include Allan Harris, who's strongest on hard-swinging numbers and shows a distinct Nat Cole influence, the Canadian Densil Pinnock, and the British Ian Shaw.

Mention of the last two underscores how jazz singing has become an international art—there have been great non-American instrumentalists from the Swing Era onward (Nat Gonella, Django Reinhardt), but, perhaps because of the language barrier, comparatively few jazz vocalists. That seems to have changed, and undoubtedly in the new century more superior jazz singers will be coming from other countries and continents. Apart from Pinnock and Shaw there are the British Claire Martin, a straight-down-the-middle swinger, and Denise Jannah, a black Dutch vocalist born in Surinam who specializes in odd time signatures.

At the millennium, then, jazz singers are both avant- and derriere-garde (to borrow Alec Wilder's term), original recipe and extra crispy, singing the standards and their own originals, stylistically indebted to the Mississippi Delta and to Rio de Janeiro, are heard in jazz clubs and cabaret rooms, were born in America and elsewhere, are male and female, and come in all colors and age ranges. Is there anyone out there singing now who is going to mean as much to future generations as

Ella Fitzgerald and Sarah Vaughan mean to us today? It's too early to tell. One thing that can be guaranteed from the vantage point of the millennium, however, is that the future looks like it's going to be a swinging place indeed.

STUART NICHOLSON

Yes, I agree with Will: we have more vocalists today. But what we have made up for in productivity we seem to have lost in individuality (and creativity). And given that so many singers—and this applies to artists working in the mainstream of jazz as well—support the same areas of stylistic inspiration, similarity in style and concept is inevitable. That's what I said in 1989 in *Jazz: The 1980s Resurgence,* and then I was talking about young musicians in the 1980s hard-bop nexus.

Same for the vocalists, only the number of role models is even smaller than the combined Blue Note and Prestige rosters of the late 1950s and early '60s—Holiday, Fitzgerald, Vaughan, Carter, McRae, and everybody is allowed a joker to add their own "indispensable favorite." They all sing the same old standards in (more or less) the same old way—I know: most of them send me their CDs. Now I have a problem with this—it's 2001, not 1958. The increasing sophistication of jazz education is a wonderful thing, but it's a mixed blessing when its production lines turn out jazz singers who all learned from the same hymn sheet. Maybe it's the *great* American Popular Song. And this *great* tradition seems to swallow a singer's identity whole unless he or she is very good. When singers look over their shoulders and see the ghosts of those who have been there before them, they turn into salt. Or at least it sounds that way. But even if they are very good, what are we left with? We are left with a warmed-over version of what's been done before— many times over—and better.

Will is right, an audience will always exist for good songs sung well. But this process is now taking us rather close to MOR music: indeed, this thoroughfare is becoming so crowded you can only cross at pedestrian walkways. As Will says of Monheit and Krall, they are younger versions of the jazz-pop chanteuse, but aren't so many of these highly touted (by their press offices) young singers who arrive in search of their fifteen minutes of fame? This is not to say MOR is bad—almost all the songbook canon recorded by Ella Fitzgerald represents MOR lieder of perfect pitch and diction. But is this what it's all about? If it is, I have a question: if art is a reflection of life, as the great sages tell us it is, then why should listening to jazz be easy when life isn't?

I think Cassandra Wilson holds an important key. After *Days Aweigh* she had the jazz world at her feet begging for more of the same. Standards. But, as Keith Jarrett once said of Miles Davis when he went electric, he did it because he *could* play "My Funny Valentine" and "So What" and all those songs. Jarrett said the sign of a great artist is to look for new challenges, and Wilson took on some of this mantle when she went M-Base and started performing her own gritty works. Good for her; some of that stuff on JMT stands up a lot better today than the critics would have us believe. And it prepared her for the next stage of her career on Blue Note: her inspired takes on Miles's electric period, for example, and her own originals. Jazz of today. And those originals are much better now. As Will says, new songs (and unfamiliarity plays a part in this) can sound anemic, but we must encourage singers to work in new directions since, yes, "Lush Life" has been done to death, but so too has so much of the *great* American popular song repertoire. Singers come and go; the repertoire remains the same. When Billie and Ella sang songs, they were singing the popular songs of their day—hell, Holiday had an aversion to singing the blues since she considered them "old-fashioned" and of the previous (Bessie Smith) generation. And she wrote her own stuff, too.

Jazz singers seem to have learned nothing from the singer-songwriters who spelled the end of Tin Pan Alley in the 1960s rock explosion. Within the context of popular music there have been some really great songs that were right for those artists, just as Wilson's compositions are right for her and Carter's compositions are right for her. It's no good looking for another Cole Porter: those days are done. This is now, and the problem with so much jazz today is that it is full of prophets looking backward.

One of the great delights of recent years has been Debbie Harry with the Jazz Passengers. She gets inside original material and brings it alive in a way I don't see and hear with many young singers. It was a superb piece of casting by the Passengers, challenging her to inhabit a range of emotions far beyond 1970s pop. Most young singers are so weighed down by the jazz tradition that in trying to negotiate a route between vocal calisthenics and passion they sound rather manufactured. In contrast, by approaching jazz singing from an entirely different perspective and unencumbered by such heavy baggage, Miss Harry sounded startlingly original.

And originality is what the late Betty Carter told me was expected of her when she started out as a singer. "When you walked out onto the stage of the Apollo or the Earle Theater in Philadelphia you knew those audiences were going to come down on you if you weren't yourself. It was a tough school: you could not go out there and be Ella or Billie or Sarah." The problem is that today, everybody wants to. But that's not the future: it's the past. The future is being explored by several singers who are writing their own material and conceptualizing their own individual take on jazz singing. Cassandra Wilson. Norway's Sidsel Endresen springs to mind: her affecting *Undertow* moves the jazz vocal into aesthetically beckoning new territory. The dynamic Beate Lech composes her own songs and, with her group, opens them up for improvisation against contemporary rhythms of European techno and house, albeit played acoustically—definitely a jazz singer of 2002. Sweden's Jeanette Lindström creates songscapes of winning beauty while Anneli Drecker has the most haunting voice I have heard in years. And Norma Winstone has been doing this for years. These singers are finding their own place in the music and taking on the challenge of creating their own repertoire, which they sing their way. Now, this might not be what audiences want. They're always going to go for something they can hum along to. It may not even be what some critics want, when they can run the Billie–Ella–Sarah–Carmen–Joker slide rule over them and come up with a score out of ten. But it does represent a way ahead for creative artists who are not much concerned with either.

BEN RATLIFF

The pinpointing of Nina Simone as ground zero for the whole jazz–folk–blues–world music thing going on right now seems right on the money. Though having said that, I'm sort of amazed that there isn't much in that category beyond Cassandra Wilson. She strikes me as a perfect indicator of the jazz problem: when a really good, sensible, zesty virus comes along, how come it doesn't result in an epidemic? (Norah Jones, whom we'll probably all be hearing about not long after this book appears, might be the next in line, but perhaps it doesn't prove much: she's being shepherded into the light by Blue Note, who are dying to duplicate what they did with Cassandra and have hired Craig Street—Cassandra's old producer—to make her album.)

Those whom the virus would infect all have their ears pointed in different directions. They're probably into Elis Regina, or cabaret singers, or reissues, or else the issues of technique they've learned in college prevent them from being easy marks for originality. I know some vocal-major types who don't buy Wilson at all. Dianne Reeves, whose records court the same general market of bourgeois bohemians but are a lot more aesthetically midwestern, sounds more authoritative to them.

TED GIOIA

Don't get me wrong: I love vocal music.

I even would go so far as to admit that jazz singers have more potential than instrumentalists to improve the state of jazz, expand its boundaries, and reclaim its popular audience.

But this potential is mostly untapped. Jazz singers are not going to take us to the promised land any time soon. They are too busy dwelling on the music's past, too content singing standards in ho-hum arrangements, too caught up in some nostalgia kick.

If I didn't hear scat singing for the next year, I wouldn't miss it. Frankly, most scat choruses are mediocre at best—if you transcribed the scat lines and played them on a horn, you would hear instantly how unimaginative they are. Very, very few scat singers today can create fresh improvised lines, and most don't even seem to try. In the jazz world, one can garner a reputation for excellence in scat singing simply by hitting the notes in tune and maintaining a sense of swing. My advice: if you are looking for creativity in melodic development, listen to horn players, check out the keyboardists, even hear Steve Turre blowing on a conch shell. But leave the jazz singers alone; they will only leave you frustrated and disappointed.

Yes, I am down on jazz singers. But the potential is real, oh so real. The promised land is sitting out there.

How do we reach it? Let me offer three pieces of advice for aspiring jazz vocalists.

First and foremost, tap into new material that takes advantage of the expressive power of words. It is not enough to be a singer; you must also be a poet. If you are not able to write your own songs, find someone who has the creative vision to do this for you. Words have tremendous power over our emotions; even spoken words set against jazz music can captivate an audience when handled correctly (hear Mark Murphy on "Bop for Kerouac" if you doubt this). Most jazz and pop lyrics fail to channel this power. Their language is flat and unimaginative. Yet when the transfiguring energy of words is married to the vitality of music, miracles can take place.

Second, look for inspiration in other vocal traditions. Ann Dyer, for example, has clearly studied the singing traditions of India, and it makes her a more powerful jazz vocalist. Brazil has produced more interesting singers in recent decades than the United States—check them out. The vocal traditions of Ireland or Indonesia or Argentina (and many other countries) are rich in content and full of implications for jazz: familiarize yourself with their beauty.

My third and final bit of advice is to let people hear more than your vocal cords: give them a glimpse into your heart and soul. Speed and pitch and range are great tools, but they are merely tools. Expressiveness and feeling are what it is all about. After a performance, you should feel exposed, feel that you have left too much of yourself in plain view. If you don't go this far, you have cheated your audience.

Each of these three areas presents a substantial challenge, perhaps even a lifetime of work. A singer who makes solid progress against each of them—as well as handles the technical demands of singing jazz—will truly earn our respect and show that the vocal art can be central to the future of jazz music, and not just serve as a relic of its past.

JOHN F. SZWED

I think it's worth a mention that in European jazz, Duke Ellington's idea of using singers to perform wordlessly (as did Adelaide Hall, Marie Ellington, and Alice Babs) is still a strong influence. Singers in Europe perform either as instrumentalists in written scores (Lauren Newton functioning as lead trumpet with the Vienna Art Orchestra, or Norma Winstone as an instrumental coequal in Azimuth), or as free improvisers (Linda Sharrock, Jeanne Lee, Maggie Nicholls, Urszula Dudziak, or Sainkho Namchylak—the Tuvan throat singer who has worked with Evan Parker and others). But Europeans also have a tradition of using folk songs, art songs, or medieval church and secular songs as the basis of jazz improvisation (Aziza Mustafa Zadeh's hip treatments of folk forms from Azerbaijan, Agnes Buen Garnas's Norwegian medieval songs with Jan Garbarek, and Tino Tracanna and Corrado Guarino's ethnic and free reworkings of the songs of Gesualdo are typical). The point they seem to be making is that there's a lot more left to sing in jazz than ballads alone.

K. LEANDER WILLIAMS

Rock 'n' roll killed the jazz singer. If jazz singing had always been difficult to get a handle on, the task became even more difficult once listeners began hearing pop through the prism of rock rather than jazz—which started in earnest after the Beatles. Folks had long accused jazz of being more about "feeling" than music, but rock took that even further by going deeper into the everyday vernacular and asserting that anyone who wrote hooks could sing them—think Carole King, Bobs Dylan and Marley, Elvis Costello, James Brown. (Ray Charles, Smokey Robinson, and Stevie Wonder were holding it down somewhere in the middle.) This new attitude took a whole lot of steam out of folks who were committed to wedding sophisticated chord changes to ingenuous turns of phrase. Audiences with jazzy aspirations quickly found that the craft makes little sense without a living repertoire.

There's probably no better indication that we're moving into what you might call the "post-rock era" than the sudden proliferation of jazz singers that Will describes. If there's a problem, though, it's kind of like what's happening in the military-industrial complex now that there's no Cold War. Singers today seem to pine for the comfort of those early changes—when the world seemed safer. That's OK if you're amazing at it, like Paula West, or if you can write a decent song or two when you put your mind to it, like Harry Connick, Jr., or if you're so damn good that you can somehow blur the distance between past and present, like Abbey Lincoln (who's also a great composer), Andy Bey, or Dee Dee Bridgewater. (I heard a young folk-pop singer-songwriter the other day who actually did that, too; some of her songs were a bit too brainy, but she did Rodgers and Hart's "You Mustn't Kick It Around" and it fit. Her name was Erin McKeown.) If you're not up to the skill of those folks, however, it's almost like being in the 1950s again.

And, unfortunately, no one has found a way to make that newfangled avant-garde vocal thing work for more than a piece or two—especially not on record. Hearing Lauren Newton, Greetje Bijma, or the recently departed Jeanne Lee live was a kick, but I don't return to their records the way I frequently return to Carmen McRae's. I'd much rather listen to "jazzy" R&B singers like Erykah Badu and Jill Scott than Cassandra Wilson, but I have hopes for a new talent named Elisabeth Kontomanou—she does a wordless world beat vocal thing with saxist Sam Newsome's group, and when she's on the music levitates. In the end, I think singers need words, though—Bobby McFerrin's success is probably the best proof of that—which leads me to believe that the jazz singer's art won't resonate with a non-nostalgic public again until someone can find a way to marry good lyrics to good melodies of the post-bop variety. Post-rock, anyone?

PETER MARGASAK

I have to admit that I don't follow jazz vocalists very closely, although I love listening to the giants. Perhaps I'm too closed-minded, but I'd rather hear Billie Holiday, Dinah Washington, Sarah Vaughan, or Helen Merrill sing standards than Jane Monheit or Diana Krall. I think it's the lack of imagination in choosing songs today that makes me feel this way.

I love Cassandra Wilson as much for her daring choice of material as her gorgeous sound, and the same goes for those recent Andy Bey albums. It's hard for singers to find new material. New tunes tend to either sound like lame imitations of things from that good old Great American Songbook, free of any contemporary relevancy, or they're forgettable pop-rock songs played with brushes. But there's a whole globe of musical traditions ripe for plunder; we hears lots of Brazilian tunes, but what about all of these great songs Susana Baca has uncovered in Peru or the ones Césaria Évora has become a Starbucks favorite by singing? These vocalists have developed an audience that intersects with fans of vocal jazz for a reason. (Of course, there's the language barrier, but solving that problem is part of the job.) As Kelvin's chapter discusses, the world makes jazz its own, so why don't we borrow from abroad in the same way?

JIM MACNIE

I realize Krall and Monheit aren't the ultimate jazz vocalists, or perhaps even the state of the art right now. But I was thinking they were adequate dispensers of some kind of respectable pleasure...until I came upon the recent Rhino video release of *Ralph J. Gleason's Jazz Casual,* that is. There, in black and white, I was reminded just how real the real deal was: Carmen McRae, backed by a trio, being about as artful as one could be while acting utterly cavalier on "I'm Going to Lock My Heart Away." Breathtaking stuff.

What I'm trying to say is that nonchalance appeals to me. The fatal wound to many of today's vocalists is the aura of formal entertainment that marks their performances as deeply as their musicality does. I've got nothing against smiles and bounce, but—and I hope this isn't just the rock fan in me talking—the level of shtick that wafts through the efforts of Reeves and Elling (both of whom I basically enjoy but never particularly listen to) reduces their impact. Even in their most informal moments, these two, and several of the others previously mentioned, somehow seem contrived. And as soon as that word enters my listening space, I'm out.

One of the reasons there's been no wildfire spread of the virus Ben speaks of is because Cassandra's breakthrough move came from the best possible motivation: a return to self. Son House and Micky Dolenz and the ever-inspiring Joni herself were such a central part of Wilson's past that it was super-obvious in her delivery. The emotional "honesty" that we're usually looking for is at the center of *Blue Light 'Til Dawn* and its followup. In the hands of others, the gauzy eroticism and bare-foot Natchezissippi vibe would have to come off as role-playing. Even though the prototype was cool, in this instance I'm glad there was no bandwagon to jump on.

As for the future: Kelvin brings up Elisabeth Kontomanou, a novel new voice on the New York scene. She and her pals Claudia Acuña and Luciana Souza have got their own mini-virus working right now: a strain of oft-wordless vocals that integrate music elements of other cultures—samba, chant, chanson—in the post-bop mix. If you stretch melodic motifs with as much natural splendor and cagey invention as Souza does, you can sate listeners who like to be touched in both the heart and the mind. Her overlooked *Poems of Elizabeth Bishop* is an indication of an experimentalist having the guts to walk the road not taken these days. I applaud that, but moreover I applaud the fact that she made that road an intriguing byway.

GREG TATE

I largely feel about jazz vocalists the way I feel about jazz guitarists: at best they're impressive but dispensable parts of my jazz experience. Exceptions to this rule are of course Louis, Sinatra, Lady Day, Betty

Carter, and Cassandra Wilson, all of whom inhabit songs in ways comparable to the best jazz instrumentalists, possessing them with so much of their own musicality and mythic properties as to never make you feel that you're listening to something that originates from a category like "jazz vocals."

PETER WATROUS

What a weird place to be if you sing jazz: somewhere between musician and entertainer. The singer, in the majority of jazz practice, has to adhere closer to pop performance standards than do saxophonists, let's say. But they also have to be working musicians. I guess that's why those who stick closer to pop—the aforementioned Jane Monheit and Diana Krall—seem from my point of view particularly distanced from jazz as I know it. Their affinity to pop, to an era of jazz as popular culture, seems particularly archaic.

But clearly people like the music of those two; jazz singers in some way are jazz's only public face. The hilariously self-righteous critical backlash to their success points out jazz criticism's fury over losing control over the discussion. The hundred thousand people who've bought Jane Monheit's newest record could care less that jazz criticism doesn't think she's cool. But let's be inclusionary: jazz singing of that type belongs in the broad context of current jazz, just like it always has. And, as always, jazz musicians and jazz companies control jazz's public face, not critics.

WILL FRIEDWALD

The classic Sinatra "concept" albums and Fitzgerald songbooks were recorded long after the golden era of American songwriting; by the LP era, Gershwin, Kern, and Hart had been in the ground for a whole generation at least. Does it matter that we want to do their songs sixty years after their deaths, rather than a mere fifteen or twenty? I don't think so. As George Avakian and others have pointed out, it wasn't necessarily the Cole Porter and the Richard Rodgers songs that were on the *Billboard* charts to begin with, when those songs were new, that is—it was just as often something like "Three Little Fishies" or the much maligned "Mairzy Doats."

In the four or five months since I wrote my main essay, I keep getting smacked in the puss with still more proof that the standard songbook and those who sing it constitute a living, vital, and thoroughly organic artform. In fact, my new book, *Star Dust Melodies: The Biography of Twelve of America's Most Popular Songs,* is predicated on the idea that there are no end of creative ways to interpret the Great American Songbook. Even in post–World Trade Center New York, the essential, traditional values of jazz singing can still be used by creative singers to produce passionate and memorable music. The jazz rhythm section, the horn obligato, the trade of fours, chordal-based scat singing, the blues form, and the bossa nova—that stuff still works when it's done right. I don't doubt that some of the elements my colleagues have mentioned—techniques borrowed from international musics, from electronics and the pop-rock world, and from the umbrella of styles referred to succinctly as jazz's avant-garde, could enhance this music even further.

8

HOMES AWAY FROM HOME

JAZZ AND THE WORLD

K. LEANDER WILLIAMS

It's easy to get a little anxious when folks start waxing jingoistic about jazz's accomplishments. Jazz, we're reminded ad nauseam, is now America's classical music, created here pretty much against all odds and then set loose everywhere, presumably so that this burgeoning melting pot of immigrants and ex-slaves might have an outlet to show off the kind of sophistication neither was supposed to be capable of. Its rhythms, inventive harmonies, and improvisational derring-do are said to reflect the wants, needs, and expectations of a populace in the throes of modernity, a nation that was looking forward while the rest of the world seemed to be looking backward—that is, until they heard jazz.

One of the most jarring things about this way of thinking—what literary folk might call jazz's master narrative—is that, to some extent, it's true. Jazz legend may contain many of the demons of hagiography that Canadian author and jazz fan Robert Fulford questions in his recent book *The Triumph of Narrative: Storytelling in the Age of Mass Culture*, but, in many respects, jazz did help introduce a sort of user-friendly American modernism to the world. Try to imagine, for example, the modern world without mambo, bossa nova, or reggae, three extraordinarily popular and far-reaching musical genomes with significant strains of jazz in their DNA. One could say the same about several other forms (South African marabi? Nigerian highlife?) now grouped for Western consumption under the "world music" umbrella.

Was jazz destined to enter the world's bloodstream? It seems so. The idiom's globalist spirit has nearly as many patron saints (think of Dizzy Gillespie, Randy Weston, Don Cherry) as there are countries on Earth. However, something expatriate American author Gertrude Stein once asked about identity may help explain jazz's ease in transit as well as its adaptability. "What's the point of [having] roots if you can't take them with you?" Stein wondered in a piece from 1936, in which she declared the United States her "country" and Paris her "hometown." Jazz began making itself at home in select cities around the world before anyone had settled on a name for the idiom, and perhaps the biggest news about jazz at the turn of the millennium is that anyone anywhere can develop fluency in it. One of its saving graces has been the fact that just about every far-flung place a jazz recording, radio broadcast, or musician has turned up, local musicians have been changed by it and wanted to claim it as their own.

However, there's a punch line. If all this talk about jazz conquest seems a tad too Cecil B. DeMille, too neatly epic, it's important that we remember that jazz desperately needed every one of those faraway hometowns. Who knows how jazz musicians would have kept growing, innovating, surviving if the global club and festival circuit that makes up much of the current jazz infrastructure were not in place? Jazz's health in its homeland has always been somewhat dodgy, which is perhaps the most one can expect of an art form created by blacks in a country that has generally viewed them with either outright antipathy or a fascination that often borders on fetishism. Pianist Oscar Peterson, who arrived in the States from his native Montreal in the late 1940s, is said to have been startled by the scuffling he witnessed among musicians he had idolized back home in Canada. Dutch saxist and arranger Willem Breuker said precisely the same thing three decades later, after a similar trip to New York to assess the scene. Jazz wouldn't really be considered legit on home turf until shortly after Breuker's visit in the late 1970s, not even—according to saxist-composer Benny Golson in Gene Lees's book *Cats of Any Color*—in the music program at Howard University, a pinnacle of higher education for African Americans.

It's hard to know where to begin plotting the course of jazz as an international music, though. It's clear that the idiom was well on the way to becoming a worldwide phenomenon by the late 1930s, but any search comes with its own chicken-or-egg conundrum: should we first address how jazz changed other peoples or how others changed jazz?

The question is made even tougher by the realization that jazz itself is a hybrid, the culmination of musical phenomena from several locales—Africa, the Caribbean, Europe—that had found their way to America by the turn of the twentieth century. One quickly stumbles into a hall of mirrors when discussing Cuba, a country whose high concentration of former slaves and proximity to jazz's Louisiana birthplace allowed it to offer significant components to the earliest "hot" music (via Jelly Roll Morton's much-bandied-about "Latin tinge"); then, once jazz had morphed from something mysterious to something nameable, from verb to noun, the island nation would become the primary source for what we've come to know as "Latin jazz," a tributary so large and distinct that it is now a parallel river.

That transition from verb to noun is particularly important in any discussion of the idiom's acceptance abroad, primarily because the verb/noun dichotomy is generally misunderstood in the States in ways that aren't possible for someone picking up the jazz trail in, say, Moscow, Tokyo, or Sydney. The misapprehension is rooted in a now infamous chapter in Amiri Baraka's *Blues People*, one in which he characterizes jazz the verb as something alive and ever evolving, and jazz the noun as something static, formalized, and easily removed from its context. Though Baraka's book rightly challenged the idea of jazz as a readily commodifiable formula devoid of funk, it's primarily his racially charged anger over what was then nounification's most audible consequence— appropriation of black music by whites—that comes through when he compares two great trumpeters, Louis Armstrong and Bix Beiderbecke. "There should be no cause for wonder that the trumpets of Beiderbecke and Armstrong were so dissimilar," he writes. "The white middle-class boy from Iowa was the product of a culture which could place Armstrong, but could never understand him."

Obviously, Baraka's fury was yet another example of how the odious racial climate in twentieth-century America stoked all kinds of tragic fallacies. But one need do little more than replace Bix's name with that of foreign trumpeters like Nigerian highlife pioneer Victor Olaiya or South Africa's Hugh Masekela or Mongezi Feza to begin questioning the veracity of the logic. No matter what we know about blues-based music's vestigial connection to West Africa, when swing washed up there at the turn of the 1940s the locals had no choice but to recognize it as a noun rather than a verb because of its foreignness and the simple fact that that's what they were told it was. Often their first encounters with the new music from America were much like Beiderbecke's, but as natives of places where vernacular melodies and rhythms were markedly different from our own, West Africans and many others of the time (Ary Barroso in Brazil, Lucho Bermudez in Colombia, Zakes Nkosi in South Africa, Lionel Belasco in Trinidad, Jean-Baptiste Nemours in Haiti) were able to expand the idiom's reach by absorbing, reanimating, and transforming the jazz impetus. (As jazz fans know, much jazz in America took advantage of outside influences and still does: witness the Andalusian passions on Miles Davis's *Sketches of Spain*, the snake-charming repetitions on John Coltrane's "India," the Japanese sonorities that pianist-arranger Toshiko Akiyoshi gets from mixing altos and flutes, the calypso breakdowns in Sonny Rollins's repertoire, and, finally, the jumpy beat of the Balkans so prevalent among a whole school of musicians on New York's downtown scene.)

With all this in mind, however, there is a point worth making about the runaway acceptance of jazz in Europe—especially since the idiom's current popularity among conservatory-bred players from Spain to Scandinavia has led some to question America's place in jazz's future. While Europe's role as nurturer, home away from home, and new frontier for jazz is indisputable, the truth is that were someone to take a trip around the world cataloging the discrete, jazz-influenced new musics that have come into being in the last fifty years, they'd probably find that Europe, while birthing scores of world-class jazz musicians and conceptualists, hasn't deviated much from the main stem's historical trajectory. It's not like in Brazil, where jazzy bossa nova begat tropicalia, or South Africa, where sax-based marabi gave us mbaqanga, or the Congo, where Congolese rumba birthed soukous, or Jamaica, where horn-drenched ska paved the way for Toots and the Maytals and Bob Marley. With the possible exception of the continent's vibrant avant-garde, jazz arrived in Europe as jazz and has taken many of its cues from elsewhere ever since, capitalizing on new developments at roughly the same time that they were introduced in other places. Mike Zwerin, an American who has covered jazz from France for decades, puts it another way in the chapter devoted to European jazz in editor Bill Kirchner's hefty anthology, *The Oxford Companion to Jazz.* "Americans taught Europeans how to play [jazz]," Zwerin writes. "Once [Europeans] learned, they distilled and added to it until they felt that they no longer needed Americans hanging around taking their gigs."

Of course, as the idiom enters its second millennium, perhaps the most we can expect from inventive jazzers on any continent is deft revamps of previous big bangs. Many of the styles I've mentioned above have been around for quite a while now, but you might not know it from the number of musicians nowadays who seem to be discovering, say, the Afro-Cuban clave rhythm for the first time. It's hard to know just how long it'll take before everyone is on the same page—or even if we all should be on the same page—but if Zwerin is dead-on when he writes that jazz's current posture has become "horizontal" where it once was "vertical" ("with so many graceful soaring spires named Pops, Prez, Bird, Duke, Monk, Trane, Miles, and Ornette"), then it's not out of the question to imagine a jazz fan's next thrill coming from Buenos Aires, and the next from New Zealand. (Both places, incidentally, are home to musicians who did solid work in New York and elsewhere before returning to teach at local music schools.) This seems to be the future suggested by the thousands of students and players who network annually at the conventions sponsored by the International Association of Jazz Educators (IAJE). (A recent one, brandishing banners that announced "Jazz: An International Language," offered among its festivities panels that addressed the parallel jazz histories of South Africa and Brazil.)

Personally, I'd love to hear more composer-bandleaders hit high marks like Denmark's Pierre Dørge and New York's Rodney Kendrick did in the mid-1990s. Dørge's *Music from the Danish Jungle* (with his long-running New Jungle Orchestra) and Kendrick's *Last Chance for Common Sense* manage to run a globe's worth of music through each artist's sensibility without getting mired in willful eclecticism or pastiche. Given their backgrounds, it's only fitting that such cohesive endeavors would come from these two: Dørge, a guitarist, apprenticed with trumpet globalist Don Cherry and kept the late South African bassist Johnny Dyani on retainer throughout his last decade; Kendrick, a pianist, hails from the Afro-blue school of aesthetics advanced by Randy Weston, Max Roach, and Abbey Lincoln. No small wonder that in one stretch Dørge can guilelessly traverse the distance from Charles Mingus–inspired tango to traditional Danish hymn to funky waltz, while Kendrick effortlessly marries earthy piano, Westonian horn charts, shrieks from North African musette, and Indian tablas. In the end, both are engaging in a sort of millennial cosmopolitanism that Gertrude Stein would have understood, moving around the world while keeping their roots within reach.

TED GIOIA

Writers often treat the globalization of jazz as mere fodder for a human interest story. The headline reads something like "Dixieland Comes to Siberia" or "King of Thailand Jams with Stan Getz"—I can validate the authenticity of both stories, by the way—and readers are dazzled by the odd juxtaposition of a new art form with venerable cultural patterns. Or, in other instances, the spread of jazz to remote areas is dealt with as just one more sign of the music's legitimization, and we are all invited to join in the self-congratulatory zeal. In this case, the headline reads "Japanese Love Jazz"—and the expected response from the reader is "Ah, shucks, aren't they swell? Aren't we swell, too?"

But these "angles" miss the key point. The globalization of jazz is not just another engaging story, another sign of the music's growing acceptance. To my mind, it is the main story, the overwhelming trend, the key evolutionary thread taking us to the music's future. If we are serious about coming to grips with the jazz of tomorrow, or even the jazz of today, this is where to start our investigation. It represents the crux of the matter, not a convenient sidebar or stopping place along the way.

Although California is my native soil and current home, I have spent several years of my life overseas, often working as a jazz musician, and have probably visited in excess of twenty-five countries during the last decade. The vibrancy of the jazz scene in these various locales is much greater and more diverse than most American-based jazz writers realize, and the quality and creativity of the music made in these places has increased enormously in recent decades. Commentators have often noted that jazz is taken far more seriously—by both players and fans—outside of the United States. The unspoken corollary, which few are willing to admit, is that this heightened seriousness now gives these musicians an advantage, an edge in their musical pursuits.

Why is this music still so little known and seldom appreciated in America? There are only two reasons for this: ignorance and arrogance. We can be forgiven our ignorance—since we have few chances to hear these artists in person, and recordings are rarely available and almost never well publicized. But our arrogance is unforgivable.

I see things changing, however. More open-minded jazz writers (including a few of my collaborators on this project) are now calling attention to the riches of this music. The U.S. jazz periodicals and editors, disc jockeys and concert promoters, are still playing it safe, preferring to feature homegrown talent in most instances. But even they will eventually see the light. Of course, the leading American jazz musicians were far ahead of everybody: for several decades the top artists—Miles, Getz, Blakey, Jarrett, Shorter, Cannonball, Metheny, and so many others—have been tapping into the rich musical talent found outside the United States. The musicians are always the first to know, aren't they? Frankly, it's time for the rest of us to catch up with them.

PETER MARGASAK

In an earlier chapter ["Black and White Turning Gray"] Jim wrote that he felt saddened by my assertion that matters of origin are becoming irrelevant. But I think Kelvin's piece does an excellent job of explaining what I was getting at in this regard. Jazz is an undeniably international music these days and, like it or not, I don't think jazz musicians in Turkey, Argentina, or South Africa spend much time considering where it all came from. At the same time I don't see the United States losing its place as the sentimental jazz capital of the world any time soon, even if its hegemonic hold, creatively speaking, is slipping. And who cares, anyway?

The more the merrier, I say. The influx of different traditions has only energized the music and raised its stakes. If American musicians aren't interested in pushing jazz further, then someone from Holland, Tunisia, or Sweden will do it.

JOHN F. SZWED

How jazz relates to the world, I suppose, depends on how one defines jazz. But even if the narrowest (and I think wrong) definition is used—that it is a semi-improvised, polyphonic music developed near the beginning of the twentieth century in New Orleans—we have to reckon with very similar musics developing at the same time in the West Indies, Brazil, and possibly Mexico and elsewhere. It's not necessary to accept Ernest Borneman's argument (that European and African music had already met in Spain by the eleventh century, and jazz therefore represents a second encounter made possible by Spanish colonization of the New World) to see the family resemblances. You need go no further than to compare the polyphony and rhythms of New Orleans Creole songs like Paul Barbarin's "Eh, La Bas" with 1920s recordings of the beguine from Martinique, or those of the choros from Brazil. Or maybe just hear the slow drag alongside the tango. Then you can follow these rhythms as they turn up slowly transformed on early ride cymbal patterns, in the left hand of Jimmy Yancey's boogie-woogie, or

156

in Lil Hardin's piano rhythms for the King Oliver band. For me, at least, jazz begins as a world music.

But even if American chauvinism will never allow for world origins, surely the role of other countries in shaping jazz must be recognized. I'm thinking of historical moments such as the acceptance of black musicians in France from World War I on, which resulted in the world acclaim of musicians like James Europe; the success of the Sam Wooding tour, which allowed fellow New Orleaners Sidney Bechet and Tommy Ladnier to meet for the first time in Moscow in 1926; the role played by Paris (and Algeria) in solidifying free jazz in the late 1960s; and even the Cold War, which, through the Voice of America, assured world acclaim for musicians like Sun Ra who had no recognition at home.

BEN RATLIFF

There are jazz musicians and there are jazz audiences. Whereas sometimes the musicians seem to have little thought or care about the people ostensibly buying their stuff—jazz does have this postwar tradition of "it's good for you, so sit there and accept it"—I think that jazz musicians are becoming increasingly clear about the idea that their audiences are curious about music from other parts of the world. And if in the past a jazz musician's momentary interest in sitar music or the milonga or whatever stayed just that—a momentary interest—now it's instant ammo for a concept album. Remember, the old small-group mainstream jazz format, especially on record, is at a sub-basement level of popularity. Any hook will do.

The marketers of world music have been hammering away at a partnership with jazz for years, and it's been through "jazz" festivals, jazz record labels, jazz magazines, and so on, that we've been able to see and hear a lot of the best (or best of the importable, translatable stuff) from other continents. Jazz musicians are exposed to these other musical cultures as a matter of course in their daily working lives. The gradual changing of jazz as a result is inevitable.

Also, musicians are going the extra mile now, spending time in other countries, learning the rhythms and instruments. New modes of communication, to sound absurdly clichéd, have made far-flung places seem closer. The average middle-class musician, even the kind who isn't a legendary bandleader or some sort of a seer, is now much more likely to get on a plane and spend enough time in Cuba or the Middle East or Africa to really learn something and bring it back home.

JIM MACNIE

Travel broadens the mind, nourishes the spirit, and, best of all, breeds inquisitiveness as much as it answers longstanding questions. So the shrinking-planet syndrome that we've been experiencing with more and more vigor during each of the century's decades has foisted our international neighbors into our backyard. Either look them in the eye and shake hands or act like a one-dimensional chooch. Those with smiles on their faces and their palms out look like interested intellectuals. The standoff boys are still putting their umpteenth spin on "All the Things You Are." While I've yet to find a space in my heart of hearts for the Balkan bounce being offered by the clique of New Yorkers that includes Brad Shepik and Matt Darriau, I sure as hell offer 'em a pat on the back for tapping a source other than "Rhythm" changes. Vijay Iyer and Rudresh Mahanthappa's South Asian inflections? (As Kelvin rightly mentions) Rodney Kendrick's post-Weston Africanisms? The Afro-Celtic thing that Lewis Nash is test-driving? The oud and berimbeu pastorals of Sam Newsome's Global Unity conglom? All are welcome, and some, most obviously Zorn's cagey rewrites and Masada's brilliant interpretations of klez themes, have already made their value quite obvious. It's irrelevant whether the moves are born of ethnic pride or chosen because their creators are bored with the same old same old—I'm not going to sweat the difference between John Benítez's reason for rocking the Cuban beat and Brian Lynch's reason for rocking the Cuban beat. I'm just going to cheer the pluralism that seems to come naturally to the most alert improvisers. If the marketing department can make hay with it, that's fine with me.

WILL FRIEDWALD

What I found fascinating about Kelvin's piece is that so many of the forms he describes as springing up around the world, from Africa to the Caribbean, at least partially in reaction to the spread of jazz, are dance forms. When jazz and big band dance music were essentially different words for the same thing, this form spread wings and planted roots all over the globe, as Cole Porter aptly described in the song he wrote for Louis Armstrong and Bing Crosby, "Now You Has Jazz." At the start of 1925, just before Armstrong began making the Hot Five series, the capitol of the music was indisputably Chicago. By 1930, it had relocated to New York, but the next stop, if not Chicago or New Orleans, was surprisingly London; the world would have regarded London as the next capitol of the music business and the dance-band world, and it probably rated higher, hot-music-wise, in most people's estimations, than, say, Los Angeles. There were great players on the West Coast, and the Central Avenue scene would be roaring by the start of the war, but at the start of the Depression, both American musicians and local talents in Britain were far better documented. The Prince of Wales himself was a connoisseur of the latest American bands and hit Broadway tunes (ironically, this selfsame fan of American Negro music was supposedly a Nazi sympathizer—try and make sense out of that one sometime).

What's interesting is the way the different parts of the world pick up on different aspects of the music in different periods—the British led the way in hot dance music of the early 1930s, the major swing stylists of the immediate prewar period were to be found in the Hot Club of France, and Scandinavia then produced one great modern jazz stylist after another in the 1950s. In the wake of Art Blakey and the Jazz Messengers, there was a great hard-bop unit in Britain named the Jazz Couriers (with a front line of Tubby Hayes and Ronnie Scott, two Sonny Rollins–influenced tenors), while South Africa gave us the Jazz Epistles with, among others, Dollar Brand and Hugh Masekela. When American jazz reached its avant-garde period in the 1960s, the arts communities of Europe and elsewhere didn't have much trouble reconciling free jazz with their own traditions of a musical avant-garde. To give credit where it's due, the late Leonard Feather, perhaps because he was born and raised in England, was in the vanguard in terms of supporting the better foreign-born players (so was Ira Gitler—the first time Ray Bryant appeared on a Prestige Record, Ira compared him to the outstanding Swedish pianist Bengt Hallberg), at a time when most of the major critics seemed bent on dismissing all non-American talent.

I also find it especially promising that many of the forms Kelvin describes around the world have absorbed jazz into local expressions of their own devising, rather than just, say, a Swahili version of Lennie Tristano. However, I have heard Polish Dixieland bands that can be described as half traditional New Orleans and half klezmer, and that, my friends, is truly frightening.

GREG TATE

Jazz is everywhere now—and not just being played everywhere from Iowa to Osaka (like almost every other musical form originating in the African diaspora, from swing to dub to hip-hop to salsa), but so fundamentally a part of the sonic infrastructure of planet Earth as to be invisible to the naked ear. As African scholar Robert Farris Thompson likes to say, the African conquest of the planet's airwaves has been complete. And as Wynton Marsalis once said about so-called world music, anybody playing a traditional folk form against a backbeat is playing African American music. As an Afrocentrically romantic African American patrimonist, I do miss the days when jazz was a predominantly and dominantly African American thing, but also recognize that a music few African Americans under the age of forty-five listen to clearly belongs to whoever shows it love, no matter where it might have originated.

The question of whether jazz is a form or a process, a laundry list or a lab experiment run amok, is one that has been thrown around since the advent of the avant-garde. Any serious listener interested in a present-day grappling with the issue will find little coming from the contemporary African American jazz camp engaged with the avant-garde legacy.

To hear what has become of the avant-garde you have to seek out the myriad Europeans who have picked up the trail after Cecil, Ayler, Ornette, et al.

STUART NICHOLSON

The speed at which jazz was disseminated throughout the world was a very twentieth-century thing. The phonograph record, able to pass unhindered through social, cultural, and territorial barriers, took the music to the farthest, and sometimes the unlikeliest, corners of the world. When Duke Ellington visited London in 1933 he was amazed to find that two sons of the then King of the British Empire, the Prince of Wales and the Duke of York, both owned very complete jazz record collections, and that the Prince of Wales was a moderately accomplished trap drummer who even sat in with the band—this at a time when the divisive British class system was at its height. By then Adi Rosner was leading the State Jazz Orchestra of the Byelorussian Republic in Stalin's Russia, and the following year Buck Clayton was leading a big band in Shanghai. In addition to James Reese Europe's Hellfighters, Lieutenant Will Vodrey's ensemble was also stationed in France in 1917–18, playing for troops and thousands of civilians, proselytizers for an early jazz in a continent fascinated by African American music. The Original Dixieland Jazz Band played a London residency eighteen months after cutting "the first jazz recording" and was even presented to royalty, as were Will Marion Cook's Southern Syncopaters, who followed in 1919 with Sidney Bechet in their ranks.

Almost from the beginning jazz went international. Music from the cultures jazz rubbed up against fed back more as a coloring, rather than significantly influencing the music's evolutionary trajectory. Yet world music influences never slipped from view, and one suspects that had that evolutionary thrust faltered, these influences might have provided a perfect fallback. A master like Duke Ellington suggested that music from other cultures might significantly enrich jazz, evolving an "exotic" songbook within his repertoire with "Caravan" (1937), "Pyramid" (1938), "The Flaming Sword" (1940), "West Indian Dance" and "Bakiff" (1943), and "Liberian Suite" (1947), a theme he continued into the LP era with suites of his impressions of foreign lands as he traveled the world. Equally, Afro-Cuban jazz has always provided an important strand of jazz, while Brazilian music in the 1960s and the World Music experiments of Weather Report and Ornette Coleman with the Master Drummers of Jajouka in the 1970s all suggested a potential for transforming jazz without actually doing so, while the global view of musicians such as Randy Weston, Yusef Lateef, and Don Cherry might well have made them emerge as key figures in the music if other developments in jazz had not assumed the importance they did.

Yet for all the talk about the globalization of jazz, American jazz continues to remain somewhat isolationist and New York–centric, as Chicago musician Ken Vandermark, winner of the prestigious Mac-Arthur Foundation "Genius" Award, points out. He told me "these retro trends" were "very much an East Coast thing that comes out of New York." For him, New York is becoming less and less relevant to developments in a jazz that is showing greater signs of vitality elsewhere, even though the Big Apple still continues to be regarded as its hub. "In the United States, in my experience, the jazz media still considers New York to be the center for improvised music in the world. It's not. It's one of the places," he asserts. "There was a time, without question, that most of the significant improvised music was either being developed in New York or being defined in New York. I would say since the late 1960s that has ceased to be true—and that's a long time ago. I think there are different reasons for that. If you are objective about it, it's pretty clear that many of the major innovators playing what I think is jazz now come out of England, Sweden, Germany, Holland, and other places from outside New York."

Although Kelvin's piece says Europe hasn't "deviated much from the main stem," Vandermark cites a number of European improvisers who have done so. Derek Bailey, Tony Oxley, Evan Parker, Barry Guy, Han Bennink, Misha Mengelberg, and Peter Brötzmann have all served as a source of inspiration for the burgeoning experimental Chicago jazz scene. "It's much more international now: New York is one of the places, it's not the only place," he continued. "Part of it is historical: so much happened in New York that the writers tend to focus on it as a trend-setting place. Large labels like Verve and Blue Note still think of New York as being the center of things. I think a lot of the writers in the United States have not been aware of what has been happening here [Chicago] or in Europe. To me the job is being aware of what is going on, and a lot of the writers still want to believe—in the United States particularly—that New York is the center of things. I don't know quite why that is when it seems pretty clear to me and the musicians I work with that the stuff is so international."

PETER WATROUS

Kelvin's piece does a nice job suggesting the music's ever-increasing decentralization, and I think it's a good time to point out that jazz, for all its nationalistic propaganda, was never as centrally located as people say it was. As I understand it, in the first decade of the nineteenth century fully half of the population of New Orleans had spent at least ten years in Havana, a good portion of those having fled the Haitian revolution earlier. That is, the fully American music was just that: a music from the Americas that came into its own here, literally speaking a different group of languages than the predominant English.

I suppose that history sets up jazz as a form that can deal with a lot of extraneous information; maybe my point is simply a reaction to the nationalistic jingoism I hear all the time to bolster the insecure. What I know is this: musicians, wherever they are, are almost always absolutely interested in music from anywhere. It's not a surprise that musicians here have borrowed from all over, nor that musicians from all over the world have borrowed from jazz, especially in the eras when jazz musicians came with oversized personalities and a ton of swing, personal and musical. Musicians are also mostly rigorous, and interested in systems, and jazz has offered all that; again, it's no surprise given the fullness of the jazz experience (learning control over harmony, rhythm, the depth of ear training necessary to play well, etc.) that jazz is slowly replacing classical music as the pedagogy of choice. It will spread because at its most basic level, it's fun to play. Sounds simplistic, but there you are. Sometimes simple things prevail.

9

OUT OF TIME

FREE JAZZ AND THE AVANT-GARDE

GREG TATE

The music/movement variously described, when not derided, by the terms *free jazz, the avant-garde, the New Thing,* and *the new black music* is often thought to represent a breaking away from a so-called jazz mainstream. But since the agreed-upon forefathers of this revolution in sound—Sun Ra, Cecil Taylor, Ornette Coleman, and Albert Ayler—all began recording in the mid to late 1950s and are therefore contemporaries of the post-bop figures responsible for developing said mainstream, the avant-garde (my preferred term for reasons to be discussed later) represents less a breaking away from than a group of artists who derived a wholly Other set of directions from the inspiration of classic bop. This revolution, as it were, now seems to have been more opposed to the conservative tendencies of their own generation than a rejection of the past. As Amiri Baraka pointed out at the time, the avant-garde actually embraced more of jazz's past than the mainstream—specifically the collective improvisation of early jazz, the timbral curiosity (curious timbres) of early swing, and the rhythmic volatility and unpredictability of early bebop.

While critics on the left and right sometimes define this movement as anti-harmonic, anti-swing, anti-standards, and, hysterically enough, either anti-European or anti-black, there is as much, if not more, compositional and stylistic range within the avant-garde's historical record and recordings as one can find outside them.

The avant-garde is neither an aberration in jazz evolution nor a frozen oddity of its history laden with 1960s-radical baggage. Like all shifts in sensibility recorded in jazz it seems completely logical from a musical and social standpoint. *Avant-garde* seems the best term to describe it because it links it with avant-garde developments in other art forms during the period (theater, concert music, painting, dance, performance art, poetry, etc.), which many jazz musicians were conscious of and sometimes even influenced by. The AACM's Joseph Jarman and Henry Threadgill both make reference to the influence of the experimental music and theater coming out of Chicago's most prominent universities.

The music to some degree did play a kind of adjunct role in the cultural nationalist politics of the day espoused by Amiri Baraka, coincidentally the avant-garde's most articulate champion in the jazz press. Problematic as these politics later became, they did provide a useful context for some of us coming to appreciate the new black music as A Black Thang.

Thanks to the peculiarities of my birth year (1957) and the African American political scene of my adolescence—not to mention the seminal influence of LeRoi Jones's epochal *Black Music*—the very first jazz concert I attended was a performance of the Sam Rivers trio and the Boston Art Ensemble at a place known as the New Colony Theatre in Washington, D.C. Home to an independent black theater company called New Black Repertory, the space specialized in productions of writers such as Baraka, Ed Bullin, Ron Milner, and others who were forging a break from the dramatic tradition of Lorraine Hansberry and James Baldwin with works that, like avant-garde jazz, disregarded genre conventions or stylistic boundaries. That the avant-garde had a home in a community bulwark like the New Colony proved that, contrary to popular belief, the music was not without African American devotees. That they were the most educated and politically conscious of their generation was only another feather in the music's cap as far as I was concerned. I was to find out, as an aspiring jazz collector and advocate, that this sizeable body of African American men and women who frequented, promoted, debated, and produced avant-garde concerts in the D.C. area would prove devoted enough to also become the first programmers and administrators of Washington's jazz-heavy Pacifica station when it got on the air in the late 1970s.

The avant-garde wasn't the only music I listened to in this period. Fusion, funk, metal, folk, soul—all the commercial staples of the era and of my peer group were in there too. But the avant-garde offered the quality of embarking on an intellectual adventure. It also became, through its openness and experimental bent, the master guide through which I toured and understood all subsequent and successive jazz history, from Ellington to Miles's black-noise Afro-futurist *Agharta* band. Ellington, already great, became more great once understood as a precursor to the large ensemble works of Ra, Abrams, Braxton, Threadgill, and Murray. Parker, already dope, became an immeasurable figure for his impact on Ornette, Jimmy Lyons, Roscoe Mitchell, and James Spaulding. The same applied to Ben Webster for his impact on Archie Shepp and Paul Gonsalves for his impact on David Murray.

The freedom espoused in this free jazz seemed a meticulous enterprise, hard-won and as fluid as that desired by Ralph Ellison's Invisible Man. It didn't imply anarchy, nor did it rule it out as an option, either. Its greatest contributions to jazz, however, aren't in the zeitgeist arena but in the musicological areas of composition and arrangement forms, repertoire, solo recitals, and expansion of the music's timbral, rhythmic, harmonic, and scalar vocabulary. Like a lot of memorable 1960s art it was disciplined and derelict, elitist and non-hierarchal, democratic and ungovernable. What it was not, thank God, was unrecorded.

Like all art, the avant-garde demands to be judged on its greatest successes rather than its worst excesses. Here then are nearly thirty indispensable artifacts of this movement, which could now be said to be in its forty-fifth year of storming the barricades: Albert Ayler, *Spiritual Unity*; Ornette Coleman, *The Shape of Jazz to Come*; Archie Shepp, *Blasé*; Cecil Taylor, *Indent* and *One Too Many Salty Swifty and Not Goodbye*; John Coltrane, *Live in Seattle* and *Sun Ship*; John and Alice Coltrane,

Cosmic Music; Tony Williams, *Life Time* and *Spring;* Tony Williams and Cecil Taylor, "Morgan's Motion" (from Williams's *Joy of Flying*); Bennie Maupin, *The Jewel in the Lotus;* Air, *Air Song;* Bill Dixon, *Considerations 1* and *Papyrus;* Anthony Braxton, *Creative Orchestra Music;* Julius Hemphill, *Dogon A.D.;* David Murray, *Low Class Conspiracy;* Art Ensemble of Chicago, *Les Stances à Sophie* and *Fanfare for the Warriors;* Eric Dolphy, *Out to Lunch;* Andrew Hill, *Andrew!!!;* Power Tools, *Strange Meeting;* Matthew Shipp, *Pastoral Composure;* Butch Morris, *Berlin Skyscraper;* Henry Threadgill, *Just the Facts and Pass the Bucket;* Sun Ra, *The Heliocentric Worlds of Sun Ra* and *It's After the End of the World;* Lester Bowie, *The Great Pretender.* Any discussion of the avant-garde's merits should probably begin in copious study of the details and carefully crafted idiosyncracies and intricacies of these recordings (or one's own variation of this list).

Because the avant-garde represents so many roads less traveled on the jazz superhighway—or traveled with less than roadworthy vehicles—the music's future lies securely in its abundant and underscrutinized past and in the dynamic relationship with the past that has been developed within the avant-garde by the AACM artists especially. Younger African American jazz artists have largely sidestepped this body of music as a resource for their own development. Perhaps this is changing with people like pianist Jason Moran, who has just released a record with Sam Rivers, and with saxophonist Mark Turner, who has spoken of a desire to inject some "fire music" into his Konitzian reveries. I would love to hear Nicholas Payton, Roy Hargrove, and others take on the challenges of interpeting Ornette's or Muhal's or the Art Ensemble of Chicago's material—even some of Tony Williams's magnificent 1960s Blue Note writing. Whatever future the avant-garde has will have to be found in the next generation, including its contribution to our sense of jazz history—one we hope will be more inclusive and less avant-phobic than Ken Burns et al.

TED GIOIA

I would like to suggest that we are in the midst of a radical transformation in how we view the concept of avant-garde in all of the arts, including jazz. It is increasingly clear to me that we are at the end of an age in which the concept of "progress" can be applied usefully to the arts. For a certain period of history, this way of conceptualizing art was valid, both for critics and for practitioners, but with each passing year the applicability of this framework becomes more and more problematic.

Does jazz progress from decade to decade? In 1940 or 1950, a critic would have clearly answered yes, but today the response would almost certainly be a vehement no. Yet our critical standards are still stuck in a time warp, and we evaluate the works of 2000 with tools that were better suited to 1950.

Let's recall that the idea that art "progresses" like a science is itself a cultural construct. The view was virtually unknown until the art historian Vasari made it current around the year 1550, and even at its most dominant, this attitude was still largely restricted to the elite classes of advanced Western societies. In most times and places, art has been viewed much differently, valued for its ability to transcend the day-to-day, to entertain, to enhance particular activities, or serve other real human needs.

Most of my research over the last several years—which I hope will eventually result in several books—has focused on precisely these often forgotten instances in which music and real life intersect: hence my fascination with work songs, healing songs, music of courtship and romance, ritual music, war songs, ballads, marches, patriotic airs, meditation music, songs of worship, and the like. My growing conviction is that these types of "genres" are not "the fringe" of musical experience, but actually represent the "heart of the matter." I would argue that even the most high-brow art music succeeds—if it succeeds at all—by reaching into people's lives and offering some promise of transcendence or enhancement.

This is not the time and place to go into the details of this perspective. But I do want to stress that the "problem" of the avant-garde in jazz is, at root, a problem of aesthetics and the criteria we use to evaluate jazz works. My belief is that the progressive approach was valid thirty to forty years ago and served as a productive platform for Ornette Coleman, Cecil Taylor, Albert Ayler, and others of that period. It also served as an aesthetic framework that could be applied meaningfully by jazz critics. But the old formula, much like Sun Ra's rocket ship, has finally run out of gas and desperately needs to be replaced by a more vibrant one. We require nothing less than a new cultural context for music-making in general, and jazz in particular.

Let me suggest one: why not take art down from its pedestal and ask it to meet real human needs—indeed, the full gamut of human needs, from escapism to spiritual transformation, from personal joy to communal solidarity, from the thrill of victory to the agony of defeat, etc., etc. I would suggest that a jazz world that valued these human ideals, instead of quasiscientific concepts, would look much different—and much better—from the one we see today.

JOHN F. SZWED

Was this not Sun Ra's whole program?

K. LEANDER WILLIAMS

The important thing to remember about music—and avant-garde music in particular—is its power to evoke, to suggest, to instigate. I think we've figured out that music by itself cannot do big romantic things like change the world, but its ability to reflect upon a given social reality can certainly prove catalytic—just think of the weight that themes like "We Shall Overcome," "Blowin' in the Wind," or Marvin Gaye's "What's Going On" used to carry. It may seem odd to link a hymn like "Overcome" to the avant-garde, but its use during the civil rights movement definitely transformed it, providing the kind of "progressive" overtones that made the song right in step with the time. Jazz avant-gardists looking for a similar rallying cry thought they'd found it in the brusque timbre of, say, Albert Ayler's tenor, but that only made sense until someone discovered that even the brashest note is just a sound, with only as much context as the player, listener, or time period gives it.

That said, I'd still like to think that music and other creative pursuits can—and ought to—provide us with examples of "progress." Part of the idea of evolutionary newness in Western culture was bound up in the fact that day-to-day realities here are truly different than they are elsewhere, in places where, say, "one" group of people live together in the same locale for thousands of years, or where science hasn't developed enough to cure diseases or offer "modern" conveniences. It may be getting harder to find inspiration in a world where it seems like we have "everything" and where instant codification of every sound is possible, but to suggest that critics, musicians, and the listening public stop asking for new sounds is kind of like of suggesting that the world is now perfect and there's nothing left for us to do. We all know that's just not true.

That could be why I don't place so much value in the much-worried-over idea that the jazz avant-garde should pack it in now that it's nearing forty years of age. I find it a bit disingenuous that many of the people who trumpet this line don't say the same thing about the "repertory"-type stuff that's going on elsewhere—most of which is much older than the jazz avant-garde. While it's true that some of the adventurous jazzers of today take their cues from the early pioneers, I defy anyone to find an ensemble from the 1960s, '70s, or '80s that sounds even remotely like what David S. Ware and Matthew Shipp are doing. Everyone knows that saxists of the 1960s swore off the piano because of chordal constraints, but Shipp seems to have pointed things in a different direction both in Ware's ensemble and in several astonishingly disparate groups of his own (from piano trios to chamber-style groups with violinist Mat Maneri). Much has been said about the jazz avant-garde's current crossover appeal among latter-day alterna-rockers, but I wasn't aware of how influential Shipp's work was becoming until I came across a recent Medeski Martin and Wood live record that had Shipp's fingerprints all over it. MM&W revisited the same kind of Shippian-avant-boogaloo on the accompanying tour, and their audiences—what you might call the jam-band constituency—went for it like catnip. I think it shows that there are far more potential avant-music fans out there than we in the jazz community like to think there are.

PETER MARGASAK

Greg writes that the avant-garde (née free jazz) served as his "master guide through which I toured and understood all subsequent and successive jazz history." I was born nine years later, but my experience was similar. Free jazz was my hook. As a fan of edgy, confrontational rock, the energy and intensity of free jazz held great appeal. Looking back, my attraction was kind of shallow; like punk rock, free jazz would annoy my parents and peers.

But that was in the beginning, and, as Greg writes, the music's openness allowed me to dig and listen far and wide. The reason I mention this process is because I see it happening all over with twentysomethings in Chicago. It's also happening in New York and, I suppose, in plenty of other locales. Greg's piece makes me think that free jazz is dormant. That's anything but the case. New York is thriving with out-music makers of many different stylistic stripes—David S. Ware, Matthew Shipp, William Parker, Charles Gayle, Rob Brown, Chris Jonas, Susie Ibarra, Chris Speed, Cuong Vu, and Daniel Carter, to name just a few—and while many of them are largely rehashing ideas from the 1960s pioneers Greg discusses, some of them are forging new approaches. Plus, that scene is nothing if not energetic.

It's the avant-garde alone that has resuscitated the Chicago scene, attracting new listeners like its New York counterpart. For many of these fledgling listeners it's just the next hip thing, but some of them will surely stick around.

Musically speaking, I think the dominance of free improvisation—whether it's heavy blowing or European-style plink-plonk—isn't enough to sustain the music. That's why composer-musicians like Jonas, Speed, and Shipp and, in Chicago, Ken Vandermark, Fred Lonberg-Holm, and the promising young saxophonist Matt Bauder are all experimenting with different structural/compositional ideas to fuel and support the improvisation.

JOHN F. SZWED

What's always amazed me about the harshest critics of free jazz is their willingness to dismiss the music without serious consideration of its assumptions and aspirations. Instead of treating it as a problematic, they see it as a problem, a threat of some kind, and dismiss it with glib comments about "craft," "professionalism," "tradition," and the lack of swing. Why not consider a few of the questions that free jazz raises: is there such a thing as pure creativity? how many restraints can you remove and still have music? how artificial and unnecessary are artistic boundaries and cultural constraints? what is swing? how distinctive and "ethnic" must jazz be to still retain its identity? is identity necessary? how is it possible for several people to play together and not limit each other's invention and creativity? and what are the limits of invention? of creativity? of music?

It might be interesting to put free jazz up against an art movement with very different assumptions. One such is Oulipo, the largely European "school" of writers that includes Italo Calvino, Georges Perec, Raymond Queneau, and Harry Matthews, and one that sees constraint as the wellspring of all creativity. For writers of this persuasion, the rules of grammar and the received forms of literature (the novel, the sonnet, etc.) are not enough to incite great writing, and extreme forms such as the acrostic, the lipogram, the palindrome, or the holorhyme are welcomed as spurs to creativity. Writers such as this have their doubters as well, and their work is accused of being artificial, cold, acrobatic, too intellectual . . . it doesn't swing. But what *does* it accomplish? What questions does it raise? What has it told us about art and creativity? (It's fascinating to me that some free jazz musicians—Anthony Braxton, for one—ultimately found their way to something akin to a Oulipean point of view in music.)

Raising questions about intentions and assumptions and the place of a movement in the larger world of art is part of responsible criticism, but it's also a way to have jazz taken more seriously outside of music.

BEN RATLIFF

We tend to think of free jazz as one long graduated tunnel, with "really out" being the stuff toward the far end that just can't quite be qualified as jazz even by the well-intentioned (like Derek Bailey's solo guitar playing) and the "more inside" being, say, Sun Ra's earlier big band work; the various degrees of outness in between are pretty easy to assign. But I think that some of the "really out" music is pretty much unattached to the rest of the compound at this point. I'm a pluralist, like everybody else in this discussion, and I wouldn't say that if not for the fact that I see the stuff from the early 1960s on Blue Note—"more inside" vanguardist records by Andrew Hill and Eric Dolphy, etc.—having more of an impact on a greater number of younger players and being part of a majority jazz culture. The legacy of Ayler, Alice Coltrane, Marion Brown, and Brötzmann has led to a new kind of late-night college radio and festivals that basically won't admit "mainstream music" (more or less all of jazz) because its organizers are afraid that they'll be diluting their brand. It's the extremely rare musician—and the very best alive fall into this group, including Greg Osby, Joe Lovano, and Keith Jarrett—who can be comfortable and committed and actually imposing playing in both traditional and free contexts.

And because I'm as much of a let's-be-friends guy as anyone else in this discussion, it bothers me that the movers of the avant-garde business—the record and festival producers, especially—take such little interest in the less "oppositional" side of jazz. Remember when Freddie Hubbard and Bobby Hutcherson played on some pretty radical records? That's the sort of thing I'd like to see. It can be encouraged, but I get the sense that nobody wants to encourage it. Like Greg, I'd love to see Nick Payton play something a little looser, but I've seen him do his mid-1960s Miles thing, and that's not completely unloose.... But rather than seeing our favorite unfulfilled virtuosos actually play the music of Muhal Richard Abrams—it won't happen, and maybe it shouldn't—I'd be more interested in having them break down their system of creating music and starting again, perhaps using (in a very open sense, so as not to produce anything like a copy) some of the strategies of the Art Ensemble, Miles, or Hemphill's *Dogon A.D.*

K. LEANDER WILLIAMS

Maybe this is an entry for the business chapter, but I tend not to challenge the choices of "niche" producers and such because it seems to me that they're usually filling a void. It's not like being shunned by a corporation that actually *has* money but can't be bothered to figure out how to spend it on something a bit more expressionistic. And even beyond that, many of the name people in jazz's less oppositional stream are simply above the price range of specialty fests. It's always back to basic economics.

JIM MACNIE

Disregarding genre boundaries (Greg's description) and removing musical restraints (John's notion) are intrepid maneuvers that many of the artists mentioned here have made their life's work. Of course, there are also those improvisers who just "play that way," operating without a wisp of iconoclastic imperative. Either way, using any and all tacks to fuse intellect with passion, avoid the obvious, examine fresh territory, and personalize your art should be applauded.

Like Peter M., I too found myself in the avant-garde end of the pool when I first jumped into jazz. After some schooling on Miles, Monk, and Mingus, my primary mentor kissed me good-bye and I headed off to what then seemed to be very alluring hinterlands of Lester's *Fast Last,* the Art Ensemble's *Certain Blacks,* and all the mid-1970s loft-scene stuff I could grab. At the time I was a community organizer, working to get some economic justice in low-income neighborhoods, and, as Kelvin offers, the music was valuable as a soundtrack to the job of derailing business as usual.

But though I still respect the era's impulse, much of its bluster now seems superfluous. Back in the day, I played *Low Class Conspiracy* on my college radio show for weeks on end, but if I was turning to an older David Murray disc these days, it wouldn't be that: too much hemming and hawing and standing on the verge of getting it on. Five bucks says the artist himself thinks so too.

Greg's closer to addressing the music's future when he references Jason Moran's current strategies. I'm listening to the disc with Rivers as I write, and its wily use of melody and rhythm makes the ramble-tamble sections that much more explosive as far as I'm concerned. Deciphering a balance between the purely free and the compellingly written have been the great contributions of Moran and his compadre/counselor Greg Osby. Go back to *Fuchsia Swing Song* and its ilk, and you find it's also something Rivers himself was a pro at.

That said, John's questions regarding pure creativity are intriguing. Can a gripping piece of music just be spouted? Is every Old Faithful eruption an everlasting spray of glory? Smitten with Evan Parker's *At the Finger Palace* and Cecil Taylor's medley "Lono: Choral of Voice (Elesion)–Lono" (1973) as I am, I once thought the answer was "Hell, yeah." But having sat through many experiments where the reaction didn't come close to substantiating the labor of the process, I'm now hedging. There is such a thing as pure creativity, but the number of artists who can steer it toward a valuable end are few. I've occasionally used Gertrude Stein's work as a parallel for free jazz, but John's Oulipo offering makes sense: constraints generate a certain kind of authority, and even as stream-of-consciousness thoughts illustrate how intricate and poetic the unfettered creative process can be, some kind of fencing—melody, mathematics, whatever—often serves the music well. Perhaps the avant-garde should have an accommodationist future.

K. LEANDER WILLIAMS

It seems to me that the "accommodationist future" you speak of is actually both the present and the past, which is to say that it's been in effect for quite some time now. In the case of the Art Ensemble, for example, *Full Force* (1979) is a markedly different record from *Certain Blacks*—and a much better one, if you ask me. The David S. Ware Quartet's two versions of "Autumn Leaves" (from 1993's *Third-Ear Recitation*) also put a new spark to some old changes. I think it was David Murray who told Gary Giddins back in the late 1970s that "the music [had] to start swinging again," and the best avant-garde albums of the last twenty years— it's even implied in the title of the fantastic Charles Gayle/William Parker/Rashied Ali date *Touchin' on Trane*—have taken Murray's plea to heart. One of the biggest tragedies of recent jazz criticism is that so few writers are willing to give contemporary avant-gardists credit for the refinement their music has been taking on for decades. Of course, at this point, many of the "futurists" have learned that it's best to pay us no mind anyway.

WILL FRIEDWALD

Greg's use of an autobiographical note in his piece struck a resonant chord with me—not least of which because he's always seemed so much hipper than I and now I find that he's only four years older than I am. My father was heavily involved in the avant-garde jazz scene of the 1960s and '70s, and the earliest jazz I remember hearing was in lofts where free blowing was the order of the day. To me free jazz basically was what jazz was, and I didn't discover other kinds of jazz until later, although my father had a wide-ranging record collection and was especially passionate about New Orleans jazz. To us, the place of free or avant-garde jazz in the history of the music was never questioned, and the relationship of George Lewis, New Orleans clarinetist, to George Lewis, avant trombonist, taken for granted. I spend more time with earlier forms of jazz now, and in that respect I may have something more in common with other second-generation participants in the 1960s cutting edge, like Joshua Redman and Ravi Coltrane—whose music can be described as somewhat more conservative than that of their fathers. Perhaps we're like the Michael J. Fox character on the 1980s sitcom *Family Ties*—his parents were 1960s radicals, yet he wears a suit and wants to get an MBA. Maybe that's too harsh an analogy, since the spirit of freedom has affected all of us. As I once wrote about

Don Cherry, the whole avant-garde movement is an unimpeachable part of what jazz is and who we all are.

STUART NICHOLSON

I'm not sure if I understand Greg properly, but he seems to be arguing that the avant-garde is the "property" of black musicians, a "Black Thang," while somehow conflating "the New Thing" with all areas of free jazz. This makes for an interesting point of view. However, I would argue for a little more critical distance. The move away from the constraints of conventional harmony toward a new form of expressionism had begun much earlier than the 1960s "New Thing." Ellington's "Clothed Woman" from 1947 was the first atonal composition in jazz, while Lennie Tristano's "Intuition" and "Digression" from May 1949 are usually cited as the first voyages into "freedom." Similar experiments continued throughout the 1950s, and a partial list might include certain of Dick Twardzik's 1954 sessions for Pacific Jazz (an acknowledged influence on Cecil Taylor); Teddy Charles, Shorty Rogers, and Jimmy Giuffre on *Collaboration West* (1954); Shelly Manne with Jimmy Giuffre and Shorty Rogers on *The Two and The Three* (also 1954); Teddy Charles on "The Emperor" from *Tentet* (1956); and Cecil Taylor on *Looking Ahead* (1958). Also note a rarely cited performance by Shelly Manne with Andre Previn and Leroy Vinnegar on "Oh Happy Day" from *Modern Jazz Performances of Li'l Abner* (1957). Nor do I associate Ornette Coleman's breakthrough in 1959 at the Five Spot in New York with the "New Thing," even though it heralded what most people accept as the beginnings of the free jazz movement. "The New Thing," to me at least, is a child of the 1960s, whose word was spread on disc by the likes of Blue Note, ESP, and Impulse!

Certainly free jazz of the 1960s was inextricably linked to the social climate from which it emerged, and which helped give it focus and momentum. For many musicians, "freedom" from conventional harmony and rhythm meant that both literally and metaphorically they were participating in the crusade for social justice or freedom. However, using an indigenous music as a vehicle of social protest was seen by some commentators as worthier than the music itself. While the avant-garde need not be immediately accessible, many albums intentionally rejected this possibility. Thus I do think we have to be cautious in our praise for certain albums from this period, as Gunther Schuller has pointed out: "For every one Coleman, there were ten lesser or no talents who sought refuge in the anarchy and permissiveness of the avant-garde."

The significance of free jazz during the 1960s was, as Max Harrison has said, the possibility of a new expressive language emerging within jazz that was wholly independent of other forms of musical expression. This elusive goal was never fully realized, although Miles Davis came close with his ambient pre-furlough 1973-to-1975 recordings. And with the rise of jazz-rock at the end of the 1960s, free jazz, looking increasingly beleaguered at the barricades of sociopolitical issues, turned inward to enclaves of true believers. Musical collectives such as the Jazz Composers Guild, the AACM, UMMA, BAG, and similar though less influential forums for the avant-garde evolved a music quite different to "the New Thing"'s energy playing (although this style did re-emerge in the New York loft scene of the 1970s). A key point that Greg misses is that these collectives stressed "inclusiveness"—not for nothing was the Art Ensemble of Chicago's motto "Black Music from Ancient to the Future." Cassandra Wilson has told me how she was particularly influenced by this outlook after working with Henry Threadgill and Air and how it influenced her music, as it did that of M-Base, in bringing a variety of ideas from a variety of sources—sometimes beyond jazz—to the table.

As free jazz entered the new millennium, Keith Jarrett came to London in July 2000 with his Standards Trio, and his group played one set of totally spontaneous, free improvisation that surprised and delighted his audience (and was recorded by ECM records). On the one hand it showed that whatever the opprobrium leveled at free jazz in the 1960s, T. S. Eliot's maxim holds true—no artist can work outside the tradition because the tradition will stretch to accommodate anything artists do (something all of us pondering the future of jazz should take account of). On the other hand Jarrett renewed the notion that free jazz today need not inhibit volatile experimentalism.

I have to say that Greg's assertion that "there is as much, if not more, compositional and stylistic range within the avant-garde's historical record and recordings as one can find outside them" might be reaching a little far given that the large proportion of free jazz compositions were open structures—of necessity, otherwise how can it be free? Certainly it might be possible to argue stylistic range, given free jazz's extensive use of manipulation of pitch and tone colors, the loosening of bop melodic and rhythmic practices, the use of shrieks and moans, the use of textures rather than preset chords, and so forth; but as to compositional range? In championing the music I do think we have to be careful in the claims we make for it. If we take the principal constituents of composition to be melody, harmony, rhythm, dynamics, form, and instrumental arrangement, then free jazz clearly struggles against more sophisticated compositional forms elsewhere in jazz, even allowing for the law of compensation and the fact that the post-impressionistic "formless" composition has now become an "established" form.

Greg also fails to acknowledge the remarkable growth of free jazz within Europe, which is playing an important role in defining the burgeoning Chicago underground—and gives some clues as to how jazz might shape up in the future. While free jazz was forced underground toward the end of the 1960s and into the '70s, a host of key American free musicians decamped to Europe (along with countless mainstream artists), including a large section of the AACM and Anthony Braxton. Here they operated within, and interacted with, a vigorous free jazz scene that had begun some ten years earlier (don't forget that the Jamaican-born London resident Joe Harriott was working along similar lines wholly independent of Ornette Coleman in the late 1950s— check out his album *Free Form*). Free jazz in Europe expanded to the point where it began to assume its own specific identity, with players such as Albert Mangelsdorff, Evan Parker, Tony Oxley, and Derek Bailey redefining the role of their instruments in jazz. Indeed, the influence of American jazz was seen as inhibiting; Peter Kowald announced an approach to freedom he called "kaputt play," the main objective of which was to "do without the influence of most Americans." Despite the intensity of free jazz excitement on albums such as Coleman's *Free Jazz* and its logical successor, Ayler's *New York Eye and Ear Control*—itself a successor to Coltrane's *Ascension*—a recording such as Peter Brötz-mann's *Machine Gun* (1968) cranks up the intensity of group improvisation to create something unforgettable—plink-plonk it ain't. Today the European free jazz scene still remains vigorous and exciting—just a couple of years ago Kevin Whitehead, for example, was amazed with what he discovered in just one small corner of Europe, the Netherlands, and wrote a book about it.

The point—and this book is about the future of jazz, after all—is that Europe has had an established audience for more adventurous forms of jazz for some forty years now. As Michael Moore, a graduate of the New England Conservatory who has distinguished himself in the Clusone Trio and now resides in the Netherlands, observes, "In America there's more pressure to be conformist, and players who were once pioneers of new music can work a lot more if they play tunes in a traditional way. In Europe there's a larger audience that grew up listening to guys like Han [Bennink] over a twenty-five-year period, and they appreciate not hearing the same thing all the time."

And here lies a clue to how the music might evolve in the future. While the American jazz mainstream seems increasingly resistant to change for a variety of reasons, jazz in Europe does not feel so constrained. Now I know there are refreshing pockets of resistance like the Chicago scene or the downtown scene, and ecstasy jazz players such as David S. Ware and Charles Gayle; but this does not match the breadth of what has happened in Europe during the last few years, where jazz has been moving forward so fast on so many fronts that even there, recent commentators have been hard pressed to keep abreast of developments. Jazz is now so big its stewardship is no longer an American preserve, and it may well be that the broadening of jazz's expressive resources, so necessary to the music's continued evolution, will come from European initiative.

K. LEANDER WILLIAMS

But with so much jazz happening everywhere, I think Peter M., in his response to my piece on jazz and the world, asked the most appropriate question: "Who cares, anyway?" Clusone 3 is—or should I say was—great. David S. Ware is great. Pierre Dørge is great. Satoko Fujii is great—and by the way, no one has said much about the Japanese avant-garde, which is also quite dynamic.

Y'know, when Jim wrote some time ago that African American creative pursuits deserve recognition or something like that, I wasn't quite comfortable with the sentiment because I kind of feel like that places too much emphasis on the tribe rather than the creativity. But I realize now that what he meant was something that this whole discussion of newness, invention, deracination, and exploratory initiative makes clear: that the notion that blacks might still take credit for what their ancestors created is problematic for a certain segment of the jazz public. No one likes to say this out loud, but if we survey the past, white guys like Getz, Brubeck, Konitz, Baker, and Tristano actually developed personal styles as a result of an odd paradox: in many cases they fell short of their initial objective, which was to sound like their black heroes. Luckily for them the pop public was essentially white and racist for a time, which meant that whites approximating black music always had more of an audience than blacks doing it for themselves. And even after Getz, Brubeck, et al., had became originals, not one of them would dare say they didn't have a debt to repay.

The reason I bring this up is because, at the turn of the millennium, what I seem to keep hearing from certain quarters is something akin to "black influences were once the lifeblood, but now they're no longer vital"—which is kind of unnerving to me not only because that's the music I dig, but because it reintroduces the kind of chauvinism that many whites rightly accused blacks of for dismissing genius players like Getz or Bill Evans. Do fans of the avant-collective Other Dimensions in Music not have a right to hew to what bassist Bill Lee (filmmaker Spike Lee's dad) calls jazz's "ancestral stream"? Or is it only fair that the balance has shifted away from the blues impetus because—as I'm constantly reminded—there are so few black faces in the audience at concerts? It seems to me that if the future of jazz—free or otherwise—is going to be pluralistic, and if we as journalists are *not* going to keep up with everything, the least we can do is understand that the old "either/or" thing should be replaced by a "both/and." I think David S. Ware is taking the music forward, while Stuart thinks—well, actually the last response doesn't make it clear who he thinks is on the cutting edge right now. Whoever it is, however, one thing is certain: as the hiphoppers like to say, "It's all good."

STUART NICHOLSON

Kelvin—don't kill the messenger. Europe continues to have very close ties to American jazz, an association that goes way back. One of the first "jazz" recordings ever made was a cylinder of "A Cake Walk" recorded in 1899 in Sweden. Whether or not this is "jazz" in the accepted sense is, to me, beside the point, which is that African American music had permeated European culture at a time when the quickest way of getting from A to B for most people was by horse. Despite instances of cross-pollination, and despite European musicians such as Stan Hasselgard, George Shearing, Marian McPartland, Victor Feldman, John McLaughlin, Joe Zawinul, and Joe Temperley making a name for themselves in the United States, Europe largely took its cues from America until the free jazz scene began developing a distinctive voice of its own.

It is only in recent times that musicians have been expressing the opinion that Europe is coming up with the most forward-looking, innovative jazz. It is not just one or two isolated voices, but the widely held consensus across a whole gang of musicians I have interviewed over the last four years that has changed my thinking: Kenny Wheeler, Bobo Stenson, Esbjorn Svensson, Bugge Wesseltoft, Ketil Bjornstat, Mike Westbrook, John Surman, Gerard Prescencer, Malik Mezzadri, Julien Lorau, Henri Texier, Nils Petter Molvaer, and a host of others. Was it Thelonious Monk who said, "If you want to know what's going on in jazz, ask a musician"?

When I was at the Toronto Jazz Festival, Jim Galloway, the festival director, said he thought American jazz "had dead-ended; the super-creative minds are in Europe now." When I interviewed Mike Brecker on May 14, 2001, in London, he talked about the sounds coming out of the ECM label, how he admired Jan Garbarek's expressive playing, and how the ECM cover art had even affected his own choice of album cover on *The Ballad Book*.

So you see, current developments beyond American shores are currently gathering momentum in a way that seems likely to impact the directions this music might take—whether you care or not.

K. LEANDER WILLIAMS

Well, I guess the most we can do is agree to disagree. I've heard most of the contemporary people you've cited, and from this vantage even their enjoyable music seems derivative on too many levels to really get into. (And I think several writers in this book have already stated how much Molvaer owes to Miles.) Did it ever occur to you that the folks you've spoken with (none of whom, based on past work, would seem to be beacons of cutting-edge jazz) might have other, perhaps more self-serving, reasons for engaging in such talk? I think I've stated elsewhere that jazz's stance has shifted from "horizontal" to "vertical," which actually means that very, very few folks anywhere are doing truly far-reaching work. If your Eurocentric vehemence seems strange to me, it's not because I'm on some sort of jingoistic tirade—though I do feel that remnants of the blues still give the best jazz its gravity (and I'm talking about Evan Parker, too). But it just seems to me that nowadays questions of identity are often used to cloud the issue, i.e., to keep us from truly assessing where jazz is going.

PETER WATROUS

It always amazes me how few people care about the avant-garde, and by avant-garde I mean the traditional jazz avant-garde that comes from

the innovations and changes wrought by a mostly black jazz intelligen-
sia in the late 1950s. I'm not talking about European or Japanese variants, or what's often termed new music, or downtown music, which
clearly owes something to that brief and beautiful explosion of creativity. After twenty years hearing music in New York the audience for the
avant-garde sometimes grew, sometimes dwindled, and sometimes borrowed audiences from rock, if the music came with a rock imprimatur.
Still, put Cecil Taylor in a concert hall, and a couple of hundred people
will show up—that in Manhattan, with its eight million souls. Not a
good ratio for a genius who's been at it for nearly fifty years and for
much of those been acclaimed, publicly and widely, as such.

Here's why *I'm* not so interested anymore: I like rhythm, and, as I got
older, I liked rhythm more and more and was drawn to rhythm genius.
I like Saturday night celebration, I like the dance floor, I like women and
men mingling, and sweating together, and the sweet humidity of sex and
the glories of movement, and while it's fine to spend an evening once in
a while in the company of mostly white males, it's not something that
I can live with too much. I got bored. I moved into the world of Cuban
swing, and Puerto Rican swing and Brazilian swing, into the glories of
our new-world mulattoism, where music and look and movement all
add up to the idea of, yes, swing, personal groove, the way of maintaining elegance in the face of all the stupid oppressions, big and little,
that fuck up the day. Sometimes I'll reach for a record from the avant-
garde, but mostly not. Simply, I love the assertion, the grace, of rhythm
and the way it makes me feel.

At the same time, I'd argue that since the avant-garde's finest cultural
moments in the 1960s, American popular culture has become progres-
sively blacker, and therefore swings harder. Spend a hour listening to
pop radio, and all you hear is black popular culture as the face of
American pop music; look at the sales of hip-hop, boy and girl groups,
black stylists like the white Christina Aguilera, and you realize that, for
popular success, a performer pretty much has to be black (and by that
I mean in intent, if not genetically). So the avant-garde is even more
marginalized; for all its brilliance, it shares even less with common
popular culture. It's become the province of an elite, and at least in
New York, a cult; the same faces show up at the same concerts. The

music and the movement have become swingless, and I don't just mean that rhythmically.

JOHN F. SZWED

I also know the loneliness of hearing music when I wished more men and women were there to listen, too—I recall seeing Captain Beefheart and Stockhausen with scarcely a woman in the house. But it's not always the avant-garde the masses pass up: I saw the Johnny Otis review and even Miles Davis's second great quartet when there were scarcely more people in the audience than on the stage. Yet, as you know, when the time and conditions are right, Cecil Taylor, Ornette Coleman, Sun Ra, Coltrane, Braxton, et al., have drawn ecstatic thousands. But what if they never drew crowds? What are we to conclude from that? That there is nothing there of musical value? That the masses are right to avoid them?

You declare your taste for rhythm, swing, dancing, sweaty sex, and music with the power to overcome the reality of everyday life. And who's going to disagree with you? But the point surely is that music is never either/or: body/intelligence, swing/not-swing, sweat/no sweat, sex/not sex, transcendence/non-transcendence. True, fans talk like that all the time, but critics?

Incidentally, what do you mean by "swing"?

K. LEANDER WILLIAMS

As for Peter's comment about "mostly white males": it's pretty obvious he's talking about an older avant-garde, because it bears very little resemblance to the one I've been witnessing over the past few years. (I'd love to hear from Peter M. on this, too, since I'm told that similar things are happening in Chicago.) Gigs these days seem to draw both sexes. The Vision Festivals staged by William and Patricia Parker each year in New York provide wonderful examples of how the cult has expanded.

PETER MARGASAK

While the scene in Chicago remains unquestionably male-dominated—in terms of both players and audience—during the last decade there have been more and more women attending concerts. Those "mostly white males" still comprise the hard core of the audience, but they are rarely alone now. Thing is, most of these newer fans don't listen to or experience the avant-garde exclusively; it's but one item on a perpetually diversifying menu. One of the most exciting things I've witnessed here is the way these different musical items play off one another. It's absolutely possible to hear new jazz ideas thoughtfully turn up in some rock band or vice versa. It ain't Utopia, but it's nice.

10

THE GHOST IN THE MACHINE

JAZZ INSTITUTIONS, INFRASTRUCTURES, AND MEDIA

TED GIOIA

Mulling over the current state of jazz, I am reminded of a visit I made some years ago to a high-tech factory. My plant tour passed through the customer service department, the warehouse, the shipping and receiving docks, the administrative offices, and other busy, if banal, hubs of daily activity. Yet the actual manufacturing process, where advanced polymer materials were produced, remained hidden from view. We repeatedly asked our tour guide to show us the place where the products were made, but he appeared reluctant to acquiesce to our demands.

Finally, after much badgering on our part, he brought us to a remote corner of the plant and paused in front of a large metal door. "Behind this door is our extremely secret manufacturing area. I will take you inside, but you must treat everything you see as strictly confidential." We readily agreed, eager to penetrate the mystery of this inner sanctum. With a bemused expression, he slowly opened the door and let us look inside.

The room was almost barren. A large vat sat in the center of the room, but it was empty and no one stood near it. Some containers of raw materials could be seen on shelves. A single worker sat in the corner, but appeared to be reading a comic book. "Is this some kind of joke?" "Where is the secret manufacturing process?" Alas, as we soon realized, there was no "mystery" to be solved. The production of these high-tech materials was bloody simple: once a day, a few chemicals were mixed together in a vat. Anyone who had the recipe could easily duplicate the entire process in a kitchen or garage. The company, as it turned out, spent most of its money on marketing and creating the right image, and almost nothing on the products around which all this mystique was fabricated.

With some degree of sadness, I am forced to admit that the jazz world today is very much like my high-tech factory. Surrounding the music we have a growing army of auxiliaries: jazz educators, scholars, critics, concert promoters, producers, disc jockeys, administrators, grant givers and grant writers, archivists, and, of course, fans. Never before have so many done so much in the name of jazz advocacy.

To cite one example: visitors to the most recent convention of the International Association of Jazz Educators (IAJE) were dazzled by the sight of some seven thousand other attendees, coming from thirty countries, filling forty thousand square feet with method books, instructional records, live demonstrations, workshops, and other events devoted to the preservation and expansion of the jazz art.

A second example: documentary producer Ken Burns recently spent almost fifteen million dollars making a nineteen-hour documentary on the history of jazz. Money for the project was raised from over a dozen different high-profile donors—including General Motors, the National Endowment for the Arts, and the Corporation for Public Broadcasting—and the results were broadcast night after night on public television, exposing millions of viewers to the wonders of jazz music. The documentary was accompanied by the release of a series of recordings, a bestselling book, and an effective marketing campaign supported by many of the most powerful businesses in America. Espresso drinkers wandering into Starbucks stores saw, heard, and almost tasted Ken Burns jazz at every turn. Web surfers logging into Amazon.com were told to visit the Ken Burns Jazz Store. Ken Burns and jazz were, for a few short weeks at least, almost anywhere and everywhere one looked.

Other examples could be cited. Universities are hiring jazz professors and establishing jazz programs. Publishers release more books on jazz in a single month now than, in the old days, were published in an entire decade. Grant money—once unavailable even to legendary jazz musicians—today is provided to greater and lesser talents alike. Nonprofit groups devoted solely to jazz music are sprouting up in every part of the country.

Truly such impressive events must indicate a renaissance in jazz music.

Don't be misled. The active music scene at the core of this hubbub is minuscule. Just like the factory cited above, the jazz world is long on image and packaging, and falls short in creating the actual product. For those trying to play this music—in contrast to those merely trying to play off it—there are fewer gigs, fewer clubs, fewer real record contracts, and fewer dollars than ever before. Do you doubt this? Talk to some of the participants at the IAJE convention and ask them about their personal backgrounds and aspirations: you will find that many, perhaps most, of them would prefer to be jazz musicians, not jazz educators, but that declining opportunities to perform and record have forced them into the (comparatively) booming world of pedagogy. Or walk into the jazz section of your local record store: true, you will see stacks of compact disks, but look more closely and you will notice that most of them contain music by artists who died long ago. Or consider that the most widely discussed matters in the jazz world during the last several years—the Ellington centenary, the Ken Burns documentary, various efforts to preserve jazz history at Lincoln Center and elsewhere, etc.—have all revolved around the music's past, not its present. Compare this to the heated jazz controversies of the 1940s and '50s, when fans vigorously debated the merits of the music that was happening then and there.

Yes, there is ceaseless activity in the jazz world, but it increasingly centers on where we have been, not where we are going. One almost senses that few really care any more where the music is heading or, even worse, are tacitly assuming that its future will be all too meager compared to its past.

What should one make of all this? I am forced to conclude that jazz as a series of institutions and enterprises is flourishing, while jazz as a contemporary form of music is suffering from exceptional neglect. The hospital is well furnished and full of shiny equipment, but the patient is still sick.

Nowhere is this odd transformation in the state of improvised music more apparent than in the ongoing debate over the role of Wynton Marsalis in the jazz world. Jazz fans have never been reluctant to debate the merits of prominent musicians: Was Hawk or Prez the better soloist? Were Bird and Diz playing real jazz? Was Ornette a genius or a charlatan? Who was hotter, Benny Goodman or Artie Shaw? These contentious discussions may have solved little, but they demonstrated the vitality of the music and the passion of its fans. Today, Wynton Marsalis is the focal point of contention among jazz people, but—strange to say!—the music on his latest recordings is seldom mentioned. Indeed, I have probably encountered, in print or spoken word, several hundred people spouting off about Marsalis during the last twelve months, and I can't recall a single instance in which one of his performances was referred to by name. Instead, it is Marsalis's role as a power broker, in making or breaking reputations, in defining the history and evolution of jazz, in handing out commissions or helping along careers, that seems to draw forth the strongest sentiments. Marsalis the musician has been eclipsed by Marsalis the institution.

But this is true not only of Wynton Marsalis. Today, jazz institutions of all sorts dwarf the music. If one listed the fifty most influential people in jazz—and put together an honest list, not some fantasy compilation—most of the names would be members of the advocacy infrastructure: critics, producers, promoters, and various movers and shakers. In 1901, jazz was shaped by Mr. Bolden; in 2001 by Mr. Burns. One played the horn; the other doesn't know how. The dismal lesson to draw from this is clear: in the current context, music making has become almost irrelevant.

Don't get me wrong. Jazz deserves support systems and institutional settings. To a certain extent, it even requires these for it to thrive in the present day. For many long decades, the jazz world was deprived of these and felt justified resentment. Not too long ago, a jazz composer could not aspire to receive a Pulitzer Prize, even though the award frequently honored classical works of dubious merit and short-lived importance; a scholar interested in jazz could not hope for a university appointment; jazz musicians would not have even considered applying for a grant or stipend. But from a position of neglect, jazz has come full circle. It is part of the establishment, with its own group of behind-the-scenes power brokers. And too often it wears its newly won laurels with a complacency that is potentially more destructive than the neglect ever was.

Who can deny that jazz is running the risk of becoming mostly a historical artifact? We have seen other arts forms and genres go down this same path: opera, epic poetry, the fugue, tragic drama, Hollywood musicals, the thirty-two-bar popular song. These continue to have an audience, but an audience that shows little interest in new works from contemporary artists. The opera fan longs to hear Verdi, Puccini, Wagner, Mozart, and can only rarely be enticed to pay for a ticket to watch a work by a living composer. And even the classic operatic works require huge infusions of support from grant-giving institutions and wealthy patrons. The similarity with the contemporary jazz world is striking.

Reversing this trend may very well be impossible. Jazz, for better or worse, owns an imposing history, one that tends to overshadow what is happening in the art form today. Nonetheless, we who love this music could do much more to ensure its future vibrancy and relevance. I could call attention to a number of relevant matters, but for the present will content myself with pointing out some specific reasons for concern and suggesting a few, modest remedies, focusing primarily on how this music is discussed, presented, codified, and taught.

Let me start by dwelling on an odd contradiction. The number of young jazz musicians is staggering, many of them boasting degrees and diplomas of various sorts, and the level of competence one finds today, even in youngsters, is striking. But competence is truly the most appropriate word. If one judges by what is presented by the dominant record companies and major jazz performance venues, the level of expressiveness and vitality in the music is at an all-time low. Then again, I am not so foolish as to judge the state of the jazz world on the basis of who is getting record contracts. I am convinced that provocative, exciting music continues to be created, but finding it is somewhat akin to searching for a diamond-tipped turntable stylus—my favorite type of needle—in a haystack. Put simply, the institutions that support the jazz world are mostly indifferent to works that do not fit into the narrowest definition of the music.

This brings me to a key point I want to make. Jazz should not be treated as a certain type of musical vocabulary. It should not be dealt with as a specific style or even as a group of styles. Its parameters should not be fixed but left open. Jazz is defined by an attitude that rejects closed systems and firm barriers, by a seeking after the fresh and vital wherever it may be found, by a mandate to express one's own particular view. Remember this is music that is built around improvisation, on spontaneous creation. Any attempt to reduce it to a body of unvarying techniques and static formulas destroys what is most constitutive in the music.

Perhaps we all agree with this view. Yet one would doubt it looking at how this music is codified and presented these days. Young musicians are taught to memorize certain licks. I have seen them labor over warmed-over phrases for ii–V progressions with the fervor of disciples memorizing Holy Scripture. Meanwhile jazz history has become a type of hagiography—it might as well be replaced with a litany of the saints. Critics, historians, educators, and other members of the jazz superstructure often embrace these static models of jazz because doing so simplifies their job of making sense of the complex and multifaceted world of improvisation. My advice: let the complexity and variety multiply. Don't try to oversimplify matters, no matter how tempting that may be. Don't try to pigeonhole musicians into a small number of accepted styles. Listen for the individual voice in the music, encourage its development, celebrate its arrival when it appears, lament its departure when it leaves.

Otherwise we will end up with a music as narrow and close-minded as our preconceptions. Back in 1976, when Albert Murray first suggested in his book *Stomping the Blues* that jazz could only thrive when infused with blues tonality, few paid much attention . . . at least at first. My initial reaction was bewilderment: I wondered how a serious writer could make such an anachronistic claim. At the time, a whole host of exciting styles in the jazz world—from ECM to AACM—were proving the wrong-headedness of this view. Could you play jazz without relying on the blues tonality? Of course you could—great musicians were doing it every day. In my own playing, I felt that it was the ultimate cop-out to overuse tired blues phrases to excite the audience; they had their place in jazz but did not constitute the essence of the music. Otherwise one was merely mimicking the most mundane mannerisms of jazz—repeating history lessons learned by rote—not creating it afresh.

Yet Murray had the last laugh. His image of the future of jazz—which bore a striking resemblance to its *past*—influenced a handful of high-profile musicians, most notably Wynton Marsalis, and proved to be a self-fulfilling prophecy. With his release of *The Majesty of the Blues* at the end of the 1980s, Marsalis initiated his personal "blue period," aiming at nothing less than the birth of a new era in jazz. And, buddy, if you had any doubts that this was a momentous event, Stanley Crouch's *ex cathedra* liner notes set you straight. Not since Jimmy Smith left the Chicken Shack, back in 1960, had the blues tonality experienced such triumph. Investigators agreed: Albert Murray's fingerprints could be seen everywhere at this crime scene.

Let's be honest: a tremendous amount of creative music continues to be made that does not fit into the Murray model. But if one judges by the music that is promoted the most aggressively by record companies; if one's view of jazz is based on what is included in high-profile documentaries; in short, if one's conception of jazz is based on pre-packaged formulas handed out by the entertainment industry and a few pundits—well, in that case, Murray looks like the great seer who predicted the future.

But is this narrow conception of jazz healthy for the music? Or is it possible that it has contributed to the stagnation we see at the heart of the jazz world?

I keep coming back to a statement Paul Desmond made in 1960, when asked about the current state of jazz. "What would kill me the most on the jazz scene these days," he explained, "would be for every-body to go off in a corner and sound like himself. Let a hundred flow-ers bloom. Diversitysville. There's enough conformity in the rest of this country without having it prevail in jazz, too." Desmond lived up to these words, refining a saxophone style that paid little heed to prevail-ing trends, and remaining blissfully unmoved by whether he was up-to-date or a Johnny-come-lately.

Over forty years later, Desmond's comments remain sound advice for the jazz world. Let us celebrate those musicians—mostly neglected and hidden from view—who are following these precepts, who are expressing their own unique twist on the improvisational art. (Many of them are found outside the United States, I would add, where their indigenous musical traditions assist in this process of individualization, but where their chances to languish in obscurity are all the greater.) The role of the support systems that surround the jazz world—the critics and historians, the educators and academics, the radio programmers and record producers—should be to reinforce these values, to resist the mindless pursuit of conformity, and to encourage the most vital currents in the music.

Yes, let a hundred flowers blossom—heck, let a thousand spring up all around the jazz world—and let each of us roll up our sleeves and start tilling the soil to help make it happen.

BEN RATLIFF

Marketing is so much more sophisticated and ubiquitous now than it was in the 1950s, when hipsters, flipsters, and finger-popping daddies presumably radared in on the secret world of jazz via a complicated system of secret handshakes and whistles, that it seems odd to protest. If the jazz world's attempts at marketing seem embarrassing, that's because there's less money to pay the marketers. A trade show is a trade show; it's definitely a pity that the IAJE is the only big event going, so that it also has to be a summit meeting on aesthetics.

I, too, run into a ton of way-better-than-competent players whose music seems cowed and conciliatory. But it's not all *The Majesty of the*

Blues out there. Who says Murray–Crouch–Marsalis is the word of God? Critics, mostly, feeling pissed that someone is trying to "own the music" and stuff it into one corner, since most of them pride themselves on open-mindedness, pluralism, and knowing what the next thing is. A lot of practicing musicians can take it or leave it. There's no proof that all jazz-playing music-school students are accepting in whole the aesthetic philosophy of Wynton Marsalis. Most of them are not being coerced to play it close to the vest, they're choosing to do so: if they're not melodically gifted, they find a safe place approximating the group sound of whomever they love, whether it's Cedar Walton or Herbie or Miles. And there are still lots of musicians going the other route, playing out and free and multicultural. They just don't end up getting the attention of major-label record companies or club owners, because their stuff is harder to make money on.

As for the impact of Wynton's recent records, I hear musicians talking about stuff on the *Live at the Village Vanguard* set. I've never spoken to another musician about Wynton's last big commissioned piece from Lincoln Center, *All Rise,* because I don't know any who heard it. Anyway, a lot of this Marsalis-as-narrow-minded-tyrant talk is starting to seem dated. For a putative blues chauvinist, Wynton is deeper into European and South American music than a lot of our loft-jazz-era warriors who concern themselves with multiculturalism and tapping into the future. There are post-Wynton trumpet players, like Irvin Mayfield and Marcus Printup, but even they are making very different kinds of artistic statements. The Lincoln Center Jazz Orchestra is a hard-working, hyper-documented, endlessly self-reflective organization, so I'm not surprised that some of those guys have splintered off and made albums that sound exactly like LCJO repertory concerts—Wycliffe Gordon, Rodney Whitaker, Joe Temperley, and a few others. But Ted Nash's new tango–New Orleans–Threadgill-esque band, Odeon, and his new record, *Sidewalk Meeting,* doesn't bother with establishing its official jazz credentials all over the place. If I'd heard it five years ago, I would have been shocked that it was made by a LCJO sideman. Now it doesn't seem like a particularly big deal.

But as long as we're making wishes rather than analyzing what exists, I'll follow suit.

To get away from structures other than Wynton-related ones, I think it would be nice if we could get a great jazz festival in New York that doesn't smack of a franchise operation; I think it could gain more public trust in the music. I think it would be great if some of the money from the Doris Duke Foundation could go to small jazz club owners, earmarking it for things like physical upgrading, commissions, practice rooms (wherever real estate permits), and recording equipment. I think we should have an equivalent—or several equivalents—to the British Council, which maintains outposts in foreign countries and sends British musicians abroad there for workshops and concerts, with the express purpose of cultural exchange. (It's worked for Wynton, after all.) I wish there were people in high levels at Universal, Dreamworks, and so on, trying to get some new jazz into film soundtracks and television shows. I wish NPR had a decent nationwide jazz program that aired new records. I wish more non-jazz indie labels were willing to take a chance on jazz groups. I wish the idiotic pricing at the top jazz clubs, and at the festivals, would just get over itself. I wish going to the Blue Note didn't sound like listening to a cheap stereo and feel like torture. I wish there were a weekly jazz program on, say, Bravo (before it had frequent commercial breaks) or HBO, where someone who wasn't necessarily a practicing jazz musician with his own vested interests and causes to defend could invite musicians to play and talk. I wish there were another mode to spread high culture across the country that didn't have the deadening effect of NPR and PBS. I wish the *New York Times* would hire a second jazz critic.

PETER MARGASAK

I think Ted is right on here. Many of his points are tightly connected to some ideas from my piece on the business of jazz. The establishment—the media, the biz, and the institutions—is more interested in jazz's past because it's easier to market. That's not going to change, and I really believe that unfortunately it's now up to musicians to control their own destiny. Unless something really strange happens, players increasingly need to make their own opportunities.

I'm convinced that people—not lots of them, but more than we have now—will respond to the music if they can find it. But the current system has no interest in making something unproven readily available. There's a greater profit margin in reissues, and, I guess, in big repertory names.

I don't want to harp on this, but from my vantage point, too much of the jazz world is uninviting to the normal guy. People may encounter the music at fancy institutions, but it's rarely intimate or inviting. Heard in a club or a café, there's a much greater chance for a real connection to occur. I know musicians need to get paid, but if the focus keeps shifting toward institutionalization, then working contemporary musicians are truly fucked. It seems to me that in its most potent eras jazz connected with people in a very direct way. As Ben said, it's all about the performance of the music.

K. LEANDER WILLIAMS

In jazz as in anything else, when there's money involved, suspicion is a must. Generally, you want to pay as much attention to the man—and in the case of jazz, I do mean "man"—behind the curtain as possible, primarily because there's so little money to go around in this biz that every new ripple comes neatly wrapped in its own agenda. But, like Ben, I can't say that I'm wrenched out of my sleep at night worrying about what Murray, Crouch, or Wynton might say or do, perhaps because life here in their home city of New York makes it pretty obvious that Jazz at Lincoln Center is just one voice among many. It's true that many of the potshots and slights in the Ken Burns documentary were drawn from what you might call the Murray template, but most of the non-jazz viewers who queried me throughout the broadcast seemed to sense that some of it was a little strange before they got to me. Wynton didn't come off terribly well, something I realized when an avant-garde musician friend told me that his mom—a woman in the dark about the jazz biz who had always kind of wondered why her relatively successful jazz-musician child had sidestepped the Wynton gravy train—called to say that the Burns thing made her proud that her kid hadn't fallen in with someone so obviously "limited." Said musician was astonished.

Whether one considers Wynton's limitations musical or intellectual, though, Ted's piece goes a long way toward explaining their genesis and the impact they've had on the jazz biz. I'm no fan of pedagogy run rampant, and though I'm also well aware that there'd be very little money to get jazzers traversing America these days without the existing network of grants and arts funding, if someone were to suddenly talk about pumping millions into a "Save Jazz" initiative it wouldn't reassure me about the idiom's health. Perhaps it's a romantic notion, but I tend to believe that jazz's hardscrabble origins had much to do with its ingenuity, necessity being the mother of invention. A loyal fan base, one that is attuned to not just what's going on in its own backyard but things elsewhere, is probably about the best endowment anyone can ask for. In the end it limits the number of agendas, middlemen, whatever, so you don't end up with this huge jazz bureaucracy that does little more than skim resources that really should be going to the most creative people.

Another writer suggested to me that the Burns film will actually take general acceptance of the music forward because it frees us critics from having to continuously re-explain chunks of jazz history. I'm not so sure, but it's interesting to contemplate. When all the new fans who bought Burns's companion box set—nearly a million, I'm told—feel that it's necessary to go out and hear music like the stuff compiled therein, it seems to me that they'll seek the safety of jazz institutions first. And if they don't like what's presented there, they'll keep searching until they find something they do like—just like nascent jazz obsessives always do. However, it'd be nice if the institutions could embrace even the types of jazz not represented in the Burns film (the companion book, by the way, covers more ground)—in order to completely serve what could be a burgeoning new jazz community.

WILL FRIEDWALD

Again, part of Ted's perspective is geographical. I don't doubt that where he is it may seem like the institutions surrounding jazz may dwarf the product itself. In New York, however, you get a different point of view: even with something like four major clubs closing in the late spring/early summer of 2001 (some permanently, some temporarily for renovations, so they say), there are at least ten venues operating nightly where one can catch major jazz seven nights a week. Here there is more jazz happening on a daily basis than the critics or the fans can possibly keep up with, and that's not only during festival time. Lincoln Center and the regularly scheduled programs built around the Carnegie Hall Jazz Orchestra don't dwarf the rest of jazz activity here; they merely complement a jazz scene that's already rich and busy.

If our institutions, such as Burns and Lincoln Center, have achieved anything, it's this: as recently as the early 1990s, it seemed as though the perception of jazz in the larger world was predicated on trends from more profitable areas of show business: when *Five Guys Named Moe* was a hit on Broadway, all the Louis Jordan records got reissued; the success of *Jelly's Last Jam* prompted a national reappraisal of Jelly Roll Morton's music; and the same happened with *The Mambo Kings* and Latin jazz. While there are mini-revivals of this or that jazz subtopic (the Buena Vista Social Club or the whole retro-lounge-swing thing, for example), it seems to me that jazz on the whole is a much more entrenched part of the big cultural landscape than it was ten years ago. It's permanent; it's not going to go away; it's something that anybody who even casually observes the music scene (at least in New York) or opens a newspaper is going to take some notice of. I couldn't say how much credit Lincoln Center and Burns may deserve for that, but the jazz institutions in place right now have obviously had something to do with it.

JIM MACNIE

Get money mongers and corporate sponsors to invest in a small space for a couple years at a time, a thorough hothouse experiment that doesn't just blow its monetary load in a two-week span of June à la the New York jazz fests? That Ratliff is thinking smart, I tell ya. Peter M. underscores my feelings, too: we'd all love jazz to have a broader audience, and we'd all love that audience to have a deeper understanding of the music's mechanics (if only to elicit bigger thrills when the tricky stuff is done correctly). And the best way to do that isn't with a massive stage and a massive PA pumping out poorly miked reed-and-rhythm-section spiel. It's to show off the music in its natural habitat: the club. Not the splashy shoulder-to-shoulder sardine can of the Blue Note, but a medium-sized art space that allows musicians a chance to test new ideas while listeners absorb all the action. Nominal admission could cover the physical overhead: electricity and computer and what have you; oil profits and ice cream profits and telecommunication profits and other corporate cashola could cover the skeleton staff and musicians' fees. Curatorial aesthetics would go beyond booking whatever major-label artist had a new record in the racks that week, moving toward an informed/committed director's view of what artistic combinations would be intriguing. New York's Jazz Gallery is in the middle of something similar right now. And I remember an early-1980s series in Worcester, Massachusetts, that had a somewhat parallel idea, too. (It's where I first caught Cassandra Wilson, scatting to Fats Navarro's "The Squirrel" in a band led by Grachan Moncur III; don't mention it to her, though, she's a bit embarrassed by the memory.) Evidently the new Lincoln Center beehive on Columbus Square will feature a clubroom that's also similar—of course they figured out their own infrastructures a long time ago. Come on, Verizon, pony up!

JOHN F. SZWED

Things are as bad as Ted says, and even worse, I'd say, because some of the institutional developments are shabby, if not fraudulent. Universities are what I know best, so I'll chiefly focus on them. We hear about jazz finally entering the academy, jazz positions being given to professors, and research centers popping up, but if you look more closely, most of it is posturing. Leaving aside the occupational/performance-oriented programs, how many universities have made a serious commitment to the music by funding jazz studies, or by hiring even one jazz professor who—like professors in other fields—does nothing but teach and research in his or her specialty? How many universities put on jazz conferences? Sponsor festivals or a concert series? Underwrite a print or online journal? Have a first-rate record, photo, film, video, or manuscript collection? A Web site with research resources? Oh, there are lots of cases of lonely souls fighting the good fight from some corner of the university, begging for funds, scuffling for space, but not much else that I've seen. Part of the problem is the academic field of music itself, which still does not take jazz seriously. Departments of music in fact often hinder efforts to develop programs in jazz by claiming they infringe on their turf, even as their turf excludes the subject.

I continue to also be distressed at the disconnection between the black community and jazz, and the role that institutions play in this. Without revisiting the forces that brought us to this situation, I want to point out how few African Americans are or have ever been faculty members in jazz programs, whether performance- or research-oriented. It's a scandal, and one that needs to be confronted wherever it exists. By the same token, the underfunded or poorly staffed jazz museums that are beginning to spring up across the country—most of which are in black neighborhoods and are viewed from outside as some kind of political payoff—are in bad need of development and support. The opposite problem—those well-funded jazz programs that are not located in the black community and that charge prohibitive admission—is of course equally distressing.

GREG TATE

My favorite idea of a jazz institution is Chicago's AACM: a composer/performer/teacher/scholar–driven organization dedicated to divining new conceptual ground for the music while encouraging the performance of new works with new instrumentation and developing new community spaces in which these manifestations can be heard. Whatever state the AACM is in now, its model is one I wish could be adopted and sustained by a collaborative body composed of the likes of Matthew Shipp, Wynton Marsalis, David Ware, Marcus Roberts, Roy Hargrove, Dave Douglas, John Zorn, Bill Dixon, Roscoe Mitchell, Henry

Threadgill, Najee.... Let a thousand competing esthetics reign, and then and only then would you have a jazz institution/infrastructure contentiously and improvisationally worthy of the name.

PETER WATROUS

Ted's piece makes me think that perhaps there are two jazzes: the one that imploded a decade ago and has generated so much official interest, and another, newer, one that so few people seem to know about, one that begs the experience of being in New York and in clubs regularly to be understood.

The first one is the noble jazz of the progenitors, the Louis–Miles–Bird–'Trane–etc. one, and it's the one that has institutions rustling around in the dusty bones, the one that warrants institutional analysis, reproduction, and canonical argument. It's the one that's officially over, the one that Wynton Marsalis pays plenty of tribute to, if unevenly. *That* jazz is safely secure in its status and really doesn't merit bickering or boosterism; *Kind of Blue* sells whether Burns labels it a masterwork or not. And really, Burns's documentary was a bit like a funeral celebration.

The other jazz is the jazz that's all over the place: the one that exists in coffeehouses, restaurants, basements, music schools, and clubs; in Europe, America, Asia, and Africa. Sometimes it has a direct connection to the jazz of the Saints, sometimes not so much. It's not a popular music anymore, and by definition there can be no founding myths to arrive from its spread. But the jazz superstructure that often bothers critics, the institutions and the academics vainly trying to be cool by repetitively proposing the avant-garde as anything more than a momentary spasm in a long history, are virtually irrelevant to this new jazz. I rarely hear any jazz musicians involved in the sort of critical huffing and puffing that embitters those in the superstructure. The new jazz musicians that I know could care less about Wynton, could care less about somebody telling them what to do. They're dedicated, like most jazz musicians have always been, to learning, playing, and making a living in a manner in which they feel comfortable.

And after the momentary centralization of jazz that Wynton brought about in the early 1980s and the inevitable reaction to it, there has been simply an explosion of disparate ideas, of thought, of play with the idea of jazz. Some of it has been dull, a chasing after the lost spirit of the Saints, and some creative. But to imagine that the academics, the institutions, have much to say about the actual workings of jazz in the here and now is to give way too much power to people who neither have it nor deserve it.

STUART NICHOLSON

I have not read a more prescient overview of jazz today than Ted's. This carefully considered piece calmly assesses the problems that ail jazz in America today. His fears become my fears and should become everybody's fears. Increasingly, young jazz musicians are becoming custodians of a music within carefully prescribed parameters, an inadvertent by-product of jazz entering academia—if you can't define the music, then how can you teach it? The open-ended definition of the music that Ted argues so eloquently for, one that allows the music to continue to broaden its expressive resources, no longer holds. Jazz is gradually being ring-fenced by educators who see limits to the art form, and a static definition of the music is emerging, one that looks backward and allows for little or no future growth.

Academicism is breeding revivalism. Jazz method books, jazz pattern books, jazz teach-yourself books are all dedicated to a style of jazz that reached its apotheosis in the late 1950s and early '60s. As Dave Liebman has pointed out, hard bop should be the calisthenics of improvisation, the warmup/workout regime before taking that leap into the future. Now the hard-bop continuum has become an end in itself.

The jazz media seem, in the main, to have abandoned their sense of antagonism toward "the business of jazz," which is to say the major record companies, for they realize they have a common interest in maintaining consumption by trying to balance older listeners' nostalgia with younger listeners' desire for the new. Some jazz magazines include "lifestyle" ads for hi-fi sets, cars, and trendy alcoholic beverages—such is the demographic the music now attracts. With the absence of any shock announcing the new in the last two decades, jazz criticism is less inclined to be "critical," more inclined to situate the music through referents, which effectively decontextualizes it. But the old problem still remains: a fear of being caught liking something other critics have decided not to like.

Where is all this leading us? The unexpected rise in the importance of the "jazz tradition" over the last twenty years, the conventions of jazz education, and an acquiescent media content with the status quo have all contributed to the creation of an American jazz mainstream that has evolved into a touchstone of craft rather than creativity, a place where like-minded musicians gather to sharpen their skills to impress other musicians, a celebration of American cultural achievement rather than a steadily evolving, developing, growing art form.

Greg appositely included a quote from Graham Haynes in his comment in Chapter 2: that the jazz era, as defined by the generations who produced swing, bebop, and the avant-garde, is over. This is correct, yet young musicians playing in these historically acceptable styles of jazz have filled the void with virtuosic recapitulation. These styles of jazz were products of their time, and this is the key to their longevity. For jazz to survive into the twenty-first century, it too must reflect its time. Which is what Graham Haynes and Bill Laswell's drum 'n' bass album, *Sacred System,* did (it also influenced Tim Hagans). It's what Haynes's albums *Transition, The Griot's Footsteps,* and especially *Tones for the 21st Century* were all about.

And here renewing jazz's lost link with popular culture becomes crucial if jazz is to exert an appeal beyond its true believers. Jazz needs to expand its audience, otherwise it will end up playing to itself, to those engaged in the infrastructure of the music Ted talks about—"the critics and historians, the educators and academics, the radio programmers and record producers." How to get that audience? Jazz has to evolve more outside the loop than inside, to a place where John Coltrane saw the future: "No limits," he said, "no limits."

CONCLUSION

A PROGNOSTICATORY *CADAVRE EXQUIS,*
COMPLETE WITH ELEGY

2002
JOHN F. SZWED

It would not seem to be a good time to speculate about the future of jazz. Having so recently departed its golden age, we are awash in reflections on the past and haunted by fears of having no future at all. But on the other hand, with no New Thing on the horizon to obsess about, maybe it is the time to be visionary.

The weight of jazz tradition at the moment seems numbingly present, its heroes oppressively beyond reach. We've already seen how this has been dealt with: some musicians have turned themselves into copy machines, reading books of classic "licks," dressing up, learning to play the blues from scales and exercises, purifying the music of its real or imagined pollutants, mining one or another of the styles of the past. Others—postmodernists, you might call them—will pay lip service to the past while making its accomplishments seem hard-bought, using conventional materials in stripped-down, abstracted, or accidentally parodic forms. Still others will say to hell with *that,* forget the traditions, and maybe go pop, or electronic, or ethnic. Some will go back to the principles instead of particulars to create their music, and regenerate it in whatever form they can. There are those who will dig in wherever they are and never change. A few will even say forward at all costs, ignore the audience, break the rules, make it new. And some individuals—in the spirit of Sidney Bechet—might even do most or all of the above in a single lifetime.

The point, really, is that jazz has always done all these things, and that's what has made it so scandalous, so marginal, so American, and so happily beyond definition and prognostication.

2017
BEN RATLIFF

...Nightclubs could have Web cameras carrying performances to your TV set, which you can watch whenever you want because of TiVo. Below the top level of jazz musicians who have a chance of winning a Grammy or being managed by Diana Krall's people, recorded music will be even more in the hands of the musicians. The notion of a "body of work" on record will be so much different from what it is now: harder to navigate, harder to document, more listening-intensive. Instead of lavish coffeetable books about Blue Note records, there will be Web-published set lists and streamable bootlegs for the fans, who will have a greater chance of being reached by the Internet.

...Jazz at Lincoln Center will still occupy its enormous new digs at Columbus Circle, but Wynton Marsalis won't be artistic director; Marcus Roberts will have taken his place, and John Medeski will be playing sold-out performances of the music of Jaki Byard in the concert hall. Their book publishing wing will have contracted all of us, at one point or another.

...MTV Jazz (sharing a channel with MTV World) will provide a middling showcase of live videos and in-studio interviews and performances, with Eric Reed, Steven Bernstein, and Erykah Badu as on-air hosts. Also on MTV Jazz, the format of this book (thesis, counterattacks, and cogitations) will be copied in a weekly critics' roundtable called "Fuckin' with Some Barbecue."

...Soul–funk–R&B hipsters like ?uestlove, Bilal, and D'Angelo will carry a torch for jazz, mentioning Dupree Bolton and Hassan Ibn Ali in interviews, stimulating enough downloads to finance full-scale explorations into their rehearsal tapes, spearheaded by whoever has been appointed to the Timbaland Professorship in Jazz at University of Virginia.

...The great jazz novel, jazz–hip-hop fusion, and jazz movie will still not yet be made.

...Jazz will become Latinized to the point of an entirely new audience emerging.

...Several extremely talented and conceptually brilliant black musicians, able to spiel learnedly about the transmission of culture from West Africa to the New World and also to illustrate it in music, will come along and utterly fascinate the fourth estate and a bit of the club-going audience. Instead of having slow-burning cult careers like Sun Ra, they will burst through the surface of national media quickly and loudly and be turned on much too quickly; only the strongest of them will be able to survive.

...Someone will revive the idea of the late-1950s Lenox School of Jazz, which will provide annual summit meetings—complete with performances that aren't beer-sponsored bonanzas making money for some nationwide promoter—for musicians from all of jazz, and a number of related fields—which by that point might include electronic improvisation—to come together and collaborate.

2020
JIM MACNIE

Since several of our essays spent a good chunk of time using the past to frame the future, I'll voice what I suspect many of us believe: change comes slow. So I'm going to count on few earthshaking amendments to the current status quo over the next two decades. There will be shifts, detours, and modifications aplenty. But don't expect true turnabouts, and don't be bummed by that news—it isn't necessarily a bad thing. As discussed, there are several creative and intriguing actions afoot in the music these days.

The jam-band/drum 'n' bass phenomenon, whether it's stemming from the post-Miles atmospherics of Stuart's beloved Nils Petter Molvaer or the racket-happy spaceprov of Medeski Martin and Wood, is drenched in possibility. Kelvin's wonderfully blunt reminder of rock 'n' roll being jazz's murderer was right on. The music's shift from the popular spectrum of the 1930s and '40s, when swing = orchestras = dancing = social music, removed young constituents from the equation. And since youth culture largely determines the prominence of most art forms and musical trends, it's desperately needed as an active participant if improvisation-based music is to regain renown. Long story short: I play Ellington for otherwise artistically sentient jazz neophytes and they hear "big band" music—they can't hurdle a tune's stylistic veneer. This may be Duke's century, but in the largest scheme of things, he remains a cultural corpse to a good chunk of citizens. (That's one reason I flew the flag for abiding with if not stressing jazz repertory in my chapter; the population at large doesn't have a grip on the music's benchmarks.) At the risk of opening the door to a dumbing down of jazz's intricacies, I'm willing to invite some fresh faces to the party.

Otherwise, count on pan-ethnic participation most noticeably affecting the music twenty years hence. Our chapter on jazz and the world only touched on the recent and keenly reported influx of Cuban and Caribbean strains. Jazz has always been a sophisticated mutt, and as the root lingo of its participants becomes broader, the options for alternatives increase. Consider that gorgeous hedged bet by Danilo Perez, *Panamonk*. Old material, new slant, great record. How old will John Benítez and Dafnis Prieto be in 2020? Early forties or so. That's just the right age for them to make truly authoritative statements after years of helping take the ever-robust clave cadences through two decades' worth of variations.

One kind of jazz revitalization will come in the form of stressing origin, in part because tradition is a deep well that is seldom tapped completely, and in part because there are so many traditions out there to tap. Brazil, Trinidad, Holland, Yemen—dollars to donuts says that some kind of ethnic folk style will bubble up when its interpreters hit New York and start spreading the word. What will happen if Ravi Coltrane gets into banghra? Perhaps the next wave of territory bands will be global. I'm big on Irish music and find several of its virtuosos to be very sharp improvisers. You can't walk away from a show by fiddler Martin Hayes without being bowled over by his sense of touch and depth of swing. And while Louis Hayes's recent Celtic/jazz experiment didn't do much for me, I'm leaving the door open to see if it matures. Hey, Rufus Harley has been dragging those bagpipes around again lately, so no stone's being left unturned.

Guess that means it's all up for grabs. Except for a few certainties. I'll still swoon for Ellington's "The Clothed Woman" and Air's "Buddy Bolden's Blues." I'll still boo-hoo about there being no duet recording between Cecil Taylor and Jimmy Lyons. And I'll still marvel at how hard it is to catch some consensus between a bunch of jazz critics. One thing's for sure: twenty years or a hundred years, the power and value of subjectivity will never change a whit.

2022
K. LEANDER WILLIAMS

I wish I thought journalists and critics would be more perceptive in a far-off time, but since many of today's writers commit many of the same dopey blunders as those thirty or forty years ago, it seems unlikely that we'll ever really get a handle on what this magical music is about. All we can hope is that great musicmakers will be as oblivious to us as they've always been.

So it's the year 2022 and, right on schedule, the public has begun scratching that nostalgic itch that casts things from two decades previous in an alluringly recidivist light. In America, at least, this would seem to suggest a populace pining for the return of Gee Dubya, but that's not the case. On the contrary, it means that the American electorate, after enduring a string of leaders who've campaigned by strapping on Stratocasters and sitting in with Kevin Eubanks on *The Tonight Show with Jay Leno,* will instead opt for another Prez who plays saxophone—

like good ol' Three-Dollar Bill Clinton (remember him?). Ravi Coltrane, now middle-aged, will be invited to the White House regularly (especially in times of crisis) in order to ease the commander-in-chief's troubled mind with note-for-note renderings of John the Father's "A Love Supreme"—the new Prez's favorite jazz album. All this will prompt Wynton Marsalis, just into his sixties, to begin showing signs that he'll be an even grumpier old man than he was a young one; Marsalis won't be able to resist grumbling about the President's apparent nonchalance toward trumpet. Meanwhile, behind the scenes, executives from the world's leading saxophone manufacturers (Selmer and Buffet in France; Yamaha in Japan; Julius Keilwerth in Germany) will meet execs from the major labels and a noted software giant in an effort to spur yet another reissue boom and boost sax sales worldwide.

Back in the 1990s the rapper Ice-T said that one day aging hip-hoppers might be found "kicking that old flavor" in jazz clubs. Many laughed at the time, but a few clubs—sensing that new jazz audiences are likely to have discovered Coltrane, Dizzy Gillespie, Charlie Parker, Miles Davis, or Sun Ra from a mention on an early rap record—will take the first tentative steps in this direction. Even the long defunct British collective Us3, the band that registered the biggest-selling Blue Note record of all time in the early 1990s with "Cantaloop (Flip Fantasia)"—a single based on a Herbie Hancock sample—will threaten a reunion. When reached for comment, Geoff Wilkinson, one of the group's cofounders, will say something about how he and British saxist Courtney Pine "always thought the group belonged at Ronnie Scott's and the Village Vanguard."

If this sounds like jazz will be on the ropes, it shouldn't. The avant-garde will no longer seem like mainstream jazz's dysfunctional cousin, primarily because of the liberal space it will be given at several branches of the new International Jazz Museums being readied in New York, Paris, Havana, Toronto, Johannesburg, and Yokohama. More cities will follow, and they'll be connected by several intercontinental radio programs and round-the-clock satellite broadcasts culled from each site's extensive video archive. Whatever their taste or level of obsession, the new jazz generation should be pretty well served.

2027
TED GIOIA

Our music in twenty-five years.... The mind reels at the thought of...
robotic jazz, clones taking solos on virtual instruments, jam sessions in
outer space, the NEA providing fans with free tickets to the Village
Vanguard....

Well, hardly.

The most striking aspect of jazz in twenty-five years will be, I believe,
the continuities with the present. Many of the great players of today
will still be performing and drawing large audiences. Musicians will still
prefer jamming on songs from the twentieth-century repertory, finding
continued inspiration in the compositions of Gershwin, Ellington, Monk,
Rodgers, Parker, Tristano, and other craftsmen of a bygone era. Singers
will still sing... often off pitch, just like today. Drummers will still drum.
Saxophonists will still complain about their reeds. In short, it will be a
familiar world.

But some things will have changed dramatically. More music from
more places will be more accessible by more people. Advances in tele-
communications will bring me into easy contact with jazz players all
around the world. I will be sitting in my home in California—yes, it
too will still exist, although it will be a bit more crowded by then—and
effortlessly check out the jazz scenes in Oslo or Ontario, Bogota or Bombay. Even more, I will be able to jam in real time with musicians in these
cities. In my car, I will no longer be restricted to the lousy radio stations
in my home town, but will listen to KLON, KCSM, WKCR, or (my first
choice) the current top hits in Bahia. On the road, on the street, at work,
or at home, the full spectrum of the jazz world will be available to me,
just for the ASCIIng.

Most people will be confused by this great opportunity to open up
their ears. After all, even with over 100 television channels, some people
still watch reruns of *Gilligan's Island*. God bless them! No, we won't be
able to transform the average Joe or Jane (or Juan or Janna) into avid jazz
fans. But an enlightened few will revel in the freedom the new technology offers.

Jazz musicians, in particular, will be delighted by the changes. They will interact directly with their audience to a far greater degree than ever before—and this will empower them enormously. Power brokers and intermediaries of all sorts will be less important. Of course, record companies, distributors, agents, deejays, promoters, and the like will still exist, but their stranglehold on the means of production and dissemination will be considerably loosened. Some musicians will still work within the old system, largely from laziness and disinclination, but more and more players—especially the younger ones—will take control of their own destiny, using technology to build satisfying careers in jazz.

Ah, the future will be bright, but not without strains of sadness. Above all, the jazz world will be beset by an unquenchable nostalgia for the past. The great musicians of the twentieth century will seem like towering artists, of mythic proportions, increasingly distant from the contemporary fray. Armstrong, Ellington, Bird, Prez—they will seem as distant as the images on the side of Mount Rushmore. Almost no one will be around who saw them perform in person, talked to them between sets, bought them a drink, or asked for their autograph. And even fewer will be left who heard Bix live, who saw Fats Waller perform, who danced to Kenton at Balboa. We will miss this direct contact with the pioneers of the music, and some—especially the old-timers—will lament the passing of a golden age. But the more vital among us will think mostly about the future, not the past, wondering what jazz might be like in another twenty-five years, and plotting about ways to make this "future of the future" even better and brighter.

2028
WILL FRIEDWALD

If no one's quoted this, then let me be the first: there's an episode of *Futurama* set in the year 3000 in which all the robots go on strike. The first reaction? "Oh no! Now who will we get to play our smooth jazz?"

Actually, I don't think jazz is going to get smoother in the next twenty or thirty years—I think it's going to get more diverse. Because so little jazz was available in the 1970s, for instance, most of the players who matured in that era tended to sound a certain way because of what they listened to growing up. Now there's so much available to inspire a creative musician, not only in terms of reissues of classic stuff (as well as offbeat old stuff that's fascinating but not necessarily anyone's definition of classic) but in terms of new music that's being recorded and circulated in a way that just couldn't happen ten years ago. (I remember not being able to find any Lester Young records when I was a kid, and being resentful that the closest thing most stores seemed to stock was Larry Young!) I can only imagine that musicians coming up today will be influenced by everyone from Dave Douglas to Joe Mooney to Ravi Shankar to Glenn Gould to Hot Lips Page.

There will be more merging and converging. There will be more historically speaking musicians who will re-create increasingly eclectic areas of the jazz past (I just heard Dean Morra, a West Coast–based 1930s revival band, playing at Lincoln Center's Midsummer Night's Swing the other night, and was surprised to hear them do "Pastorale" by Spike Hughes and his All Negro Orchestra as well as "Annie's Cousin Fanny" by the Dorsey Brothers, two works I never thought anybody would revive). But I feel that there will be less division between revivalists and other forms of jazz. Current examples: David Murray playing Ben Webster isn't more Murray than Webster, and even Slide Hampton's *Tonight Show*–style orchestration of *A Love Supreme* for the Carnegie Hall Jazz Band, which sent most Coltrane purists running for the exits, riveted me.

The combination of diversification and musical/technical convergence has to be good for the music, not only in terms of content, but in terms of the way the music as a whole is perceived. Right now, according to *Billboard*, it seems that basically the only kind of music people listen to is 1) traditional-style, clean-cut teen icons and virgins à la VH1; 2) hostile ghetto youth in turned-around baseball caps; and 3) old dudes in cowboy hats whose woman done left them with no gas in the pickup truck. Yet as more and more people hear more and more different kinds of music—and thanks to the new technologies, they'll have to work hard if they want to avoid it—they will listen to more different kinds of stuff. Jazz will evolve as it always has and pop will hopefully get more interesting too, absorbing more jazz and world influences.

I've already used this famous Ellington bit, but it bears repeating here. At certain performances late in his career—this in the 1970s when people were already beginning to think about the millennium—Ellington would pose the question, "What will jazz sound like in the year 2000?" His answer was: a lot like Louis Armstrong singing "When the Saints Go Marching In."

2032
STUART NICHOLSON

Thirty years from now is a period roughly equivalent to that between Louis Armstrong's epic solo on "Weather Bird" and Ornette Coleman's *The Shape of Jazz to Come*. A long period in terms of jazz history, but not so long that with any sort of luck I might still be around to check things out.

First there's the dear old repertory brigade, convinced they are playing "the real jazz" yet conscious of a limit to their art. This movement will continue to grow apace, if only for logistical reasons. Simply put, with so many young musicians being produced by colleges and universities, most will never reach the vanguard of jazz but will wish to practice their art, if only in modest humility, rather than keep in step with the zealous reformers. For them, performing stage-band versions of Fletcher Henderson, Duke Ellington, and Count Basie tunes and playing in the adopted voices of jazz's posthumous heroes will give them an identity that they would, perhaps, be hard pressed to find elsewhere in the music.

The new legitimacy conferred upon the repertory movement by the Ken Burns *Jazz* documentary and bestselling jazz history, and the forthcoming citadel now being erected at Columbus Circle, former home of the Coliseum, in New York City as a shrine to jazz's past, will make this movement appealing to private and public funding—after all, Ken Burns had no problems raising eighteen million dollars. Jazz concerts will become sponsored by the likes of General Motors since jazz will be seen as "modern" (in Wynton's sense of the word) and American (as opposed to "European" composers such as Bach, Beethoven, and Mozart). The comfortable middle-aged will dress up and go in order to see and be seen. Affluent white audiences, whose only contact with members of the black community is at a check-out till or in the work environment, will be able to congratulate themselves on their liberal-mindedness in honoring black achievements by listening to concerts of the music of Armstrong and Ellington. There will be free afternoon concerts that grade-school students are required to attend, since listening to jazz will be one more item on the school curriculum, alongside learning math and reciting conjugations. Most large cities will boast a jazz repertory orchestra surrounded by an infrastructure akin to a symphony orchestra. Touring soloists, adept at imitating Cootie, Tricky Sam, Buck, Lester, Roy, et al., will perform with these orchestras in regular concerts. It'll all be quite boring.

Then there will be another kind of jazz, where adventurous musicians will be pushing the envelope, bringing all sorts of influences—world and dance—within a music that defies category but people can dance to and have a good time. To find this music you need to go to hole-in-the-wall nightclubs catering to young audiences and be prepared for loud music. The repertoire crowd will look down on this music, decry it, saying it doesn't deserve to be elevated with the dignity and cachet the term *jazz* can bring. The music will be highly rhythmic, the virtuoso soloists will have evolved a new language, yet it will be fun, good-time music. The record business, now long gone after MP3s made it cease to be viable, will no longer be around to dilute and mainstream this music from the margins.

Earnest grad students will prepare their degree theses on how this music seems to echo the origins of jazz—the slow drag, the stomp—when people considered jazz a dance music, and when it was always to be found at the wrong end of town. Could it be history is repeating itself, they will ask—just as New Orleans music brought together the several strands of vernacular, popular, and classical music of the day, could this one be bringing together the strands of music relevant to the year 2032? Could that original spirit of jazz still be alive and creating a music for the people—a social music, inclusive and creative, and continually evolving—just like jazz always used to?

2042
PETER MARGASAK

Four decades from now the hard bop that's remained jazz's most visible form—for nearly five decades—will finally be heard as a style from the past, although it won't yet appear on symphonic bills like the works of Ellington, Morton, and Waller. Of course, musicians will still be playing it, but more as an act of nostalgia replete with blue serge suits and skinny neckties. Citizens of the Far East and Australia, among the most devoted jazz listeners the world has ever known, will frequently squabble over the music's purity, engaging in heated debates over whether a laptop computer should be heard in a tune written by Woody Shaw: is it sacrilege or just a sign of inevitable musical evolution?

Some musicians will still release commercial studio albums, although mostly as promotional devices for Internet radio, but the majority of recordings will be ordered directly from the artist's Web site. Consumers will order custom-made albums culled from live performances, Internet broadcasts, and sessions recorded in home studios.

And, just as likely as all of this, I will be finishing my second term as president of the United States.

[NO DATE]
PETER WATROUS

The future of jazz will look like this: a couple of people in class studying historical models. After class they'll go home and play the music, the same way math or chess clubs meet and deal. Occasionally, like in chess, someone will come out of the ranks to become famous in the loose community of chess players and, with enough charisma, perhaps attract attention outside the small world of those obsessed. That'll be rare, though.

Finally, why should jazz be anything but a skill learned by those few who care, and probably have no interest in making what they play attractive to anyone but those familiar with the language already? It'll drift away into a coma, albeit an intelligent coma. But as a popular music, well, I doubt it. It doesn't even have the bulk of orchestral work and compositions that make classical music a viable repertory art—I mean, how many times will someone pay a pile of money to hear the "Far East Suite"? The best and brightest will go into popular music, or if that's too desperate a world, they'll become doctors and lawyers. Jazz will be a hobbyist's music. Every day it becomes so.

What can reverse this? Only the unimaginable, the dire, or . . . I haven't a clue since the runaway train of popular culture flattens pretty much anything that I can live with. But then it won't go away, either; like boxing and venereal disease, it'll hang on. A few days ago, Diana Krall broke the pop top ten. The same day, I was speaking to someone, educated, mature, etc., who had never heard of John Coltrane. So jazz will keep on going, losing half its ranks every ten years, and therefore getting smaller but never disappearing.

R.I.P.
GREG TATE

My first flippant response to this was that my ouija board is broke and my tarot card reader's on crack. My second, less flippant, response was that I'm far less interested in the future of jazz than the future of Black-folk and the future of Kingfish Bill Clinton's Harlem. I have always believed jazz came from the future anyway—a tachyon beam from some post-liberated alternate Black reality where the burden of oppressive racial subjectivity had been eradicated and people of African descent practiced freedom without having slavery flashbacks. On the other hand, I also believe that, to paraphrase Blakey again, no niggas, no jazz. Meaning if somehow, some way, this generation of African American youths of all classes aren't encouraged to bring all their hip-hop musicality and technology in the thing, jazz may as well be dead: a thing alive in name but certainly not in Negroidal vitality and invention.

ABOUT THE AUTHORS

WILL FRIEDWALD is the author of six books, including *Jazz Singing, Sinatra! The Song Is You,* and *The Good Life* (with Tony Bennett). His two current projects are *Star Dust Melodies: The Biography of Twelve of America's Most Popular Songs* and *A Biographical Dictionary of Jazz and Pop Singers,* both forthcoming from Pantheon Books.

TED GIOIA is a jazz pianist and music historian. He is the author of *The History of Jazz* and *West Coast Jazz.*

Brooklyn-based critic **JIM MACNIE** has written about pop and jazz for twenty years. He is the managing editor of VH1.com.

PETER MARGASAK is a staff writer at the *Chicago Reader.* His work has also appeared in *Down Beat, Jazz Times,* and the *New York Times.*

STUART NICHOLSON is the author of several books on jazz, including highly acclaimed biographies of Ella Fitzgerald, Duke Ellington, and Billie Holiday. He has written extensively on jazz for newspapers and magazines in both the United States and Europe.

BEN RATLIFF has been a jazz and pop critic for the *New York Times* since 1996; his work has also appeared in magazines including *Lingua Franca, Artforum, Metropolis, Spin,* and *Rolling Stone.* He lives in Manhattan with his wife and two sons.

JOHN F. SZWED is Professor of African American Studies, Anthropology, Music, and American Studies at Yale University. He is a contributor to the *Village Voice* and *The Wire* and is the author of *Space Is the Place: The Lives and Times of Sun Ra, Jazz 101,* and a forthcoming biography of Miles Davis.

GREG TATE. *Village Voice* staff writer and author of the collection *Flyboy in the Buttermilk,* is also the leader of the fourteen-member improvisational aggregate Burnt Sugar/The Arkestra Chamber. This spring will see the publication of his anthology *Everything but the Burden or How Blackfolk Became Fetish Objects,* an exploration of the influence and appropriation of African American culture in the twentieth century.

PETER WATROUS wrote about music for twenty years.

K. LEANDER WILLIAMS has two porkpie hats, one for winter and one for summer. He is a staff writer at *Time Out New York* and has contributed to several publications, including the *Village Voice, Rolling Stone,* the *New York Times, Artforum,* and *Vibe.*

ABOUT THE EDITOR

YUVAL TAYLOR was an editor at Da Capo Press for eight years; he is now the editor of A Cappella and Lawrence Hill Books, both imprints of Chicago Review Press. He also edited *I Was Born a Slave: An Anthology of Classic Slave Narratives.*

CONTRIBUTOR INDEX

GENERAL INDEX

ALSO AVAILABLE
FROM A CAPPELLA BOOKS

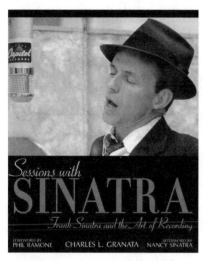

SESSIONS WITH SINATRA
Frank Sinatra and the Art of Recording
by Charles L. Granata, Foreword by Phil Ramone, Afterword by Nancy Sinatra

"*Sessions with Sinatra* is written from the heart: a refreshing and accurate portrait of the wonderful relationship Frank had with musicians, and the depth of his understanding of music. Chuck Granata's impressive study captures the true spirit of the beautiful human being I knew Sinatra to be. In musical terms, this book's got chops!"—Quincy Jones

$29.95 • 256 pages, cloth, 100 B&W photos
ISBN 1-55652-356-4

GIL EVANS: OUT OF THE COOL
His Life and Music
by Stephanie Stein Crease

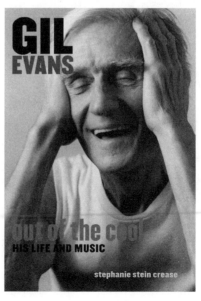

"When writing about a musical figure, the greatest triumph an author can achieve is to stir within readers a desire to hear and savor the subject's music. Stephanie Stein Crease has accomplished this with her beautifully constructed biography of jazz arranger Gil Evans. Crease captures the musician's soul, and she does it by dissecting Evans' music as thoroughly as she analyzes his psyche."
—*Variety* magazine

"Without question one of the most important jazz biographies in recent years."
—Stuart Nicholson, author of *Ella Fitzgerald* and *Billie Holiday*

$26.95 • 400 pages, cloth, 27 B&W photos
ISBN 1-55652-425-0

BOSSA NOVA

The Story of the Brazilian Music That Seduced the World
by Ruy Castro, Foreword by Julian Dibbell

"This book makes a golden era of Brazilian history accessible to a generation who never knew the poet pioneers of this Brazilian jazz form."—*The New York Times*

"This chatty, vivacious account of bossa's development in Rio and Sao Paulo in the fifties...is never boring as it follows the comings and goings of an Altmanesque cast of night-club pianists, newspaper columnists, students, diplomats, and poets in a milieu as free-wheeling as Fifty-second Street at the birth of bebop."—*The New Yorker*

$26.00 • 400 pages, cloth, 35 B&W photos
ISBN 1-55652-409-9

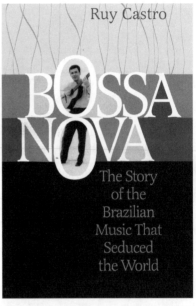

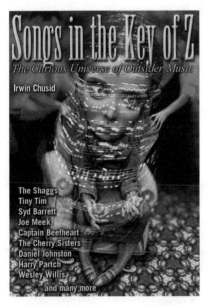

SONGS IN THE KEY OF Z

The Curious Universe of Outsider Music
by Irwin Chusid

"This book is filled with memorable characters and their preposterous-but-true stories. As a musicologist, essayist, and humorist, Irwin Chusid gives good value for your entertainment dollar."—Marshall Crenshaw

"Chusid takes us through the musical looking glass to the other side of the bizarro universe, where pop spelled backward is... pop? A fascinating collection of wilder cards and beyond-avant talents."—Lenny Kaye

"Guaranteed: this book will take readers to record stores searching for Chusid's list of musical miscreants."—*Library Journal*

$16.95 • 304 pages, paper, 60 B&W photos
ISBN 1-55652-372-6

Available at your favorite bookstore,
or from Independent Publishers Group at (800) 888-4741.
www.ipgbook.com